THE PETRINE MINISTRY

THE NEWMAN PRESS
SIGNIFICANT SCHOLARLY STUDIES

The Newman Press imprint offers scholarly studies in historical theology. It provides a forum for professional academics to address significant issues in the areas of biblical interpretation, patristics, and medieval and modern theology. This imprint also includes commentaries on major classical works in these fields, such as the acclaimed Ancient Christian Writers series, in order to contribute to a better understanding of critical questions raised in writings of enduring importance.

THE PETRINE MINISTRY

Catholics and Orthodox
in Dialogue

Academic symposium held
at the Pontifical Council for
Promoting Christian Unity

Edited by Cardinal Walter Kasper
Translated by the Staff of the Pontifical Council
for Promoting Christian Unity

The Newman Press
New York/Mahwah, N.J.

Cover design by Lisa Pomann
Book design by Lynn Else

Library of Congress Cataloging-in-Publication Data

Ministero petrino. English
    The Petrine ministry : Catholics and Orthodox in dialogue : academic symposium held at the Pontifical Council for Promoting Christian Unity / edited by Walter Kasper ; translated by the Staff of the Pontifical Council for Promoting Christian Unity.
        p. cm.
    Symposium held May 21-24, 2003.
    Includes index.
    ISBN 0-8091-4334-8 (alk. paper)
    1. Papacy and Christian union—Congresses. 2. Orthodox Eastern Church—Relations—Congresses. 3. Catholic Church—Relations—Orthodox Eastern Church—Congresses. I. Kasper, Walter, 1933- II. Title.

    BX324.3.M4713 2005
    262'.13—dc22

                                                                            2005001971

First published in English in the United States of America by
THE NEWMAN PRESS
An imprint of Paulist Press
997 Macarthur Boulevard
Mahwah, New Jersey 07430

www.paulistpress.com

Printed and bound in the
United States of America

CONTENTS

Contents

PRESENTATION

Cardinal Walter Kasper, President of the PONTIFICAL COUNCIL FOR PROMOTING CHRISTIAN UNITY, convened an academic symposium in Rome from May 21 to 24, 2003, on the theme of the Petrine ministry.

The background to this initiative can be traced to the Encyclical Letter *Ut unum sint* (n. 95) and the request of Pope John Paul II to study the question of the Petrine ministry with other Christians with a view to "seeking—together, of course—the forms in which this ministry may accomplish a service of love recognized by all concerned."

In the years following the promulgation of the Encyclical, the PONTIFICAL COUNCIL FOR PROMOTING CHRISTIAN UNITY received various studies and contributions from the other Churches and Ecclesial Communities on the aspiration expressed in *Ut unum sint.* These were gathered to form the basis of a summary and a reflection presented to the Plenary Session of the Council (November 2001).[1]

Furthermore, after the promulgation of the Encyclical in 1995, the theme of the Petrine ministry in its implications for dialogue with the other Churches and Ecclesial Communities resonated throughout the ecumenical community and in various research initiatives by institutes and research centers focusing on the theological and historical aspects of the issue.

Lastly, the question of the Petrine ministry, which had also been looked at by the Pontifical Committee of Historical Sciences (symposium in 1989) and by the Congregation for the Doctrine of the Faith (1996), is a recurring theme in relations and official dialogue between the Roman Catholic Church and the majority of the other Churches and Ecclesial Communities.

The symposium, which was held in the offices of the Pontifical Council for Promoting Christian Unity, aimed at furthering study on the theme with a view to offering a contribution to a reflection in the

---

1. "Petrine Ministry, a Working Paper." Information Service, no. 109 (2002/I–II), 33–47.

1

ecumenical perspective. As well as five Catholic experts and eleven delegates representing a range of Orthodox Churches, the symposium featured eight speakers who presented papers, from both the Catholic and the Orthodox points of view, dealing with the themes of the symposium, which an opening address by Cardinal Walter Kasper introduced.

List of Speakers

Introduction to the Theme and Catholic Hermeneutics of the Dogmas of the First Vatican Council
>Cardinal Walter Kasper
>President of the Pontifical Council for Promoting Christian
>>Unity

The Biblical Foundation of Primacy
>Monsignor Dr. Joachim Gnilka
>Emeritus Professor of the Katholisch-Theologische Fakultät, Ludwig-Maximilians-Universität, Munich (Germany).

>Reverend Professor Theodore Stylianopoulous
>Emeritus Professor of the Holy Cross Greek Orthodox School of Theology (Brookline, United States, Greek Orthodox Archdiocese of America).

Primacy in the Church Fathers
>Professor Vlassios Phidas
>Lecturer at the Faculty of Theology of the University of Athens (Orthodox Church of Greece) and the Institut de Théologie Orthodoxe d'Études Supérieures of the Orthodox Center of the Ecumenical Patriarchate Chambésy of Chambésy (Switzerland).

>Reverend Professor Vittorino Grossi
>Lecturer at the Augustinianum Patristic Institute of the Lateran Pontifical University (Rome).

The Role of the Bishop of Rome in the Ecumenical Councils
>Professor Vittorio Peri
>Retired staff member of the Vatican Apostolic Library; member of the Joint International Commission for Dialogue between the Roman Catholic Church and the Orthodox Church as a Whole.

Reverend Professor Nicolae Durã
Lecturer at the Faculty of Theology of Bucharest (Orthodox
Church of Romania).

*The Question of the Roman Primacy in the Thought of Saint Maximus the
Confessor (Communication)*
Dr. Jean-Claude Larchet
Theologian, patrologist (Serbian Orthodox Patriarchate).

Recent Discussions on Primacy in Relation to Vatican I
Reverend Professor Hermann Joseph Pottmeyer
Emeritus Professor of the Katholisch-Theologische Fakultät,
Ruhr–Universität Bochum (Germany).

Recent Discussions on Primacy among Orthodox Theologians
H.E. Professor Johannis Zizioulas
Metropolitan of Pergamon (Ecumenical Patriarchate),
Patriarchal Theological Counsellor, President of the Academy
of Athens, Orthodox President of the Joint International
Commission for Dialogue between the Roman Catholic Church
and the Orthodox Church as a Whole.

List of Orthodox Delegates at the Symposium

Ecumenical Patriarchate
As well as the speaker for the fourth topic, the Metropolitan of
Pergamon, H.E. Johannis Zizioulas, the Reverend Deacon
Maximos Vghenopoulos (Phanar, Istanbul).[2]

Greek Orthodox Patriarchate of Antioch
Mr. Albert Laham.

Serbian Patriarchate
Dr. Jean-Claude Larchet.[3]

---

2. Reverend Professor Boris Bobrinskoy (Institut de Théologie Orthodoxe
Saint Serge of Paris), delegate of the Ecumenical Patriarchate, cancelled his attendance due to ill health.
3. The Holy Synod of the Serbian Patriarchate had also nominated H.E.
Atanasie, Bishop of Zica, who was unable to attend due to pastoral commitments.

Patriarchate of Romania
> As well as the speaker for the third topic, Reverend Professor Nicolae Dură, H.E. Petronio Salajanul, Assistant Bishop of Oradea; Reverend Dr. Ioan Ica Jr., of the Faculty of Theology of the University of Cluj and member of the delegation of the Patriarchate of Romania in the Joint International Commission for Dialogue between the Roman Catholic Church and the Orthodox Church as a Whole.

Orthodox Church of Greece
> As well as the speaker for the second topic, Professor Vlassios Phidas, Professor Petros Vasileadis of the Faculty of Theology of the Aristotle University of Thessalonika.

Orthodox Church of Bulgaria[4]
> H.E. Dometian, Metropolitan of Vidin.

List of Catholic Experts at the Symposium[5]

Monsignor Roland Minnerath of the Faculté de Théologie Catholique, Université Marc Bloch of Strasbourg, France;

Monsignor Ivan Dacko, delegate of the Ukrainian Greek Catholic Church;

Reverend Professor Gerhard Podskalsky, SJ, of the Philosophisch-Theologische Hochschule Sankt Georgen–Theologische Fakultät (Frankfurt) and of the Pontifical Oriental Institute;

---

4. An invitation to nominate delegates had also been extended to the Patriarchate of Moscow, which subsequently cancelled its attendance.

5. The symposium was also attended by the Secretary of the Pontifical Council for Promoting Christian Unity, (Bishop) Brian Farrell, the Under Secretary, Monsignor Eleuterio F. Fortino, and staff members of the Oriental Section of the Council.

Reverend Frans Bouwen, MAfr (Missionaries of Africa, White Fathers, Jerusalem); Consultor of the Council; member of the Joint International Commission for Dialogue between the Roman Catholic Church and the Orthodox Church as a Whole;

Reverend Professor Dimitri Salachas, staff member of various Pontifical Universities; member of the Joint International Commission for Dialogue between the Roman Catholic Church and the Orthodox Church as a Whole.[6]

In consideration of a possible continuation of the study and joint reflection on the theme of the Petrine ministry, the participants all agreed in affirming the importance that this be undertaken within the framework of the Joint International Commission for Dialogue between the Roman Catholic Church and the Orthodox Church as a Whole, expressing the hope that the Commission may presently resume its work.

The positive experience of the symposium also encouraged participants to envisage a similar encounter on the theme "Ecclesiology of Communion and Primacy."

---

6. Reverend Professor John F. Long, SJ, Consultor of the Pontifical Council for Promoting Christian Unity, and Reverend Archimandrite Ignace Dick, Protosyncellus of the Greek-Melkite Archbishopric of Aleppo, also Consultor of the Council, both cancelled their attendance for different reasons. Reverend Professor John Long contributed to the publication of the proceedings.

Introduction to the Theme and Catholic Hermeneutics of the Dogmas of the First Vatican Council*

Walter Kasper

On behalf of the Pontifical Council for Promoting Christian Unity and in my own name I wish to welcome you most cordially to this Symposium on the Petrine ministry. I am grateful to you for having accepted so willingly my invitation and am thankful to the Patriarchs and synods of your Churches for sending you to our meeting. This response seems to me a very positive sign showing that we are together on the same path and are trying to find together a solution even for such a difficult and thorny issue as that of the Petrine ministry. May God's Holy Spirit accompany us in these days of reflection and discussion.

The great interest of so many people in our meeting over the last weeks makes it clear that our Symposium is understood and welcomed as an encouraging sign. We are responsible for the task that has been entrusted to us by our Churches and for the expectations that are placed in our meeting. The Pontifical Council and all its staff wish you a most pleasant stay in Rome and will do their best to make this Symposium successful. Please feel free to share with us your comments and wishes.

---

* Original text in Italian.

We are well aware that human capacities are insufficient and that we depend on the help of God's Holy Spirit for the success of our endeavors. Especially in these weeks before Pentecost, we should anchor our hope in the Holy Spirit, that He may enlighten our understanding with his wisdom so that we can find the way towards one another; may He fill our hearts with His love so that we can also have the courage of setting on this journey towards each other.

I.

Before making some introductory remarks on the subject that we are focusing on, I wish to briefly draw your attention to three points concerning the character of our Symposium.

1. The invitation to the Symposium was extended by the Pontifical Council for Promoting Christian Unity to the major Eastern Sister Churches and was graciously accepted by them. Therefore the context in which our Symposium takes place is an ecclesial one. As Church theologians, we do not take part in the discussions in a private capacity but as theologians of our Church and as witnesses of her tradition.

2. Despite its ecclesial nature, this Symposium is not an official Church initiative; its character is academic. Our place is not the bishop's chair but the professor's. In other words, the Academy and the Aeropag.

This has a twofold consequence. First of all, we cannot—and do not want to—take any decisions on behalf of our Churches. We rather wish to make our contribution to a better and deeper understanding that could possibly help our Churches to find a solution. Second, we do not intend to be a parallel initiative to the International Theological Commission between the Roman Catholic Church and the Orthodox Churches, and even less to replace it. On the contrary, we hope that this International Theological Commission may resume its activity soon. The work of our Symposium is not a substitute for that of the International Commission but rather an additional contribution that could be used by it.

3. Because of its academic character, this Symposium is not a public event. It is limited to its participants. Especially journalists do

not have any access. Nevertheless, in order to avoid awakening the impression of a secret gathering and raising misplaced speculations, we have informed the public on the fact that this Symposium is taking place, on its participants and topics, but no information was given on its contents. Of course, each one of you is free to give interviews. But please bear in mind that the discussion takes place here and not in front of the public. The possible decision to give the press some general information should be taken unanimously by the participants, not now but at the end of our Symposium.

II.

After these remarks on the character of our Symposium, I wish to say a few words on its subject.

We all know that there are questions among our Churches needing to be discussed and solved. Nevertheless, between the Orthodox Churches and the Roman Catholic Church there is especially one serious dogmatic and canonical problem: the question of the Petrine ministry claimed by the Bishop of Rome. Pope Paul VI and, after him, Pope John Paul II have already recognized and clearly expressed that, for non-Catholic Christians, the papal ministry is the major hindrance on the path towards unity. On the ecumenical level, the question of the primacy of the Bishop of Rome is one of the most difficult issues, but it is also one of the most important and urgent to be faced.

The question of papal ministry is much more than a theoretical one. It is much more than a theological and canonical problem. It stirs emotions on both sides. The fact of being in favor of papal primacy is one of the most fundamental characteristics of the very identity of Catholics. Likewise, its refusal belongs to the very identity of many Orthodox and Protestants. This is why it is a very emotional issue.

Nevertheless, there have been important developments in the last decades. Of course, the Churches are still quite far away from a consensus. But the atmosphere in which the question has been discussed has changed remarkably. The conviction that there should be a kind of ministry of unity in the Church, especially in today's global world, is growing at the ecumenical level. The desire of a visible center of unity has been expressed in different ecumenical dialogues. But the current concrete form of primacy in the Catholic Church is not acceptable for all the other Churches.

In order to dissipate this tension, Pope John Paul II, in his Encyclical Letter *Ut unum sint* (1995), made a revolutionary step for a Pope.[1] He said that he was aware that "the Catholic Church's conviction that in the ministry of the Bishop of Rome she has preserved...the visible sign and guarantor of unity, constitutes a difficulty for most other Christians, whose memory is marked by certain painful memories." He also added: "To the extent that we are responsible for these, I join my Predecessor Paul VI in asking forgiveness."[2]

Being aware of his "particular responsibility" for Christian unity, the Pope affirmed that he is willing to "find a way of exercising the primacy which, while in no way renouncing what is essential to its mission, is nonetheless open to a new situation." He prayed "the Holy Spirit to shine his light upon us, enlightening all the Pastors and theologians of our Churches, that we may seek—together, of course—the forms in which this ministry may accomplish a service of love recognized by all concerned."[3] Finally, the Pope invited Church leaders and theologians to engage with him "a patient and fraternal dialogue on this subject."[4] He has repeated this invitation on many occasions and underlined that we do not have any time to lose.

What should this discussion focus on, then? Clearly, the Pope does not want to bring into question the Petrine ministry and the dogma of primacy and infallibility. He wants to look for new forms of exercising the Petrine ministry without renouncing its essence. Thus the Encyclical Letter distinguishes between this unchangeable essence and the changeable forms. But this very distinction is a prob-

---

1. This step had been prepared by several declarations by Pope Paul VI and by Pope John Paul II himself. Cf. J. A. Radano, "*Ut unum sint*: The Ministry of Unity of the Bishop of Rome," *Angelicum* 73 (1996): 327–29.

2. *Ut unum sint*, 88.

3. Ibid., 95.

4. Ibid., 96.

lem because non-Catholic Churches often deny that there is a Petrine ministry at all or they disagree on the question of what is the essence of the Petrine ministry and which are the forms that can change. Hence the question is not purely a practical or pragmatic one but a theological one.

It involves a series of theological problems, such as the biblical foundation, the historical development in the first and second millenniums, and the interpretation of the doctrine of the First and Second Vatican Councils. In these dogmas as well, one needs to make a difference between the content and the historical formulations.[5]

Therefore, the task of our Symposium is clear. We should not focus on making practical suggestions but rather on making a theological contribution on the theological presuppositions for such an answer to the Pope's question that, hopefully, will help the Churches to solve the concrete problems and to move closer to that unity wanted by Christ for his disciples.

III.

We are not starting from scratch with our reflections. A discussion on the Petrine ministry had already taken place before the Pope's Encyclical Letter. I am not referring simply to the centuries of old controversies but also to the recent ecumenical discussion. The question was already touched by the International Theological Commission in the last chapter of the document of New Valamo (1988) "The Sacrament of Order in the Sacramental Structure of the Church."[6] After *Ut unum sint*, such discussion has turned from a brook into a great river. There have been official replies from Churches (e.g. the Church of England and the Church of Sweden) and a wide range of theological contributions in books, magazines, conferences, and symposia. The question of the Petrine ministry has been dealt with also in several of our dialogues with other Churches and Ecclesial Communities. Furthermore, a short time after the Encyclical, the Congregation for the Doctrine of the Faith and the Pontifical Council

---

5. Second Vatican Council, Pastoral Constitution *Gaudium et spes*, 62.
6. *Growth in Agreement II* (Geneva 2000), 678–79.

for Promoting Christian Unity organized symposia on the question and published its results.[7]

With the help of the Johann-Adam-Möhler Institute in Paderborn (Germany), this Pontifical Council has gathered all these contributions, made its own analysis, presented and discussed it during its last Plenary Assembly in November 2001, and finally published its results.[8] With this report we can say that the first phase of our discussion is over. With our Symposium we wish to start a second phase, where we hope to be able to deepen the question. In the report on the first phase, we have pointed out and analyzed the existing problems so far; now, in the second phase, we should try, step-by-step, to head towards a solution.

IV.

After these brief preliminary remarks on the nature, theme, and background of our symposium, I would like to offer an initial contribution. I would like to pose the question: How can the dialogue go on in its second phase? Is such a dialogue at all possible, and is it possible to expect it to be successful and to bear good fruit? The Catholic Church is dogmatically bound to the First and Second Vatican Councils, which she cannot give up; also the Orthodox Churches are de facto bound by their critique of, and opposition to, these dogmas. What is the room for maneuver, then? Can there be an honest solution?

In what follows, I want to offer the answer from the Catholic perspective and in terms of Catholic ecclesiology. In doing so, I am well aware that Eastern ecclesiology has a different approach,[9] which does not mean that the two ecclesiologies are necessarily contradictory; they can be understood to be complementary.[10]

---

7. *Il primato del successore di Pietro: Atti del simposio teologico, Roma, dicembre 1996* (Vatican City, 1998); *Il ministero Petrino e l'unità della Chiesa* (Venice, 1999); *Il primato del successore di Pietro nel ministero della Chiesa* (Vatican City, 2002).

8. *Information Service* (2002/I–II) 29–42.

9. Cf. J. Meyendorff et al., *The Primacy of Peter in the Orthodox Church* (London, 1963); O. Clément, *Rome autrement: Un orthodoxe face à la papauté* (Paris, 1997).

10. Y. Congar, *Diversité et communion* (Paris, 1982), 108–13.

According to the Catholic understanding, the path to be undertaken involves the rereading and the re-reception of the dogmas of the First Vatican Council. Rereading and re-reception are not an *escamotage* [slight of hand]. It means to interpret the teaching of the First Vatican Council on the primacy and infallibility of the Pope according to the "normal" and common rules of dogmatic hermeneutics. According to these rules, dogmas should be abided by in the sense in which the Church once declared them.[11] But in the Catholic view, this does not imply an irrational and fundamentalist compliance with a formula. In fact, according to the First Vatican Council, faith and understanding belong together. Catholic teaching therefore recognizes a progressive deepening in the understanding of the truth that was revealed once and for all.[12] There is a history of dogmas in the sense of a history of understanding and interpretation, and there are corresponding theological rules of interpretation.[13] In this context, Ratzinger speaks of the need for a rereading,[14] Congar and others speak of a re-reception of the First Vatican Council.[15]

The concept of reception, which has often been neglected in the past, is fundamental for Catholic theology, particularly for ecumenical theology and the hermeneutics of dogmas.[16] Such reception and re-reception do not mean questioning the validity of the affirmations of a Council; rather, they mean its acceptance on the part of the ecclesial community. This is not a merely passive and mechanical acceptance; rather, it is a living and creative process of appropriation and is therefore concerned with interpretation. It is not my intention to discuss in this

---

11. "Hinc sacrorum quoque dogmatum, is sensus perpetuo est retinendus, quem semel declaravit sancta mater Ecclesia, nec umquam ab eo sensu alterioris intelligentiae specie et nomine recedendum est" (*DH* 3020). Cf. *DH* 3043.

12. *DH* 3020; Second Vatican Council, Dogmatic Constitution on Divine Revelation *Dei verbum*, n. 8.

13. Cf. W. Kasper, *Die Methoden der Dogmatik* (Munich, 1967).

14. J. Ratzinger, *Das neue Volk Gottes* (Düsseldorf, 1969), 140.

15. Y. Congar, op. cit.

16. Cf. Y. Congar, "La réception comme réalité ecclésiologique," *RSPhTh* 56 (1972): 369–403; A. Grillmeier, "Konzil und Rezeption," in *Mit ihm und in ihm* (Freiburg i. Br., 1975), 309–34; W. Beinert, "Die Rezeption und ihre Bedeutung in Leben und Lehre," in W. Pannenberg and Th. Schneider, *Verbindliches Zeugnis* (Freiburg-Göttingen, 1995), 2:193–218; G. Routhier, *La réception d'un concile* (Paris, 1993).

context the entire body of dogmatic hermeneutics, and I will confine myself to an exposition of only four rules that are decisive for the interpretation of the dogmas on the primacy and infallibility of the Pope.

1. A first rule for such a rereading and re-reception of the Petrine ministry is the integration of the concept of primacy in the whole context of ecclesiology. This rule was formulated by the First Vatican Council itself. It affirmed that the mysteries of faith are to be interpreted "e mysteriorum ipsorum nexu inter se," that is, according to the internal context binding them together.[17] The Second Vatican Council has expressed the same idea with the help of the doctrine of the hierarchy of truths.[18] Therefore no dogma should be considered as isolated but should be interpreted taking into account the whole doctrine of the faith. Especially it should be interpreted on the basis, in the context, and in the light of the basic Christian dogmas on Christology and the Holy Trinity.

This integration of the primacy had already been suggested by the First Vatican Council. The Council describes the meaning of primacy in the Proemium to the Constitution *Pastor aeternus*. It affirms that, according to God's will, all faithful should be kept together in the Church through the bond of faith and love. It then mentions the famous quotation that is now at the basis of today's ecumenical commitment: "ut omnes unum essent." Finally, it refers to Bishop Cyprian: "ut episcopatus ipse unus et indivisus esset," Peter was called to be "perpetuum utriusque unitatis principium ac visibile fundamentum."[19] An article recently published by the Congregation for the Doctrine of the Faith presents again this formulation in its fundamental importance for a *theological* interpretation of the *juridical* declarations on the doctrine of primacy.[20] Thus, the unity of the Church is the raison d'être and the context of interpretation of the Petrine ministry.

---

17. *DH* 3016.

18. *Unitatis redintegratio* 11: "When comparing doctrines with one another, they [i.e., theologians] should remember that in Catholic doctrine there exists an order or 'hierarchy' of truths, since they vary in their relation to the foundation of the Christian faith."

19. *DH* 3050ff.

20. P. Rodríguez et al., "Natura e fini del primato del Papa: Il Vaticano I alla luce del Vaticano II," in *Il primato del successore di Pietro nel ministero della Chiesa* (Vatican City, 2002), 81–111.

Because of the outbreak of the Franco-German War, the First Vatican Council was not able to proceed with the integration of primacy into the whole ecclesiological context. This process remained uncompleted, since it only managed to define the primacy and infallibility of the Pope. This led later to unilateral and unbalanced interpretations. Nonetheless Vatican I had affirmed that the primacy does not cancel but confirms, strengthens, and defends the direct authority of the bishops.[21] Pope Pius IX explicitly highlighted this when he confirmed the declaration of the German bishops against the dispatch of Bismarck. In this way, Pius IX defended himself against extreme interpretations and defended the position of the bishop as the ordinary pastor of his diocese.[22] Even the formula considered scandalous in the ecumenical perspective, that the Pope is infallible "ex sese, non autem ex consensu Ecclesiae,"[23] had already been interpreted during the Council by the speaker of the Doctrinal Commission in a purely juridical sense, in the sense that definitions did not require juridical ratification from a higher source,[24] but, in theological terms, it is not a question of an infallibility that is separate from the faith of the Church.[25]

The Second Vatican Council took up the question and took a second step towards the integration of primacy into the whole doctrine of the Church as well as into the whole collegiality of the episcopal ministry. This Council also reaffirmed the importance of the local Church, of the sacramental understanding of the episcopal ministry, and, above all, of the understanding of the Church as *communio*. This has revived synodal elements, especially at the level of synods and bishops' conferences.

Nevertheless, the Second Vatican Council was not able to reconcile fully the new elements—which in reality correspond to the oldest tradition—with the statements of the First Vatican Council. Many issues have remained unconnected. Sometimes there is mention of the existence of two different ecclesiologies in the texts of the

---

21. DH 3061.
22. DH 3112–3117.
23. DH 3074.
24. Cf. Mansi, *Amplissima collectio conciliorum*, 52:1317 A–B.
25. Ibid., 36 C–D.

Council. This has led, since the Second Vatican Council, to a controversy on interpretation, to some degree continuing even today. In this sense, the Second Vatican Council, too, has remained an uncompleted Council. The integration of the Petrine ministry in the whole of ecclesiology, the relation between the universal and the local dimensions of the Church, the applicability of the principle of subsidiarity, and other questions raise theological and practical questions that have not yet been definitively resolved.

When one takes seriously that the Petrine ministry is constitutive within the Church and that all other ministries have to be in communion with it though they are not derived from it but have their own sacramental root, then a one-sided pyramidal conception of the Church is overcome and a communal one prevails, where the different institutions and ministries have their respective irreplaceable roles and are in an interplay with each other. Such a communal view, which makes room for the freedom of the Spirit, could result from a fuller reception of the Second Vatican Council.[26]

2. The second principle of dogmatic hermeneutics concerns the rereading of the First Vatican Council in the light of the whole tradition and the integration of that Council within this tradition as a whole. The texts of the First Vatican Council itself already pointed out this route. The introduction to the Dogmatic Constitution *Pastor aeternus* described it as the intention to interpret this teaching "secundum antiquam atque constantem universalis Ecclesiae fidem" and defend it against mistakes.[27] Clear mention was made of the declarations of the previous Popes and of the preceding Councils.[28] The First Vatican Council even appealed to the consensus between the Church in the East and the Church in the West.[29] The Second Vatican Council reinforced especially this last point when it mentioned the legitimacy of the particular tradition of the Oriental Churches[30] and recognized that they can rule themselves according to their own law.[31]

---

26. Such a view seems to correspond with the Orthodox view as described by O. Clément, *Rome autrement: Un orthodoxe face à la papauté* (Paris, 1997), 59–64, 107.

27. *DH* 3052.

28. *DH* 3059.

29. *DH* 3065.

30. *Unitatis redintegratio*, 14.

31. Ibid., 16.

Such indications express an important concept, valid for all Councils: the Church is the same in all centuries and in all Councils; this is why each Council is to be interpreted in the light of the whole tradition and of all the Councils. The Holy Spirit, Who guides the Church, particularly its Councils, cannot contradict Himself. What was true in the first millennium cannot be untrue in the second. Therefore the older tradition should not be simply considered as a first phase of a further development. The other way round is also true: the later developments should be interpreted in the light of the wider older tradition. Therefore the First Vatican Council should be seen in the context of the older Councils. Thus the first millennium's ecclesiology of communion, reaffirmed in its validity by the Second Vatican Council, constitutes the hermeneutical framework for the First Vatican Council.

In the meanwhile, especially after Cardinal Ratzinger's conference in Graz, the normative importance of the first millennium has been widely recognized also in Catholic theology.[32] But it is essential to understand it correctly. It is clear that it is not a question of simply going back to the first millennium or reverting to an "ecumenism of return."[33] Such a return to the first millennium is impossible, in any case, for historical reasons: divergent views already existed in the first millennium, and so it cannot offer us any miraculous solution. Moreover, significant developments have taken place in the second millennium not only in the Catholic Church but also within the Eastern Churches.[34] Why should we suppose that the Spirit guided

---

32. J. Ratzinger, *Die ökumenische Situation—Orthodoxie, Katholizismus und Reformation: Theologische Prinzipienlehre, Bausteine su einer Fundamentaltheologie* (Munich, 1982), especially 209: "As for the doctrine of primacy, the claims of Rome in the face of the East should not be greater than those formulated and lived in the first millennium" (Cf. *Istina* 20 [1975]: 87–111; also L. Bouyer, ibid., 112–15). On the subject: M. Maccarrone, ed., *Il primato del vescovo di Roma nel primo millennio* (Rome, 1991).

33. J. Ratzinger, *Kirche, Ökumene, Politik* (Einsiedeln, 1987), 76f.; 81ff.

34. On the Orthodox side, mention should be made, in this context, of the end of the Roman—i.e., Byzantine—Empire, at which point there was no longer an emperor who in a certain sense was the coordinator of unity; as well, some of the Patriarchates and autocephalous national Churches are of relatively recent origin. It should also be borne in mind that the majority of the Orthodox Christians in the diaspora live in the Western world.

the Church only in the first millennium? And did not the first millennium already contain the foundations of what developed in the second, which is true of the Eastern tradition also?[35]

Therefore today, at the dawn of the third millennium, we cannot turn back the clock of history; but we can interpret the different events of the second millennium in the light of the first one in order to open the door to the third millennium. The Second Vatican Council had already initiated the interpretation of the First Vatican Council within the wider horizon of *communio* ecclesiology.

A corresponding reception on the part of the Churches in the East has not happened so far. Such a reception would not imply a mechanical acceptance or a submission of the East to the Latin tradition: it would entail a lively and creative process of appropriation into one's own tradition. This would enrich the tradition of the Eastern Church and give it a greater degree of unity and independence that is currently lacking. Also, the Latin tradition would be freed from the constraints in which it found itself in the second millennium. The Church as a whole—as the Pope has expressed many times—would start breathing with two lungs again. This implies that integrating the other tradition and vice versa could lead to different forms and expressions in the exercise of the Petrine ministry, as occurred in the first millennium and as occurs today in the Oriental Churches in full communion with Rome.

3. We come now to a third hermeneutical principle: the historical interpretation.[36] As is the case for all dogmas, so also for the First Vatican Council it is fundamental to make a distinction between the unchangeable binding content and the changeable historical forms. This principle was clearly expressed by the Second Vatican Council: "The deposit and the truths of faith are one thing, the manner of expressing them is quite another."[37] Hence it would be wrong to take

---

35. From the Orthodox side, cf. J. Meyendorff, *Orthodoxy and Catholicity* (New York, 1966), 49–78; O. Clément, op. cit., Paris, 1997.

36. H. J. Pottmeyer, *Die Rolle des Papstums im dritten Jahrtausend*, Quaestiones disputatae 179 (Freiburg i. Br., 1999).

37. *Gaudium et spes*, 62. This sentence takes up the speech Pope John XIII delivered at the opening of the Council (*AAS* 54 [1962], 792). It was further developed by the Declaration of the Congregation for the Doctrine of Faith *Mysterium Ecclesiae* (1973), in *DH* 4539ff.

the formulations of the First Vatican Council as the only possible way of expressing what the Petrine ministry concretely means and what is permanently binding in it.

The Fathers of the First Vatican Council experienced specific historical conditions that led them to formulate things the way they did. The Council majority saw the Church besieged from all sides and in an almost apocalyptic situation. They were traumatized by the Enlightenment, the French Revolution, the absolutism of modern states, by Gallicanism and Episcopalism, and wanted to make sure that the Church would remain capable of action even in extreme situations. This is why they reverted to the modern idea of sovereignty: they defined the primacy of the Pope in terms of an absolute sovereignty, in such a way that he could act even if he were to be prevented from communicating with the Church. Their statements on primacy were especially conceived for extreme and exceptional situations.[38]

The understanding of the primacy in the sense of sovereignty does not mean—even according to the First Vatican Council—that the Pope's power is unlimited. It is limited in several ways: by revelation itself and by the binding tradition, by the sacramental structure and the episcopal constitution of the Church, and by human rights given by God. Therefore the problem is not the dogma of the First Vatican Council itself but its maximalist interpretation both by its Ultramontane advocates and by its critics.[39] This has turned what was considered an exceptional situation into a normal one. The exceptional case has been, so to say, stretched in time and made permanent. Therefore we should agree with Cardinal Ratzinger when he says that the centralized image given by the Church until the Council did not stem directly from the Petrine ministry. The uniform canon law, the uniform liturgy, and designation of the episcopal chairs by the central power in Rome—all these are elements that do not necessarily belong to the primacy as such.[40]

If we separate the declarations on the primacy of jurisdiction from their historical forms, then we find their binding essential meaning,

---

38. H. J. Pottmeyer, op. cit., 44ff.

39. Ibid., 66ff.

40. J. Ratzinger, *Das neue Volk Gottes*, 142.

that the Pope is free to act according to the specific and changing necessity of the Church. The primacy should therefore be interpreted in the light of the needs of the Church and applied accordingly.[41] In this sense, John Paul II, in *Ut unum sint*, speaks of the need to find ways of exercising the primacy according to the new ecumenical situation of today.

4. A fourth and last hermeneutical principle is the interpretation of the Petrine ministry in the light of the gospel. The importance of this principle has been highlighted especially in the dialogue with the Lutherans, but also Catholics agree on its significance.[42] Real value in the Church belongs to what has its foundation in the gospel and not to what is only a human invention.

In this sense, the Catholic Church is convinced that the primacy is founded in the testimony of the Bible and ultimately in Jesus Christ himself. Mention should be made not only of the well-known Petrine references in the New Testament (especially Matt 16:18f.; Luke 2:32; John 21:15–17) but also of the fact that Jesus gave Simon the name *Képhas* (John 1:42), meaning "rock," thereby explaining his function in the Church. Furthermore, mention should be made of the privileged role of Peter among the twelve as their spokesman and representative, and his role as leader of the early community in Jerusalem, as well as the entire Petrine tradition in the Bible (especially 1 and 2 Peter) which goes beyond the earthly existence of Peter, extending into the postapostolic and postbiblical era and tradition.

While it is true that historical interpretation of the Bible provides a firm basis, historical interpretation alone does not provide the ultimate foundation for our belief. In its original meaning, the gospel is not a book but the message witnessed in the Bible and, in the power of the Spirit, also proclaimed and believed in the Church. Therefore the Bible witness cannot be cut off from this witness of the living

---

41. *Il Primato del successore di Pietro*, 501f; cf. W. Brandmüller, "Natur und Zielsetzung primatialer Interventionen im zweiten Jahrtausend," ibid., especially 377ff. Also remarks by D. Valentini, ibid., 381ff.

42. *Dei verbum*, 21: "It follows that all the preaching of the Church, as indeed the entire Christian religion, should be nourished and ruled by Sacred Scripture." It is worthwhile noting that the Council sees Sacred Scripture in the context of tradition and the doctrine of the Church; cf. *Dei verbum*, 7–10.

Church tradition. Thus today a purely historical understanding of the gospel, which looks only for the exact historical meaning of the words of the so-called historical Jesus, is obsolete. Historical exegesis is certainly legitimate, helpful, and fundamental, but theological debate cannot be in a narrow sense biblistic and should not separate the Scriptures from the living tradition. It should take into account both Scriptures and tradition, employing a spiritual and theological hermeneutics.[43]

In this sense, the faithfulness of the community of Rome despite persecution and the confrontation with Gnosticism, its steadfastness against Marcion, and its contribution to the final establishment of the biblical canon, together with the role of its bishops, who very early took over responsibility for the unity of the Church beyond the Roman community, were all factors that convinced the early Church that in the church of Rome and in its bishop the promises given to Peter are realized and still at work. And so, from the third and fourth century on, the Church referred to the biblical witness, which is given especially in Matt 16:18.[44]

However, such a historical and, at the same time, spiritual interpretation entails not only finding the formal biblical foundation of the Petrine ministry but also highlighting its meaning and exercise according to the Gospel, that is, its interpretation not in the sense of power but in the sense of service. Indeed, the Gospel says: "Whoever wishes to be first among you must be your slave" (Matt 20:27). This aspect is reflected in the expression *servus servorum Dei* used by Pope Gregory the Great.[45]

---

43. All this is meant with the difficult and complex term *ius divinum*. It is widely recognized that the *ius divinum* does not exist in a pure and abstract sense but concretely is translated into history through the *ius ecclesiasticum* and the *ius humanum*. In this sense the *ius divinum* comprises what has acquired its definitive value, on the basis of the Holy Scriptures, in the history of the Church, guided by the Holy Spirit. Cf. K. Rahner, "Über den Begriff des "jus divinum" im katholischen Veständnis,' in *Schriften* (Einsiedeln, 1962), 5:249–277; G. A. Lindbeck, *Primacy and the Universal Church* (Minneapolis, 1974), 193–208; J. Freitag, "Ius divinum—ius humanum," *LThK* 5 (1996): 697ff.

44. J. Ludwig, *Die Primatsworte Mt 16,18.19 in der altkirchklicheh Exegese* (Münster, 1952); W. Kasper, *Dienst an der Einheit* (Düsseldorf, 1978), 82–88.

45. *DH* 3061.

Pope John Paul II has emphasized this dimension anew. He has referred to the martyr bishop Ignatius of Antioch, who described the primacy of Rome as the "primacy of love."[46] Thus, the Pope himself has given an important indication for a new interpretation of primacy inspired by the gospel. His interpretation is not a jurisdictional one based on the idea of sovereignty; it is a spiritual one based on the idea of service—a service to unity, a service and sign of mercy and love.[47]

This closer reference to the Bible has brought it about that the commonly employed language now substitutes, for the expressions *papal ministry* and *papacy*, the terms *Petrine ministry* and *Petrine service*. This linguistic change is quite telling. It seeks to give the papacy—developed throughout history and in part also burdened by history—a new interpretation and reception in the light of the gospel, not renouncing its essential nature but setting it in a new, wider spiritual understanding on the theoretical as well as on the practical level. The Petrine ministry is *episkopê*; that is, it is a pastoral service following the example of Jesus the good shepherd, who gives his life for his flock (John 10:11). In this sense Peter admonishes his fellow elders: "Tend the flock of God that is in your charge, exercising the oversight, not under compulsion but willingly, as God would have you do it—not for sordid gain but eagerly. Do not lord it over those in your charge, but be examples to the flock" (1 Pet 5:2–4).

In this sense we can say that the Petrine ministry should be interpreted theologically as *episkopê*. Such an interpretation of the juridical formulations would correspond to the intentions expressed in the Proemium of the First Vatican Council,[48] taken up also by the Second Vatican Council.[49] Pope John Paul made reference to this interpretation in *Ut unum sint*, placing such juridical formulations in a biblical and theological context. This could constitute an ecumenically useful approach.

Such a pastoral understanding of *episkopê* does not exclude authority in the biblical sense of *exousia*; a primacy of jurisdiction and a pastoral primacy of service cannot be mutually substituted or placed

---

46. Ignatius of Antioch, *To the Romans*, prologue.
47. *Ut unum sint*, 88–93.
48. P. Goyert, "Primato ed episcopato" in P. Rodriguez et al., op. cit., 133ff.
49. Second Vatican Council, Dogmatic Constitution *Lumen gentium*, 18.

in opposition, as some theologians propose.[50] For pastoral responsibility without the means to carry it out would be void and would not help the Church in the urgent situations in which she would most need it. Rather, the question is how the service of *episkopê* in the spirit of the gospel can be carried out with *exousia*. This question concerns, in different ways, both our ecclesiological traditions.

In conclusion, I would say that with the help of such an interpretation in the light of the four hermeneutical principles outlined above, it is possible to uphold the binding and unchangeable essence of the Petrine ministry and, at the same time, open and explore a pathway and prepare a new spiritual reception in our own Church that—as we hope—can facilitate a broader ecumenical reception as well. My hope is that, as was the case in the first millennium, the Petrine ministry may take a form that, although differently exercised in the East and in the West, could be recognized both by the East and by the West within a unity in diversity and a diversity in unity. I have no illusions. I am aware that the path ahead, on the basis of human measures, may yet be long. But I still hope that when we patiently and at the same time courageously do what we can do, God's Spirit will help and accompany us to reach what He has in mind for the full visible unity of the Church.

---

50. As does H. Küng, *Die Kirche* (Freiburg i. Br., 1967), 545, 558.

THE MINISTRY OF PETER—
NEW TESTAMENT
FOUNDATIONS*

Joachim Gnilka

Preliminary Observations

A dramatic incident from earliest Christian history is related at Gal 2:11ff. The scene is Antioch, the second most important early Christian community after Jerusalem, and we are told about a controversy between Cephas and Paul concerning table fellowship between Jewish and Gentile Christians. Strict Jewish Christians reject this table fellowship because the Gentile Christians do not observe the Jewish dietary regulations. Cephas, who had initially shared table fellowship with the Gentile Christians, without any inward reservations, is influenced by persons who come from Jerusalem, and he abandons this table fellowship. Paul sees this as a threat to the unity of the Church, and he contradicts Cephas before the assembled community: "I opposed him to his face, because he stood self-condemned." This so-called Antiochene incident remains a matter of dispute among exegetes to the present day. Some interpreters see it as an overture to the Reformation, especially because Paul's doctrine of justification may have played a role in this controversy. W. Schenk observed: "Tell me how you interpret the Antiochene incident, and I will tell you what kind of Christian you are."

Although this incident remains important, one must not overinterpret it, as happens when two thousand years of Christian experi-

---

* May 21, 2003 (morning session). Original text in German. English translation by the author.

ence are projected back into the text. Paul respected Cephas's authority, but he understood himself as an apostle with rights equal to those of Peter. He saw this unity as based in the unity of the gospel, and this is why he evaluates his conflict with Cephas as follows: "But when I saw that they were not acting consistently with the truth of the gospel..." (2:14). Nevertheless, the gospel is entrusted to human beings, and it is they who have to care for its unity. It is this concern that leads Paul to challenge Cephas.

If we wish to learn something about the position of Simon Peter in earliest Christianity, we must bear in mind the following characteristic of our sources: they do not present us with any community constitution in which Peter's position would be set out; they are far from thinking in the constitutional and juridical terms in which many people today are accustomed to think. At most, one can see buds of ideas that will later blossom into reflections on canon law. In many respects, our sources are full of holes.

The Gospels present stories and narrations which mix up narrative accounts with proclamation of the Good News. The letters limit themselves mostly to suitable solutions directly dealing with problems arising in particular communities. Nevertheless, a recapitulation of the New Testament is significant for the formulation of our problem, because for our reference we have the New Testament documents as witnesses for the foundation of the early Church and for the valuable writings of this period. Now I intend to approach the person and the ministry of Peter in the light of the New Testament. It refers to the time during which he accompanied Jesus like and along with other disciples, and in contrast to the post-resurrection period of the early Church. I will conclude with some final considerations.

1. Simon, the Exemplary Disciple

Simon, like his brother Andrew, hailed from Bethsaida. Both of them were fishermen. He settled in Capernaum following his marriage. All the four evangelists ascertain his significant role within the circle of the disciples. About Simon, we have been sufficiently informed, whereas the rest of the Twelve are often mentioned only by their names. The repeated mentioning of his name can be an indication of his esteem because none of the Gospels is written by him. The synoptic authors present him as first disciple along with Andrew. Luke 5:1ff. concentrates on the history of the vocation of the disciples with special focus on Simon, concluding with the words of Jesus to him: "Do not be afraid; henceforth you will be catching men." In John 1, Simon is not mentioned as first disciple, rather he comes to Jesus through the mediation of his brother. However, according to John 1, Jesus confers on Simon a new name at the very first encounter: "You are Simon son of John. You are to be called Cephas (which is translated Peter)" (1:42). Conferring of this name finds mention also in Mark 3:16; Luke 6:14; Matt 10:2; 16:18, but the ecclesiastical promise is attached only to the last reference. Paul recognizes this name too. Mostly he calls him Cephas, once Peter, but never Simon.

The very name Cephas/Peter deserves our closer attention. The Aramaic name was Kepha, grecized as Cephas and translated into Greek as Peter. Peter means stone, sling stone (F. Passow), Kepha means "stone" and "rock." Besides, there are other meanings (arch, dome) which are of less importance. To me, the concept of precious stone for Kepha seems more appropriate (G. Dalman). I assume that the earthly Jesus gave Simon the name Kepha, but still without any ecclesiological implications. Conferring of a new name indicates his specially chosen position. It is in this sense that Simon can be called the first disciple.

Simon comes forward repeatedly as spokesperson of the disciples. In most cases his questions were directed to Jesus' teachings having halachic character, which means, pertaining to the life of the discipleship and the community, levitical purity (Matt 15:15), temple tax (17:24ff.), forgiveness (18:2), reward for following Christ and the false ambition (19:27ff.). It is again in the name of discipleship that he confesses the faith in Jesus as Messiah, in Mark 8:29. There are three occasions on which Jesus preferred to treat him equally with James and John. These three had been chosen to be witnesses of the transfiguration on the mountain (Mark 9:2), raising up of the daughter of Jairus (5:37), and the agony of Jesus in Gethsemane (14:33). Jesus' reproach to the sleeping disciples had been addressed to Simon personally: "Simon, are you asleep? Could you not keep awake one hour?" (14:37) His failure was depicted unvarnished. Jesus had cursed him with "Satan" because he was rebellious against the plan of suffering (8:33), but he himself renounces Jesus before the servants and maids of the high priest. His denial of Jesus was so intensively portrayed as to mean that he might even lose his discipleship. He relied totally on being reaccepted by Jesus through his grace. Certainly, his imminent martyrdom is already indicated in John 13:36: "Where I am going, you cannot follow me now; but you will follow afterward." It is more evident in 21:18: "When you grow old, you will stretch out your hands, and someone else will fasten a belt around your waist and take you where you do not wish to go." We should not ignore the typical character of Simon. He is portrayed as the exemplary disciple who confesses and denies; proves to be loyal and is also as cowardly as the others.

Simon is specially depicted as an exemplary disciple in the circle of the Twelve. Forming of the circle of the Twelve is to be understood as a symbolically prophetic act of Jesus which points to the eschatological restoration of the twelve tribes of Israel. Mark 3:14 makes known the function of the Twelve, namely, to be with him and to extend their support to him in his ministry of proclaiming the kingdom of God and of casting out devils. As his companions, they are supposed to bear witness to him. Hence, Mark mentions their presence in significant contexts (4:10; 6:7; 9:35; 10:32; 14:17). But this common function which all of them share affects Simon particularly. If Peter is the first disciple and is specially mentioned at the end of the Gospel, apart from the other disciples, as addressee of the Easter message which the women brought (16:7), it is to be seen in the context of the witnessing function.

2. The Petrine Ministry

The ministry of Peter, as commissioned to him, can be understood only in the framework of discipleship. He shares this ministry with other disciples. He does not exercise it alone as the absolute authority. This element is important, even though it is true that he is entrusted with a special mission, as seen in different prominent passages. When we closely observe the individual passages, their connections appear relevant and important. Moreover, all these passages refer to the postresurrection situation, for the ministry of Peter has to do with the community, the Church. And the Church comes to exist only after resurrection, primarily through confession of faith in Jesus as the crucified and risen Lord.

We see an exception to this postresurrection nature of his mandate in Luke 22:31ff. Jesus emphatically addresses Simon in Luke's farewell words: "Simon, Simon, listen! Satan has demanded to sift all of you like wheat, but I have prayed for you that your own faith may not fail; and you, when once you have turned back, strengthen your brother." The idea of being sifted in Satan's hand signifies hard trials in discipleship. In the ministry of Jesus the disciples might have already experienced such trials, above all during the passion. So, supported by the prayers of Jesus, Simon should strengthen this community of brothers and sisters in faith. This is the only passage which directly speaks of his relationship to his companions. The clause "when once you have turned back"—possibly a later addition out of consideration for his denial—brings back Simon into the circle of the disciples, just because he himself was weak in faith. It reveals to him that ultimately it is not he who supports the discipleship, but the Lord.

Thus we come to the *locus classicus* of the ministry of Peter, Matt 16:17–19. The text is well constructed in three verses.

Blessed are you, Simon son of Jona!
For flesh and blood has not revealed this to you,
but my Father in heaven.

And I tell you, you are Peter,
and on this rock I will build my church,
and the gates of Hades will not prevail against it.

I will give you the keys of the kingdom of heaven,
and whatever you bind on earth will be bound in heaven,
and whatever you loose on earth will be loosed in heaven.

This composite text presents a combination of different images and traditions. First of all, Simon is addressed with the unique blessing formula and "Bar-Jona." It follows the conferring of the name, in whose interpretation we discover the Church-founding words and the promise of the victory over the underworld. In the Greek text we can recognize the origin of the already conferred name. The name Petros ("stone, precious stone") is reinterpreted as Petra and it attains an ecclesiological significance. Unambiguously, Petra means "rock." In the third verse we have the word "keys" in combination with binding and loosing. In fact, the image of the keys requires an explanation in relation to closing and opening functions. But it is not usual, however, to attribute the functions of binding and loosing to keys.

Beginning with the concept of rock, we translate "Petros" as rock. Simon is the rock upon which Christ wants to build his *ecclesia*. Today there is a widespread agreement in the understanding that "rock" refers to the person of Simon and not to his faith. A. Schlatter commented on the false personifying of the faith, as it may correspond to a logic other than what is found in the Bible, because Jesus entrusts his work to a person and not to an idea. The concepts of rock and of building are very common in the New Testament and among the Jews (Qumran). For example: Christ is the stone which the builders rejected and became the cornerstone (Mark 12:10f.; cf. Ps 118:22). Similarly, according to 1 Cor 3:10 Jesus Christ is the foundation, which Paul had laid in founding the community of Corinth, upon which others build. In Eph 2:20, the Church is built on the foundation of apostles and prophets, whereas Christ is presented as the keystone. In describing the heavenly city of Jerusalem, the wall of the city rests on twelve foundations, which carry the names of the twelve apostles of the lamb (Rev 21:14). The significant picture in Matt 16:18 reveals that the rock-foundation of the Church is an individual apostle. And Christ is the architect of the *ecclesia*, which he calls his Church. Hence, it concerns the new messianic community, united in the faith in Jesus, the Christ and Son of God. This refers to the universal Church and not to any particular local or provincial community. What requires our close observation is the future and postresurrection perspective: "On this rock I will build my church." This perspective, going back to the earthly life of Jesus, safeguards the insight that the community can come into existence only after the resurrection.

It is not, however, clear in which manner Simon should be the rock (foundation) of the Church. In view of this, we must consider the content of the promise: the gates of Hades will not overpower the

Church. Hades refers to the kingdom of death. On the principle *pars pro toto*, gates of Hades represent the entire kingdom of death. Avoiding any picturesque description, it means: the destructive powers of death cannot prevail over the messianic community. It is an eschatological community until the end of times. Probably there exists a mythology behind this message, which can be verified from the Jewish texts. It goes back to a cosmic origin. Accordingly, God had founded the earth on the temple rock, the stronghold on which the world is created. The temple rock is also presented as a dike against the primeval floods. The double functions, of foundation stone and of shutter of the underworld, reach in Matt 16:18 congruence with the Jewish mythology. So, the temple rock can be identified with Abraham, the forefather of the Jews: "Look, I have found a rock, upon which I can make and set up the world," says God on seeing Abraham, according to Jalqut Schimeoni I § 766. In the light of this Jewish text, it becomes explicit that in Jewish biblical tradition, extraordinary things could be demanded from individual persons. Consequently, we can understand these texts whenever we come across them in the New Testament, only if we are open to these concepts as already having a long history behind them.

If we wish to know more precisely how Simon Peter had fulfilled the task entrusted to him, it should be answered: he did it as guarantor and guardian of the gospel. He had forged the gospel and legitimated it. The introductory blessing words of "Simon Bar-Jona" speak for it. He becomes blessed because he was endowed with the revelation of God. Relying upon his own capability he could not attain it. He was not enabled for it by "flesh and blood." It was the heavenly Father of Jesus who had enabled him for it. The peculiar style of this blessing deserves closer attention. Generally, individuals are blessed in the Bible when they achieve something significant or fulfill a certain condition. Very seldom we come across this form of extolling without preconditions. For example: "Happy are you, O Israel! Who is like you, a people saved by the LORD, the shield of your help" (Deut 33:29). Simon Peter was likewise blessed, not because of his achievements, but because he received the revelation as a gift. Moreover, I guess that it presents a form of investiture on the recipient of revelation. It means that Peter would be associated with the Gospel of Matthew in a very special way. He should be understood as its guarantor and guardian. We have to take into account that the author of this Gospel formulated the blessing text elaborately so that it might have its place in the literature.

Against this background—Peter as guarantor and guardian of the gospel—the function of the power of keys can be conferred on him. This image is also old, as it can be traced back to ancient Egypt. One who opens and closes has to provide also for the security of those who come in and go out. Already an interpretation of this idea is considerably expounded in Isa 22:22. Eliakim here receives the control of the royal house of David with the following words: "I will place on his shoulder the key of the house of David; he shall open, and no one shall shut; he shall shut, and no one shall open." So too, Peter receives the authority over the kingdom of heaven along with the keys. He does exercise this authority here on earth, and not as heaven's gatekeeper according to the cliché. As guarantor and guardian of the gospel, he gives the message and the teaching of Jesus to the people and entrusts them with the keeping of the same. Thus he provides them the means of access to the kingdom of heaven. This idea occurs in the Gospel of Matthew in relation to 23:13. "But woe to you, scribes and Pharisees, hypocrites! For you lock people out of the kingdom of heaven. For you do not go in yourselves, and when others are going in, you stop them." In fact Peter enters in their place. Conversely, if we look at the task given to Peter, which is especially that of opening the gates of heaven, it is clear that his ministry is to be described as something positive.

Binding and loosing constitute a pair of complementary concepts, which points principally to captivity and to setting free in the Old Testament. Isaiah 58:6: "to loose the bonds of wickedness." The early Christians in their missionary preaching might have originally used this verse. For the missionaries the idea of binding and loosing constituted the basic standard of Christian life; the consequence of acceptance or rejection of their message determined the salvation of mankind (E. Käsemann, P. Hoffmann). Here we could compare it with Luke 10:16: "Whoever listens to you listens to me, and whoever rejects you rejects me, and whoever rejects me rejects the one who sent me." The concept of binding and loosing in this context could clearly refer to the last judgment. But in Matt 16:19, it is the Jewish rabbinical understanding of binding and loosing that is significant (*asar/sera*). Accordingly, binding and loosing means as much as prohibiting and allowing, as related to decisions concerning discipline and teachings. Acceptance of these teachings in heaven has its effects already in the present time.

If we pay attention to the functions of Peter—rock of the Church, shutter of the gates of Hades, powers of the keys, binding and loosing—everything is rooted in the Gospels. He is the authoritative founder, guardian, and reliable interpreter of the Gospel. Here we find an important difference; a function given once for all and given for the first time (F. Hahn). It means, in his destiny to be the rock of the Church, he cannot be replaced. It is indelibly proper to him. Just as, according to the Jewish mythology, Abraham is the temple rock, which is once laid and on which the world rests, so too Peter is the rock of the Church.

Besides Peter, now there are the Twelve and other apostles. They also founded the permanent apostolic gospel. If Eph 2:20 acknowledges apostles and prophets as the foundation of the Church, it speaks of their ministry of founding the gospel, which gave direction to the entire edifice. 1 Corinthians 15:1–11 speaks explicitly of the ministry of all the apostles. All of them together founded the gospel. It is true, here also Cephas is mentioned at the first place, but with equal rights follow the Twelve, then James and all the apostles and lastly Paul. He considers the unity of the Church as preserved in the Gospels and as proclaimed by all disciples. Moreover, what is said about Peter is also applicable to the apostles already mentioned. Their function cannot be repeated or replaced. The gospel can be founded only once, after which it is interpreted and proclaimed.

The results of the ongoing research testify that the Gospel of Matthew originated in Syria, probably in Antioch. It means that the tradition of Peter's ministry began in the Syrian church. We can see a completely similar tradition in the supplementary chapter of John's Gospel. It could also suggest that this Gospel originated in the Syrian region. If we follow the pericope John 21:15ff.—taking the postresurrection perspective into consideration—Jesus entrusted Simon Peter with the shepherd's ministry over the Church. Christ speaks of his lambs, his sheep, which can be compared to Matt 16:18, "I will build my church."

In the Gospel of John, the ministry of Peter finds its foundation in chapter 10, where Christ presents himself as the good shepherd. Remarkably, in the narration of the huge haul of fish, John presents an Easter story. It is Peter who draws the extremely filled net onto the land. The mysterious number that might have been 153, along with the comment that the net was intact even with so many fish, may refer to the fullness of number. Possibly the huge number stands for all the peoples of the world. As the Fourth Gospel contains many background meanings, I like to maintain that this special fishing of Peter symbolizes the unity of the Church and Simon Peter might be considered as its guardian. The theme of unity occupies an important place in the Fourth Gospel.

The outstanding position of Peter faces a peculiar competition from the disciple who is described as "the disciple whom Jesus loved." This beloved disciple leans on the breast of Jesus at the last supper, which means, Jesus had a special place for him. He stands at the foot of the cross and the crucified Lord entrusted his mother to him. Simon Peter and the other disciples were absent. Most remarkable is the running of Simon Peter and the beloved disciple towards the tomb of Jesus on Easter morning. The beloved disciple reaches the tomb first, but lets Peter go in before him. It is said about the beloved disciple that he believed already at the tomb (John 20ff.). As I have already mentioned, in John's Gospel Simon Peter is not the first disciple, but he comes to Jesus through his brother Andrew. The two first disciples are Andrew and another disciple whose name is not announced. One can guess that it speaks of the beloved disciple himself, who is not described with this name at the first meeting.

Returning now to the central passage, Matt 16:17–19, we distinguish between the unique and unrepeatable commission of Peter to be the rock of the Church, and his very first assignment to the power of the keys and the exercising of the power to bind and to loose. If we look into the Acts of the Apostles, there are examples of how he exercised such powers. He takes a decision in the critical case of Ananias and Sapphira and also in the case of Simon the magician (5:1ff.; 8:18ff.). As a rule he functioned together with others. On the Feast of Pentecost he raised his voice together with the eleven (2:14) and he appeared repeatedly accompanied by John (3:1ff.; 4:13). He played a leading role in the community at Jerusalem. Paul confirms this as he visits Cephas in Jerusalem after his Damascus experience (Gal 1:18). He might have handed over the community leadership to James in order to dedicate himself to the mission among the Jews. As found in Gal 2:9, Paul and Barnabas together with James, Cephas, and John (sic!) make a resolution in the gathering of the apostles. This concerns Peter and Paul. Paul is entrusted with his mission to the Gentiles and Peter is set apart for the Jewish mission (2:7f.).

We notice in Matt 18:18 that the power of the community to bind and to loose is exercised within the community. "Whatever you bind on earth will be bound in heaven, and whatever you loose on earth will be loosed in heaven." A process of expulsion from the community should be undertaken if a sinner is not ready to change his ways, after being reprimanded thrice. Here the local community is in focus. Binding and loosing thus means the imposing and lifting of a ban respectively. This juridical text is certainly framed in response to pressing appeals for forgiveness. It is Peter who raises the question how often he should forgive his brother who sins against him. And his answer is: seventy times seven (18:21f.).

At the end of the Gospel, the resurrected Lord instructs the eleven apostles and commands them that they should in turn teach the people to keep all that he had commanded them. This demands commitment to the gospel of Jesus. This command had been earlier given to Peter, the guarantor and guardian of the gospel. We see also in the Gospel of Matthew, which emphasizes the person of Simon Peter as unique, that his commission is deeply rooted in the ministry of the other apostles, even extending to all in the community.

Summary

The most prominent duty concerning the ministry of Peter is to strengthen the brothers and sisters in faith.

He preserves the tradition of the gospel and reliably interprets it. The very fact that this apostle becomes very prominent in the Gospel of Matthew speaks for its origin in Jesus. Here one may remember the sermon on the mount which is in the same Gospel.

The New Testament not only advises but also demands the collegial exercising of the Petrine ministry even though Peter remains the head. It is to be considered that the leading of the universal Church by Peter is testified in the Gospel of St. John, the Gospel which emphasizes the Spirit of God strengthening every Christian.

The ministry of Peter has to present the unity of the Church, a unity to be understood as the unity under the gospel.

References

E. Dinkler, *"Die Petrus-Rom-Frage,"* Theologische Rundschau 25 (1959): 189–230, 289–335; 27 (1961) 33–64.

O. Cullmann, *Petrus,* 2nd ed., Zurich, Stuttgart, 1960.

P. Hoffmann, *"Der Petrus-Primat* in Matthäusevangelium," in *Neues Testament und Kirche* (Festschrift R. Schnackenburg) (Freiburg, 1974), 94–114.

W. Schenk, *"Das 'Matthäusevangelium' als Petrusevangelium,"* Biblische Zeitschrift 27 (1983): 58–80.

F. Hahn, *"Die Petrusverheißung Mt 16.18f,"* in Exegetische Beiträge zum ökumenischen Gespräch (Göttingen, 1986), 185–200.

P. Stockmeier, *"Papsttum und Petrus-Dienst in der frühen Kirche,"* Münchener theologische Zeitschrift 38 (1987): 19–29.

J. Gnilka, *Das Matthäusevangelium,* Herders theologischer Kommentar zum Neuen Testament 2 (Freiburg, 1992), 46–80.

Summary of Discussion

There is a variety of "ministries of unity" to be found in the New Testament: Petrine ministry, Johannine ministry, Pauline ministry, ministry of James, and so on.

A certain specific role of Peter is recognized by almost all: a role as a spokesman or a representative for the Twelve. But does this role imply a specific authority, and more precisely an authority over the other apostles? Does Peter have a ministry of unity? Is he the only one to have a ministry of unity?

For the Orthodox participants, this ministry of unity is exercised not only by Peter but also by others, for instance, by Paul. The ministry of Peter is always very closely linked to that of the other apostles; Peter belongs to the group of the Twelve and cannot be put above them. Because of that, the specificity of a Petrine ministry, in both theory and practice, is not so clear in the New Testament.

For the Catholic participants, the existence, necessity, and specificity of Peter's ministry are more clearly affirmed in the New Testament. Peter is presented as the guarantor of the faith and of the unity of the early Church. Though Paul claims equality with the other apostles, he goes to consult Peter in Jerusalem so as to receive confirmation of the authenticity of his ministry. The disciple whom Jesus loved (John 21), who is at the center of the Fourth Gospel and refers to the more charismatic communities of Johannine tradition, nonetheless underlines the necessity of an effective bond between these communities and the universal Church, represented by Peter. There is more New Testament evidence on the necessity of a Petrine ministry, however, than on the way this ministry should be exercised. As to the succession in Petrine ministry, there also remain some questions regarding both the necessity and the mode of this succession.

All agree that there is a certain distance or difference between the New Testament affirmations and later historical developments investing Petrine ministry with a more precise significance and a more juridical outlook. Though these developments cannot be based on or proved by the New Testament alone, they can be seen as being in line with the New Testament, as an unfolding of the New Testament affirmations. For the Orthodox, however, these "unfolding links" with the New Testament are less obvious; they find them more optional than necessary.

All agree that a distinction should be made between a modern scholarly interpretation and the patristic interpretation of the New Testament, particularly when it comes to the interpretation of chapters such as Matt 16. This hermeneutical problem should be kept in mind.

CONCERNING THE BIBLICAL FOUNDATION OF PRIMACY*

Theodore Stylianopoulos

Introduction

Let me begin by expressing my gratitude for the privilege of participating in this academic symposium on the Petrine ministry. I am especially thankful to His Eminence Walter Cardinal Kasper for the opportunity to offer the present contribution on an issue that has immense implications for the unity of the Christian churches. We laud the spirit of Pope John Paul's encyclical *Ut unum sint*, in which primacy has been explicated in distinctly biblical and pastoral terms as a ministry of love, unity, and service. We welcome His Holiness's invitation to all Church leaders and theologians to engage with him in "a patient and fraternal dialogue...leaving useless controversies behind...keeping before us only the will of Christ for his Church and allowing ourselves to be deeply moved by his plea 'that they may all be one...so that the world may believe that you have sent me'" (John 17:21) (*Ut unum sint*, 96).

As an Orthodox theologian, I acknowledge that the Orthodox Church has long nurtured profound respect for a qualified primacy of the church of Rome and its revered pontiff, in spite of acrimonious controversies in the relations between the two churches especially during the second millennium which still impact negatively on the memory of many Orthodox Christians. As far as the principle of primacy is concerned, the Orthodox tradition itself has fostered various forms and levels of primacy among the Orthodox churches and their

---

* May 21, 2003 (afternoon session). Original English text.

leaders from ancient times. These levels of primacy include canonically defined privileges as well as responsibilities under the term πρεσβεςα ("privileges of seniority") rather than the term πρωτειον ("primacy"). These terms may imply subtle but significant differences of nuance between "privileges" and "rights." Nonetheless it is well known that, in both theory and practice, concepts and structures of authority, hierarchy, and primacy, albeit qualified by conciliarity, parity, and the consensus of the whole Church, are intrinsic to Orthodox life and thought.[1]

In dealing with the subject of Petrine primacy, contemporary Orthodox scholars have engaged the question from various historical, political, and theological viewpoints. However, the weight of analysis has primarily focused on the witness of tradition rather than that of the Scriptures. Even in cases where key texts of the New Testament have been debated as to their significance for or against the Petrine primacy, reliance is usually grounded in the interpretations of those texts by the church fathers.[2] Only in rare instances do we find critical exegetical analyses based on the contextual witness of the biblical texts themselves in the manner of international biblical scholarship.[3]

---

1. For a broad perspective on these matters, see the articles by Metropolitan John (Zizioulas) of Pergamon, Prof. Dumitru Popescu, and Prof. Nicolas Lossky in *Petrine Ministry and the Unity of the Church*, ed. James F. Puglisi (Collegeville: Liturgical Press, 1999), 99–135; Bishop Kallistos Ware, "Primacy, Collegiality, and the People of God," in *Orthodoxy: Life and Freedom* (Oxford: Studion Press, 1973), 116–29; John Meyendorff et al., eds., *The Primacy of Peter in the Orthodox Church* (Crestwood: St. Vladimir's Seminary Press, 1992); and a collection of articles on the catholicity of the Church in *St. Vladimir's Theological Quarterly* 17, nos. 1–2 (1973). See also the significant points of agreement on leadership, Church order, and the mystery of the Church between Orthodox and Anglican theologians in *Anglican-Orthodox Dialogue: The Dublin Agreed Statement 1984* (Crestwood: St. Vladimir's Seminary Press, 1985), especially 15–19.

2. For example, Dumitru Popescu, "Papal Primacy in Eastern and Western Patristic Theology: Its Interpretation in the Light of Contemporary Culture," in *Petrine Ministry and the Unity of the Church*, 99–113.

3. Veselin Kesich, "The Problem of Peter's Primacy," *St. Vladimir's Seminary Quarterly* 4, nos. 2–3 (1960): 2–25; and John Karavidopoulos, "Le rôle de Pierre et son importance dans l'Église du Nouveau Testament: Problématique exégétique contemporaine," *Nicolaus, rivista di teologia ecumenico-patristica* NS 19 (1992): 13–29, originally in Greek as "Ο ρολος του Πετρου και η σημασια του στην Εκκλησια της

And even in such cases one can detect an inclination toward what is perceived to be the normative interpretation of the church fathers. The fact is that the question of the relationship between critical biblical scholarship and the patristic exegetical heritage is still unsettled in contemporary Orthodox theology. Because of this state of affairs, my own task of dealing with the biblical aspects of primacy calls for a brief disclosure of the present paper's hermeneutical presuppositions, not least for the judgment of my Orthodox colleagues.[4]

1. Hermeneutical Remarks

Exegesis has been called an exercise in humility. To do exegesis is to set aside all bias and attend with utmost care to the biblical text in all its literary, historical, as well as theological implications. At the exegetical level there need not be separate cases of Orthodox or Roman Catholic or Protestant exegesis but simply a common exegetical concern to listen carefully to the voices of the biblical texts, to honor their historical and theological witness, and to work out significant convergences of interpretation. Professor Karavidopoulos rightly critiques the extreme polemical positions of the past and seeks to present a more objective analysis of the Petrine texts in the New Testament (Matt 16:17–19; Luke 22:31–32 and John 21:15–17).[5] Of course honesty requires the acknowledgment that personal commitment to our respective traditions makes total objectivity virtually impossible. Yet the difficulty of achieving full objectivity is no argument for

---

Καινης Διαθηκης: Συγχρονη εξηγητικη προβληματικη," ΔΕΛΤΙΟ ΒΙΒΛΙΚΩΝ ΜΕΛΕΤΩΝ NS 10 (January–June 1991): 47–66; P. Boumis, "Η Πετρα του Πετρου," ΘΕΟΛΟΓΙΑ 51 (1980): 146–157, and George Galitis, "Συ ει Πετρος," ΓΡΗΓΟ–ΡΙΟΣ ΠΑΛΑΜΑΣ 55 (1972): 193–97. The latter is a homiletical encomium to Peter given on the Feast of Saints Peter and Paul.

4. For a fuller account of my own efforts to bridge critical biblical studies with the tradition of Orthodox theology, see Theodore Stylianopoulos, *The New Testament: An Orthodox Perspective* (Brookline: Holy Cross Press, 1997), vol. 1.

5. J. Karavidopoulos, "Ο ρολος του Πετρου," 47–48. Nevertheless, he states that "it is self-evident that the attempt to understand the biblical references to the apostle Peter will be based mainly on the Orthodox exegetical tradition," 48, without raising the consequent hermeneutical and moral obligation of completely impartial exegesis.

abandoning the ideal or for pursuing it with less vigor. On the contrary, sound critical study, whether of biblical or patristic sources, constitutes a test of integrity for theological scholarship and a source of hope for constructive work. What is encouraging is that critical scholarship has already demonstrated a revolutionary impact on the way many of the controversies of the past are now seen in a new light, for example, concerning Scripture and tradition, word and sacrament, as well as the issue of the Petrine primacy itself.[6]

Another hermeneutical consideration arises from that fact that modern biblical studies have shown beyond the shadow of doubt that the Gospels are "Easter documents" written from the perspective of the resurrection faith of the early Christians. The formation of the Gospels entailed a fairly free and dynamic process driven by the use of the oral tradition about Jesus in the early Christian congregations as well as by the theological interests of the individual evangelists. Therefore, as in the case of Jesus himself, and in spite of divergent scholarly opinions about details and methodology, a hermeneutical distinction must in principle be allowed between the "Peter of history" and the "Peter of faith." However, much of scholarly work in this area has not only been extremely conjectural but also notably contradictory in its conclusions. My own hermeneutical assumption is that the Gospels provide trustworthy historical memories of Peter's relationship to Jesus and to the other disciples. Just as in the case of Jesus, so also in the case of Peter, I am inclined to see essential continuities between the pre- and post-Easter situations. Moreover, the canonical status of the Gospels requires that full attention should be

---

6. On the issue of primacy, see the collaborative ecumenical approaches as evidenced by Raymond E. Brown et al., eds., *Peter in the New Testament* (Minneapolis: Augsburg/Paulist Press, 1973); the Anglican–Roman Catholic Commission's *Final Report*, ed. H. R. McAdoo and Alan C. Clark (Cincinnati: Forward Movement Publications, 1982); the papers of the Lutheran-Catholic Dialogue in Paul C. Empie and T. Austin Murphy, eds., *Papal Primacy and the Universal Church* (Minneapolis: Augsburg Press, 1974); *Episkope and Episcopate in Ecumenical Perspective*, Faith and Order Paper 102 (Geneva: WCC, 1980); William R. Farmer and Roch Kereszty, *Peter and Paul in the Church of Rome: The Ecumenical Potential of a Forgotten Perspective* (New York: Paulist Press, 1990); and most recently James F. Puglisi, ed., *Petrine Ministry and the Unity of the Church*, op. cit.

given to the interpretation of the texts as we have them rather than to seek to revise or rewrite them without sufficiently secure evidence.

Modern biblical studies have also demonstrated the diversity of the New Testament books pertaining to many issues, such as Christ, Spirit, Church, Law, Israel, and no less church order. In similar manner, the New Testament presents a variegated witness regarding the role of Peter. One has to contend not only with diverse portraits of Peter but also significant omissions about his role. This indisputable diversity therefore raises the hermeneutical concern that no text can be taken in isolation, either to be estimated as if it carried overwhelming importance or to be ignored as if it bore no comparative value. Rather, it is the case that the whole witness of the New Testament must be assessed in terms of its parts and the parts in terms of the whole, which is an old and wise exegetical principle. In addition, of crucial importance is not only the question of the role of Peter in the context of various and developing forms of leadership in the early Church, but also the nature and quality of Christian leadership itself as exemplified and taught in various biblical texts. Indeed, it is poignantly ironic that in Church history we have not a few instances of disputes over "who was the greatest" (Mark 9:34), when the Lord Jesus by word and deed had set down a ministerial leadership of an entirely different spirit.

A final hermeneutical factor has to do with the relationship of Scripture and tradition—the authority of the canon and the authority of the Church. Unless one insists on old biases, or espouses revisionist theories that devalue both the scriptural canon and the ancient Christian tradition, critical studies have conclusively affirmed an organic interdependence between Scripture and tradition to such an extent that they can no longer be played off against one another. We read statements such as "to acknowledge the authority of the canon is to acknowledge the authority of the tradition which gave rise to it."[7] And again, "the early Church did not think of the authority of scripture apart from its relationship to the theological tradition expressed in the rule of faith or apart from the use of Scripture in Christian

---

7. Harry Y. Gamble, "Canon: The New Testament," in *Anchor Bible Dictionary*, ed. David Noel Freedman (New York: Doubleday, 1992), 1:859.

worship."[8] These hermeneutical judgments urge serious attention to both the relevant biblical texts and their use in the ongoing community of faith that received, interpreted, and applied them. The work of the Spirit in the Church by no means ceased after either the composition or the collection of the New Testament books. In spite of major controversies in Church history, it would be theologically absurd to claim that Christ failed in his promise to be with his Church always. From this perspective, the ministry of Peter and the question of primacy cannot be finally decided on the basis of the New Testament alone. Rather, the witness of the tradition as a whole must be taken into serious consideration as long as that tradition is judged to be not contradictory to the biblical witness. Although we have our historic differences, our cherished theological positions, and our respective optic standpoints, the common hermeneutical challenge is to dialogue with sufficient integrity and critical judgment, neglecting neither Scripture nor tradition, that the Spirit himself may lead us toward a mutually acceptable understanding of the truth regarding key issues, including the Petrine ministry.

2. Primacy in Matthew 16:16–19

The New Testament speaks of many kinds of primacies. There is the primacy of God's kingdom and righteousness (Matt 6:33). There is the primacy of one Lord, one faith, and one baptism (Eph 4:5). There is the primacy of the gospel (Rom 1:16–17; Gal 1:6–9; 1 Cor 15:1–11). There is the primacy of hearing and obeying God's word (Matt 4:4; Mark 7:13; Luke 1:28; Heb 4:12–13). There is the primacy of love (Matt 5:43–44; 22:36–40; Rom 13:8–10). There is the primacy of mercy (Matt 9:13; Luke 15:7; 23:43; John 8:11). There is the primacy of sacrificial service (Mark 9:35; 10:42–45; John 13:12–17). There is the primacy of humility (Matt 11:29; Mark 18:4; Luke 14:11; Phil 2:3–8). An inquiry into the Petrine primacy must never lose sight of the significance of all the above primacies that provide the deeper and broader context for the discussion of our subject.

---

8. Rowan A. Greer, "Biblical Authority in the Early Church," in *Anchor Bible Dictionary*, ed. David Noel Freedman (New York: Doubleday, 1992), 5:1027.

The role of Peter in the New Testament has been extensively investigated.[9] The present paper is no place to enter into any sort of detailed exegetical analysis of the evidence and all debated positions. In general there is wide agreement that, in spite of a mixed portrayal, the figure of Peter enjoys a preeminence among Jesus' disciples and in the early Church. John P. Meier sums up the critical consensus on the "historical Peter" as follows. Peter is among the first to be called, the most actively engaged in exchanges with Jesus, the most visible spokesman and leader of the disciples and of the first Christians, and thus the most prominent figure among the Twelve. Peter was known by the nickname of Cephas or "Rock," but it is not certain whether the nickname was attributed to him by Jesus, who in any case gave it a new significance, or was already known to others prior to contact with Jesus. At a pivotal point in Jesus' ministry, not necessarily the same as that of the surnaming, Peter made a profession of faith about the messianic dignity of Jesus. However, the language of the confession and Jesus' words in answer to Peter (Matt 16:16–19) are heavily influenced by the post-Easter Christian tradition. Jesus' rebuke of Peter playing the role of "Satan" is historical but not necessarily the present context in Matthew and Mark where it is reported. Peter's denial of Jesus at the time of the passion is also historical but the precise circumstances are obscure. Peter claimed to have seen the risen Jesus and apparently became the rallying figure of the Jerusalem church in the early days. After several imprisonments he left Jerusalem to do missionary work in such places as Antioch, perhaps Corinth, and later quite probably Rome. According to Meier, the overall picture of Peter in the New Testament is that of a complicated person with strengths and weaknesses. Peter was energetic and fervent but also given to doubt and panic. He was a bold leader of the early Church but also capable of reversals in Church policy (Gal 2:12). We hear so much about him in the New Testament because he

---

9. In addition to sources cited above, see Pheme Perkins, *Peter Apostle for the Whole Church* (Columbia: University of South Carolina Press, 1994; reprint, Minneapolis: Fortress Press, 2000); Timothy Wiarda, *Peter in the Gospels* (Tübingen: Mohr Siebeck, 2000); and John P. Meier, *A Marginal Jew* (New York: Doubleday, 2001), 3:221–25. The latter assesses the whole scope of the question of discipleship, the Twelve, as well as the role of the individual disciples in the ministry of Jesus.

was the most prominent and influential member of the Twelve during Jesus' ministry and in the early Church. Next to Jesus, Peter is the most fascinating figure in the Gospels and, in spite of his weaknesses, an important bridge between Jesus' ministry and later in the early Church.[10]

Orthodox biblical scholars and theologians would easily accept the above minimal critical consensus on Peter and more. For one thing, no Orthodox scholar has ever raised doubts about either the authenticity of the key Petrine texts of Matt 16:16–19, Luke 22:31–32, and John 21:15–19 or the historical reliability of the Book of Acts. For another, Peter's preeminence among the disciples and his leadership role in the early Church, especially together with Paul, are typically exalted in the Orthodox tradition. The interest of Orthodox scholars has been to register two major concerns regarding Peter's "primacy." One concern is about the nature and extent of that primacy. Granted that Peter enjoyed prominence, even certain precedence, among the disciples and in the early Church. But does that status necessarily entail authority above and over the Twelve? Does the role of Peter imply an institutional office intended to guide and govern the universal Church? The other concern is about the nature of the succession of Peter's dignity and function. Is there evidence in the texts that the role of Peter is to be succeeded by one bishop in a single local church—Rome? Granted that the apostolic pastoral authority to teach and guide, as well as the sacramental powers, indisputably continue in the life of the Church by virtue of God's providence and presence. But does it follow that these attributes pass on to individual leaders in particular churches that alone can claim apostolic founding? If Peter's role could be conceived of in terms of succession, does this dignity belong to the bishop of Jerusalem, or Antioch, or Rome and why? Those questions are of course central for all inquirers, whether Orthodox, Protestant, or Roman Catholic. Our task is to bring the key points of debate into conversation and cautiously draw the relevant conclusions arising from the Petrine texts.

The main text is Matt 16:16–19, which is distinctly Matthean in redactional formulation. Here Peter's confession is fuller than that

---

10. J. P. Meier, op. cit., 221–45, 629–30.

reported in Mark (Mark 2:29), possibly reflecting Matthew's accent on Jesus as Son of God (Matt 14:33; 11:27). Also, we have evidence of Matthean expressions such as the reference to "the living God" (Matt 16:16; 26:63) and especially the plural "heavens" in Matthew (cf. Matt 16:17–19). Above all, the solemn words of Jesus addressed to Peter occur only in Matthew, although the Gospel of John in a different context clearly echoes the tradition concerning the surnaming of Simon as Cephas (John 1:42).[11] Those solemn words of Jesus in Matthew include: a) a blessing on Peter as one given a special revelation from God to perceive the mystery of Jesus; b) the surnaming of Simon as "Rock" in a play of words presupposing the original Aramaic; c) a declaration that Christ would build his invincible Church upon that rock; d) and a promise that Christ would give to Peter the "keys of the kingdom," that is, authority "to bind and loose" matters on earth with the full approval of heaven.

It is well known that liberal scholars dispute that the above pronouncements are logia of Jesus, while conservative scholars tend to find historical substance in them. Rudolf Schnackenburg writes: "Whether and how [these] statements, combined in 16:18–19, were bound together in the (Jewish-Christian) tradition adopted by Matthew is disputed in scholarship. Rarely are they recognized as declarations of the earthly Jesus."[12] Even on the assumption that these words are largely shaped by Christian tradition, the interpretations concerning their import can be contradictory. For example, some see in Matt 16:16–19 an exaltation of Peter as "chief Rabbi of the universal church" in the context not of Rome but of Antioch where the development toward a monarchical episcopate may be on its way.[13] Others view the intended impact of this text as being just the opposite: the diminution of Peter's traditional prominence in the community of Antioch ca. 85 AD by means of a pattern of praise and

---

11. Of course, that this tradition is well established in the early Church is evident from Paul, 1 Cor 1:12; Gal 1:18; etc.

12. Rudolf Schnackenburg, *The Gospel of Matthew*, trans. Robert R. Barr (Grand Rapids: Eerdmans, 2002), 160. John P. Meier, op. cit., 229–35, reviews the evidence on both the conservative and liberal sides.

13. Raymond E. Brown and John P. Meier, *Antioch and Rome: New Testament Cradles of Catholic Christianity* (New York: Paulist Press, 1983), 67–68.

dispraise.[14] To pursue such hypothetical questions is beyond the scope of this paper. More direct to our task is an examination of the exegetical currents on primacy, particularly pertaining to Matt 16:16–19, as they have relevance for the ecumenical discussion of our subject.

Jesus names Simon as Cephas or Rock. What is the significance of this nickname? Dumitru Popescu sums up the standard view of Orthodox scholars based on the majority opinion of the church fathers. In Matt 16:18 Peter as Cephas or Rock signifies the confession of faith by Peter, a faith that belongs to all the apostles and has specifically in mind the divinity of Christ who is the supreme Rock. Partly on this basis Popescu concludes that the Orthodox tradition relates primacy not to Peter himself but to the See of Rome.[15] In similar fashion George Galitis and John Karavidopoulos find that the meaning of "rock" has to do with the confession of faith and the fundamental content or truth of that confession on which the Church of Christ is built.[16] The prominence and leadership of Peter are not disputed but understood as being not different in kind from that of the other apostles.

Two Orthodox scholars have gone a bit further. In his commentary on Matthew, Panagiotis Trembelas,[17] following A. Plummer's exegesis, affirms that Peter, too, may be viewed as the rock of the Church. The fact the Christ himself is the foundational cornerstone of the Church is not reason to deny that Peter himself can indeed function as rock, yet, no more than the rest of the apostles (Eph 2:20). The crux of the matter is still the confession of faith. Peter is the first confessor, the foundation upon which others are added and thus the Church is built on the confession of all believers. Likewise Peter's prerogative of the keys (meaning according to Trembelas both admission

---

14. Arlo Nau, *Peter in Matthew: Discipleship and Dispraise* (Collegeville: Liturgical Press, 1992), 24. I owe this reference to T. Wiarda, *Peter in the Gospels*, 22–23. According to that literary schema Peter walks on the water but sinks (Matt 14:22–33), he confesses Jesus but then objects and is severely rebuked (Matt 16:13–23), he is a member of the inner circle but is terrified (Matt 17:1–13).

15. D. Popescu, *Papal Primacy*, 107, 110–13.

16. G. Galitis, "Συ ει Πετρος," 195; and J. Karavidopoulos, "Ο ρολος του Πετρου," 55–57.

17. P. Trembelas, Υπομνημα εις το κατα Ματθαιον Ευαγγελιον (Athens: Zoe Brotherhood, 1951), 315–17.

to the kingdom and authoritative judgments about conduct) carries the authority of the risen Christ, the supreme holder of the keys (Rev 1:18). But, again, this authority was granted to all the apostles (Matt 18:18). Trembelas quotes with approval Bengel's older observation that if the keys were given only to Peter and the bishop of Rome, then the bishop of Rome, after the death of Peter, would be the shepherd of the surviving apostles, with authority over them, something utterly unthinkable.

The bond between Peter's confession of faith and Peter himself has been advocated by another Orthodox scholar, Canon Law Professor Panagiotis Boumis[18] of the University of Athens. Boumis argues that it is absolutely necessary to see unity and concord between the two traditionally opposed interpretations on the grounds of both exegetical and ecumenical requirements. According to Boumis, "rock" must by all means be applied to Peter himself as well as to the confession of faith by Peter. Ecumenically, it cannot be that all the voices on opposing sides have been completely wrong and without foundation for so long, or that the divine providence has permanently allowed an irreconcilable conflict on such a crucial issue of unity without the possibility of resolution. Exegetically, the answer is that the change of words from Πεστρο to πεστρα, as well as the use of the conjunction και instead of the more restrictive δε in Matt 16:18, allow the harmonious coexistence of many "rocks" including Christ, Peter, and the rest of the apostles at their particular level of dignity and function.[19] For Boumis, there is no need to oppose Peter and his confession of faith, but to hold the two together as one comprehensive truth.

Veselin Kesich, the Serbian Orthodox biblical scholar and now retired professor at St. Vladimir's Orthodox Theological Seminary, is the first Orthodox theologian to stress the particular significance of

---

18. P. Boumis, "Η Πετρα του Πετρου," 147–57.

19. Professor Boumis seems to forget that the Aramaic word for "Cephas" in both instances is exactly the same. Also, it is doubtful that the argument on the basis of the Greek conjunctions is decisive. Boumis does not pursue the consequences of his thesis about the unity of Peter and Peter's confession of faith for the question of the later claims of primacy but presumably assumes the traditional Orthodox interpretation of primacy.

"rock" applied to Peter himself. He is aware of Oscar Cullmann's[20] novel step among Protestants, and cites him favorably. Kesich writes:

> But only Peter was promised that the church would be built upon him, both on him personally and on the rock of his faith, since there is no difference between *Petros* and *petra* in Aramaic. Cephas stands in Aramaic for both Greek words. There is a formal and real identity between them. Thus Peter's faith and Peter's confession cannot easily be separated from Peter himself. And this *petra* is not simply Peter's faith, underlying his confession, but may also be taken as referring to Peter personally.[21]

Nevertheless, just as in the case of Cullmann, Kesich insists that Matt 16:16–19 provides no evidence of any notions of succession or any basis for the later claims of the jurisdictional powers of the papacy.

That Orthodox scholars have gradually moved in the direction of affirming the personal application of Matt 16:17–19 to the apostle Peter must be applauded. From the standpoint of critical scholarship, it can no longer be disputed that Jesus' words to Peter as reported in Matt 16:17–19 confer a special distinction on Peter as "rock"—the foundation on which Christ promised to build his Church. To be sure, Jesus addresses his question to all the disciples in the plural and Peter answers on behalf of all as their representative. However, just as Simon speaks directly to Jesus, Συ ει ο Χριστος etc., so also Jesus declares directly to Simon, Συ ει Πετρος," etc., bestowing only on him the distinction of being Cephas/Rock, no mere semantic attribution without substance.[22] It is exegetically neither possible to separate Peter from his faith, nor to diminish his prerogatives by exalting the importance of his confession of faith. Likewise, the privileges

---

20. Oscar Cullmann, *Peter: Disciple, Apostle, Martyr,* trans. Floyd V. Filson (New York: World, 1958), who finds a postresurrectional background behind Matt 16:17–19.

21. Veselin Kesich, *The Problem of Peter's Primacy,* 6. The bold is in the original.

22. Wolfgang Trilling, *The Gospel according to St. Matthew,* trans. Kevin Smyth, ed. John L. McKenzie, 2 vols. (New York: Crossroad, 1978–1981), 2:61.

accorded to Peter can be played off against neither the primacy of Jesus as the foundation of the Church, nor the fact of the shared character of those prerogatives with the rest of the apostles. These points are now conceded by conservative Protestant biblical scholars as well. For example, D. A. Carson candidly states: "if it were not for Protestant reactions against extremes of Roman Catholic interpretation, it is doubtful whether many would have taken 'rock' to be anything or anyone other than Peter."[23] Carson adds the insight that "rock" in Matt 16:18 cannot mean Jesus because in this context Jesus is said to be the builder of the Church, not its foundation.[24] As far as the text of Matt 16:16–19 is concerned, whether it can be demonstrated to represent logia of Jesus or an early Christian tradition preserved and developed in the community of Matthew, we can indeed speak of a Petrine function, a special mandate and commission to Peter,[25] which is distinct in some undefined manner from that of the other disciples.

But what is the nature of Peter's special role as "the rock" upon which the Church is built? A key word in the context is εκκλησια (Matt 16:18; cf. 8:17), almost certainly presupposing the Hebrew *qahal*—the assembly or community of Yahweh. There is no conclusive way to settle the question whether or not Jesus used this word. However, what must be emphasized is that the concept of community is quite conceivable within Jesus' ministry as part of his act of selecting the Twelve and his overall vision concerning the restoration of Israel in the end time.[26] To the degree that Jesus raised the messianic question, and that his ministry carried messianic import, it is quite likely that the historical Jesus sought to gather a community around him. In line with classic Jewish messianism, there can be no

---

23. D. A. Carson, "Matthew," in *The Expositor's Bible Commentary*, ed. Frank E. Gaebelein (Grand Rapids: Zondervan, 1984), 8:368. Similarly, Donald A. Hagner, "Matthew 14–28," in *Word Biblical Commentary*, ed. David A. Hubbard and Ralph P. Martin (Dallas: Word Books, 1995), 33B:470–71.

24. Ibid. My emphasis. Of course Carson is careful to deny that thereby the uniqueness of Jesus as foundation of the Church is in any way compromised.

25. The position of Roman Catholic scholars, for example, Trilling, op. cit. 60–61, and Schnackenburg, op. cit. 156ff.

26. This case is powerfully made by N. T. Wright, *Jesus and the Victory of God* (Minneapolis: Fortress, 1996).

Messiah without a messianic people.[27] And Peter was to be "the rock"—the firm ground and security—on which Jesus' community was to be established. Nevertheless, the primary builder of this new community was Jesus himself. The community was Jesus' ("my church"), not Peter's. The invincible might against which the powers of hell would not prevail derives from Christ, not Peter, and belongs to the Church (εκκλησιαν/αυτης), not to a Petrine office. Jesus and the Church are greater realities than Peter. Peter's function was to serve in some distinctive but undefined way as Jesus' representative or helper in building the community. Moreover, for Matthew, and here we must agree with Schnackenburg,[28] the promise "I will build my church" envisions both Jews and Gentiles after Easter. This promise anticipates the Church in its universal nature—one people under the Messiah. A similar universal element may perhaps be found in Jesus' triple mandate to Peter to feed and shepherd "my lambs" (John 21:15–17; cf. 10:16; 11:52; 17:20–21). Still, thus far, we can discern neither the precise nature of primacy, nor any idea of succession as a necessary part of the Petrine commission.

The context of Matt 16:17–19 speaks of the gift of "the keys of the kingdom" and the conferral of authority to "bind and loose" things on earth. These two aspects are closely related. For Matthew, the kingdom can be no other than God's rule breaking into history through the proclamation of the good news by Jesus and the disciples (Matt 4:17; 10:7). Proclamation of the kingdom results in a reality that involves raising up disciples, baptizing, and passing on Jesus' teachings in community (Matt 28:19–20). Thus, the keys of the kingdom and the conferral of authority to "bind and loose" clearly suggest that Peter in some way is authorized to function as Jesus' representative and instrument in carrying out Jesus' mission of proclamation of the dawn of God's kingdom and of the building up of Jesus' community. Here we can follow the view of Donald A. Hagner who speaks of Peter's "office and function" as "the" scribe trained for the kingdom (Matt 13:52), even the primary custodian and guarantor of the tradition of the teaching of Jesus, the one able to admit or exclude a person from the eschatological community of

---

27. Carson, op .cit., 369. So also many other commentators.
28. Schnackenburg, op. cit., 159.

salvation.[29] However, in spite of the centrality of the gospel, we need not agree with Hagner that "binding and loosing" have to do only with the gospel as a word of grace and judgment.[30] In Matt 18:18 the authority to "bind and loose" has to do with matters of communal discipline. And in John 20:23 the commission has to do with the conferral of the power of forgiveness. Thus one need not restrict the authority of "binding and loosing" to any single element but view it as inclusive of evangelical, doctrinal, sacramental, pastoral, and administrative powers. In addition, we must note that the gifts and powers granted to Peter carry divine authority and approval. It is by God's revelatory initiative that Peter makes his confession of faith. It is Christ who confers on Peter a special role in building his Church on the rock that is Peter. And Peter's exercise of the powers of "binding and loosing" bears the seal of heaven (i.e., God). In those respects the authorized prerogatives and responsibilities of Peter rightly may be called divine and sacred. From the standpoint of Matthew's Gospel, according to Trilling, "these are not human institutions which have evolved from below, but a divine order from on high. They are among the salutary blessings of the new covenant."[31]

Now the issue arises as to whether or not the above prerogatives and duties are exclusively Peter's. If Matt 16:16–19 was our only testimonial, then we might be inclined to adopt such a view. But of course the question has to be answered in the light of the whole Gospel of Matthew and beyond that of the entire New Testament. It is a paradoxical fact that apart from Matt 16:17–19, Peter's status is not particularly accentuated in the Gospel of Matthew. For Matthew, just as for the other evangelists, Peter is the leader and spokesman of the disciples, but precisely one among them who shares their strengths and weaknesses. His faith and confession of Jesus is the faith and confession of all (Matt 14:33). The power of "binding and loosing" is granted to all (Matt 18:18). Although the context of Matt 18 may involve matters of discipline in a local community, the fact

---

29. Hagner, op. cit., 471–75.

30. Ibid., 473. So also Carson, op. cit., 373.

31. Trilling, op. cit., 65. Schnackenburg, op. cit. 157, notes that the keys of the kingdom, symbolizing right and power, indicate that "Peter exercises his authority on earth in harmony with Jesus, who remains the Lord of his church."

remains that Jesus' authoritative words are addressed to all the disciples who had raised the question about "who is the greatest in the kingdom of heaven" (Matt 18:1). In this context the final arbiter of communal discipline is not Peter, or any single leader who may have succeeded Peter, but the community as a whole (Matt 18:15–18). The parallel power of forgiveness granted to all the disciples (John 20:23) indicates that the community's authorization to "bind and loose" need not be restricted to disciplinary matters. Moreover, at critical points in the Gospel of Matthew, such as the sending out of the disciples (Matt 10:5ff.) and the great commission (Matt 28:16ff.), Peter is given no special attention, much less a distinctive role. The powers to preach, teach, heal, forgive, baptize, pastor, and build up community are granted to all the disciples. In the eschatological kingdom, they will all "sit on twelve thrones, judging the twelve tribes of Israel" (Matt 19:28).

Yet it is true that, as Trilling points out,[32] there is no contradiction that in Matt 16:19 the authority to "bind and loose" is given to Peter and that in Matt 18:18 it is given to the Church. The unity is marked by the subject matter and that both charges come from Jesus. Peter is the first among the disciples but, precisely for that reason, one among the others. From this perspective, according to Trilling, Ephesians can speak of the Church "built on the foundations of the apostles and the prophets" (Eph 2:20) without mentioning Peter. Trilling, a Roman Catholic scholar, draws the following weighty inference about succession: "If the apostolic office lives on in the church, the Petrine office must also live on in it. Otherwise the church would not be faithful to the constitution which Jesus gave to it."[33] We need to keep this deeper principle in mind. But neither should we lose sight of the paradox that in Matthew, apart from Matt 16:17–19, the idea of a Petrine authority qualitatively distinct from the authority of the other disciples is not evident. The logia of Jesus

---

32. Trilling, op. cit., 64–65, 96. Similarly, Schnackenburg, op. cit., 177, writes: "There is no contradiction between the assignment of the power of binding and loosing on one occasion to Peter and then to the community that is in concord with Peter...[but] how the community is formally constituted plays no special role for [Matthew]."

33. Trilling, op. cit., 64.

in Matt 16:17–19 do not reverberate in Matthew's Gospel. Indeed, the evangelist in certain places seems to emphasize a kind of communal egalitarianism (Matt 18:1–4, 18–20; 20:25–27; 23:8–12) that by implication decisively qualifies matters of status, rank, and authority. Is the evangelist conscious of the paradox or is he combining traditions in his Gospel without sufficient literary and theological integration? The answer is a matter of conjecture. We may conclude that, as far as the Gospel of Matthew is concerned, whatever particularity of a Petrine primacy exists—and certainly its specific definition and forms receive no mention—it must be seen in the light of the closest possible sharing of authority and power with the Twelve in the context of the greater reality of the community of faith. In other words, Peter's special role in Matthew is very close to one who functions as *primus inter pares*.[34]

3. Primacy in Paul and Luke

Inquiry into the nature of the Petrine primacy must lead to other landscapes of the New Testament beyond the Gospel of Matthew. The earliest witness to the tradition is represented by the apostle Paul. Paul certainly knew the nickname Cephas, his most frequent reference to Peter.[35] Paul also knew the tradition of Peter as the first witness to the resurrection of Jesus and the authorized leader of the Christian mission to the Jews (1 Cor 15:5; Gal 2:8). When Paul went to Jerusalem some three years after his conversion, it was Peter who received him for an extended visit, acting as a kind of bridge between Paul and James (Gal 1:18–19). This fifteen-day visit, quite apart from personal matters, was particularly significant because "Peter served Paul as a *source of tradition about Jesus*."[36] Furthermore, at his second visit to Jerusalem, Paul willingly submitted his gospel and therefore his own apostolic ministry among the Gentiles to the judgment of the

---

34. This of course is the standard Orthodox position. This is also the conclusion of the Protestant biblical scholars Carson, op. cit., 368, and Hagner, op. cit., 468. Hagner adds that Peter functions as a representative of the disciples and of the whole Church, without specifying implications of such ecclesial representation.

35. 1 Cor 1:12; 3:22; 9:5; 15:5; Gal 1:18; 2:9–14.

36. Raymond Brown et al., op cit., 23. The emphasis is in the original.

Jerusalem apostles (Gal 2:2, 9), no small matter given Paul's sense of apostolic vocation and freedom. From Paul's viewpoint, therefore, Peter was a figure of considerable magnitude and influence not only in Jerusalem but also more widely in the early Church (Gal 2:11; 1 Cor 1:12; 3:22; 9:5).

Is there a Petrine primacy in Paul? Was Peter truly Cephas for Paul? The answer is yes and no. For Paul, Peter served as a secure contact with the Jerusalem church and as a source of knowledge of the historical Jesus. For Paul, Peter enjoyed a primacy in Jerusalem insofar as, by common agreement, he had been "entrusted" with the gospel to the Jews just as Paul had been "entrusted" with the gospel to the Gentiles (Gal 2:7–8). Peter was one of the prominent leaders of the Jerusalem church, the reputed "pillars," although interestingly James heads the list in Gal 2:9. Perhaps at the writing of Galatians James had assumed the leadership of the Jerusalem church. Most important of all is that Peter, along with James and John, acted as arbiters in the matter of the Gentile mission and the agreed division of labors in the Christian mission between Paul and the Jerusalem leaders (Gal 2:9) during the earliest years of the Church.

However, Paul's own sense of direct apostolic authorization from the risen Christ is absolutely clear and viewed as in no way inferior to that of Peter and the others (Gal 1:12ff.; 1 Cor 9:1; 15:8ff.). When the truth of the gospel was at stake, with James apparently being the leader of a different vision, Paul did not hesitate to deliver a vigorous public rebuke of Peter about the implied reversal of policy toward Christian Gentiles (Gal 2:11–14). There is in Paul no idea whatever of other apostolic figures, and certainly no notion of a single universal leader, possessing keys of authority and exercising supervision over his largely Gentile congregations, for whom Paul himself was the leader and slave (2 Cor 4:5).[37] As his letters everywhere attest, his own view and practice of leadership was defined by a self-effacing sense of teamwork, an astonishing flexibility, and a delicate balance in the use of authority and persuasion, all in the service of Christ and the gospel. Thus Paul's remarkably humble move to lay

---

37. A striking image invoked by C. K. Barrett, *Church, Ministry, and Sacraments in the New Testament* (Grand Rapids: Eerdmans, 1985), 39, who has some insightful things to say about ministry in the New Testament.

his gospel before the Jerusalem leaders, to whose reputed position he could refer with a touch of disdain (Gal 2:6, 9), was due more likely to other reasons than any formal obligations to a primacy claimed by Peter or others. For Paul, the importance of Jerusalem is shown by his recurrent visits there despite personal dangers as a perceived apostate. To bring the gifts of Gentiles to Jerusalem was a crucial part of "magnifying" his ministry for the conversion of his fellow Jews (Rom 11:13–14; 15:25ff.; 2 Cor 9:12–14). Above all, Paul's profound understanding of the oneness of the gospel (1 Cor 15:11) and unity of the Church as the body of Christ (1 Cor 10:16–21) made the prospect of a divided Church of Jewish and Gentile Christians unthinkable. As far as Paul is concerned, to the extent that a Petrine ministry was operative in the early years of the Church, it was a matter of commission to service and pastoral usefulness in a particular historical situation, and not a matter of a permanent and universal authority not shared by other apostolic figures.

The preeminence of Peter as leader of the apostles and in the early Church is also evident in Luke-Acts, a two-volume work written during the last third of the first century. Although Luke does not preserve, and perhaps does not know, the tradition about Peter surnamed Cephas, his Gospel presents a favorable portrait of Peter that smoothly fits with the picture of Peter's career in Acts.[38] In particular, Luke omits Jesus' harsh rebuke of Peter as Satan reported in Mark and seems to underscore Peter's role as witness to the resurrection (Luke 24:12, 34). Notable is that Luke's version of the prediction of Peter's denial, seen in a context of cosmic struggle with Satan, is accompanied by Jesus' promise of restoration and a charge to "strengthen your brothers" (Luke 22:32). This role is clearly fulfilled in the Book of Acts where Peter functions as the leader and spokesman of the Jerusalem church in the early years. Luke's Gospel gives no evidence of any distinct prerogatives granted to Peter, such as to be the "rock" of the Church and to "bind and loose" matters in the community. The mission charge by the risen Jesus is addressed to all the disciples without differentiation (Luke 24:44–49; Acts 1:8). As in the Gospel of Matthew, the eschatological privilege of sitting on the twelve thrones

---

38. Raymond Brown et al., op. cit., 127ff.

judging the twelve tribes of Israel is granted to all (Luke 22:30; cf. Rev 21:14).

Can we speak of a Petrine primacy in Acts? Peter takes the initiative in the election of Matthias, but does not himself make the decision (Acts 1:15–16, 23–26). He delivers the Pentecost sermon but yet "standing with the eleven" (Acts 2:14). He is clearly the leader and spokesman of the early Christian community, but the Twelve and the entire Church select the seven deacons as an attempt to settle the dispute between the "Hebrews" and the "Hellenists" (6:1–6). Peter is the one to discipline Ananias and Sapphira (Acts 5:1ff., 8ff.), but the apostles together dispatch both Peter and John to oversee the mission in Samaria (Acts 8:14). The crucial outbreak of the mission to Gentiles by God's initiative occurs through Peter's reluctant contact with Cornelius (Acts 10). But then Peter had to give account to rank and file Christians (Acts 11:1–3) and later to "the apostles and the elders" at the apostolic council (Acts 15:6ff.). At this council, it is James who seems to have the primary voice (Acts 15:13–21), while the community participates in the process (Acts 15:22ff.). For Luke, the apostle Peter is a major figure in the early Church but Paul in particular is the "vessel of election" (Acts 9:15), the great hero of the Christian mission and an exemplary shepherd (Acts 20:17–38). As the story of Acts progresses, James seems to take the reigns of the Jerusalem church (Acts 15:13ff.; 21:18), while Peter vanishes from the scene with no explanation about his future work or role in the Church that remains speculative at best.[39] From the Lucan perspective, leadership is a communal enterprise featuring a number of major figures, including Peter, James, Paul, and Stephen, as well as the participation of the presbyters and the community as a whole. The witness of Acts highlights the prominence of Peter but

---

39. Ibid., 48–49, offer three possible interpretative options for the evidence of Acts regarding the role of Peter: a) that Peter and the Twelve were never really local leaders, a position held by James, but were concerned with a kind of universal leadership; b) that Peter was a local leader upon whose departure James took his place, with no issue of universal leadership being in question at all, and c) that Peter was a universal leader operating from Jerusalem, a position transferred to James at some point. My opinion is that the witness of Acts favors the second option.

provides no evidence of primacy as status and authority superior to those of other apostolic leaders.

4. Primacy in Other New Testament Texts

We must also briefly examine the later New Testament tradition, namely, the Gospel of John, 1–2 Peter, and the Pastoral Epistles. In the Gospel of John we find echoes of the Cephas tradition (John 1:42) and the confession of faith by Peter (John 6:68). However, no special privileges accorded to Peter are reported in these contexts. A striking feature in the Gospel of John is the parallelism between Peter and the beloved disciple, especially chapters 13–21. The beloved disciple is presented in more favorable light because of his loyalty to Jesus and his insight at crucial points.[40] The intent of the comparison is to show neither rivalry between the two, nor the superiority of the beloved disciple. The beloved disciple himself bears witness to Peter's abundant haul of fish (John 21:11, 24) and to Jesus' restoration of Peter as a shepherd of Christ's flock (John 21:15–17),[41] a role fulfilled by Peter in the earliest years of the Jerusalem church. Does John 21:15–17 imply a special universal pastoral authority granted to Peter? The passage in isolation could be read in that fashion. If so, it should also be noted that the flock is Christ's flock, pastoral authority is rooted in love, and the emphasis is put on Peter's responsibility, not the flock's obedience.[42] In the larger context of the Fourth Gospel, however, Jesus addresses his Easter commission to the disciples as a group (John 20:21–23). That Peter carries higher pastoral authority (primacy) than the beloved disciple is not a credible interpretation of

---

40. Pheme Perkins, op. cit., 96–97, lists the reasons for the special standing of the beloved disciple: he is closer to Jesus than Peter at the Last Supper; he grasps the significance of the empty tomb; he stands at the foot of the cross along with Jesus' mother; he perceives the risen Jesus on the lake shore, and he lives a long life of witness and leadership. In contrast, 98–101, Peter remonstrates against the foot washing; he uses the sword; he denies the Lord, but yet is restored as a shepherd of Christ's people, a ministry sealed with martyrdom.

41. See Barrett, op. cit., 48–49. Moreover, Jesus' words in John 21:21–23 undercut a spirit of rivalry or question about superiority.

42. Raymond Brown et al., op. cit., 142–43.

witness of the Fourth Gospel. A more reasonable position is to view the parallelism between Peter and the beloved disciple as a way of highlighting the leadership of the beloved disciple in comparison with Peter's known prestige in the wider Christian tradition.[43] Just as Peter is the revered leader of others, so also the beloved disciple is the revered leader of his community. Unless one wants to speculate that significant historical facts were forgotten or deliberately altered, the witness of John, just as that of Luke, gives no support to the principle of primacy as superior privilege and authority, that is, Peter being a special successor to Jesus in a qualitatively different way from the status and role of the other apostles.[44]

The letters of 1–2 Peter are testimonials to the prestige of Peter probably in Asia Minor (1 Pet 1:1; 2 Pet 3:15). Whether or not the authenticity of these letters can be established,[45] they underscore the ongoing preeminence of Peter in the Christian tradition in intriguing comparison with Paul. First Peter reflects a core Pauline theme[46] and is addressed to Christians in areas that include the Pauline mission. Further, by the adoption of the Pauline letter form and consequently the Pauline pattern of maintaining authority by means of apostolic letters, 1–2 Peter remake Peter "in the image of Paul."[47] First Peter presents Peter as a "copresbyter" giving authoritative instructions to other "presbyters" on how to shepherd God's flock under the authority of Christ the chief shepherd (5:1–3). This letter attests to a post-Pauline situation in which, just as in the case of the Pastorals (and

---

43. Ibid., 138–39. However, Savvas Agouridis in an essay, "Peter and John in the Fourth Gospel," in his book Αρα γε Γινῶσκεις Α Αναγινωῶσκεις (Athens: Artos Zoes, 1989), 132–37, advocates the thesis that the Fourth Gospel emphasizes the "superior authority" (yet not primacy) of the beloved disciple in order to counteract Peter's prestige and authority among Christian groups in Asia Minor which have misunderstood the Synoptic tradition, 137. This essay was first published in *Studia evangelica*, IV, ed. F. L. Cross (Berlin: Akademie, 1968).

44. So also Perkins, op. cit., 103.

45. Perkins, op. cit., 120, and many other Roman Catholic and Protestant biblical scholars treat 1 Peter as pseudonymous. Second Peter is almost universally regarded as pseudonymous.

46. The theme of sharing the suffering and future glory of Christ (1 Pet 1:6–7:11; 2:21; 3:18; 4:13; 5:9–10).

47. Perkins, op. cit., 125.

Luke), "presbyters" have gained prominence as community leaders.[48] The comparison with Paul is more direct in 2 Peter where Paul and his Gentile converts are explicitly mentioned (2 Pet 3:15–16). Second Peter, although marked by a very different form and outlook, portrays Peter as the privileged eyewitness of Jesus' transfiguration (2 Pet 1:16–19) and therefore an authoritative interpreter of Paul, even a guardian of the faith, over against heretical readings of a collection of Paul's letters (2 Pet 3:16).

Is there a Petrine primacy in 1–2 Peter? The evidence from 2 Peter is more convincing in this regard. According to Orthodox theologian Jerry Klinger, Dean and Professor of the Orthodox Section of the Christian Theological Institute of Warsaw, 2 Peter provides the "first sign" of the idea of primacy in the developing tradition around the early second century, yet an idea claimed for both Peter and Paul in their respective traditions.[49] Raymond Brown and his group similarly discern a "Petrine magisterium" in 2 Peter, outstripping a parallel "Pauline magisterium" claimed by the Pastorals as protection against heretical teaching (2 Tim 1:13; 4:3–4).[50] Brown and the ecumenical group also note that, while Peter and Paul are the most important figures in the development of the canonical tradition, one could as well speak of a "James magisterium" in the developing apocryphal tradition.[51] From this perspective, we may see in 1–2 Peter the first intimations of a developing tradition of Petrine primacy, yet in the larger

---

48. Raymond E. Brown and John P. Meier, op. cit., 138–39. Of course the growing status and authority of presbyters in the development of Church order is disputed. Barrett, op. cit., 41–42, argues that "presbyter" in 1 Peter is not a technical term but signifies merely "older man."

49. Jerzy Klinger, "The Second Epistle of Peter: An Essay in Understanding," *St. Vladimir's Theological Quarterly* 17, nos. 1–2 (1973): 189. Klinger finds that 2 Peter, in contradistinction to Matt 16:18, John 21:15–17 and Luke 22:32 (Jesus' prayer for Peter's steadfastness in the faith), anchors Peter's authority to the transfiguration as the highest degree of enlightenment into the Christian mysteries. Perkins, op. cit., interprets the witness of 2 Peter in this way: "Peter is once again remade in the image of Paul. Peter can become the universal shepherd in the larger church if his letters provide the basis for a resolution of the controversy over the interpretation of Paul's letters," 125.

50. Raymond Brown et al., op. cit., 155–56.

51. Ibid.

context of divergent Christian traditions that variously exalt a plurality of prominent figures, including Peter, Paul, James, and John.

As far as the church of Rome is concerned, we may note that at the end of the first century Clement of Rome addresses the Corinthians with a sense of authority but writes on behalf of the whole Church, not in his own name. Clement cites both Peter and Paul as luminous examples of steadfast suffering in the face of persecution and martyrdom (*1 Clement* 5.2–7), but makes no reference to any special privileges accruing thereby to the bishop of Rome. Clement refers to the idea of apostolic succession (*1 Clement* 42.4–5), but gives no evidence of being a monarchical bishop. When Ignatius of Antioch writes his letter to the Roman Christians, he addresses the church of Rome as a whole, not a single leader of distinct authority. According to Raymond Brown and John Meier, the single-bishop structure did not arise in Rome until nearly the middle of the second century.[52] In their view, by the 80s and 90s of the first century, Antioch (Matthew) and Rome (*1 Clement*) were invoking the image of Peter as a "symbol of the center" between the contrasting positions of James and Paul. Peter exercised a wider apostolate in the early Church than that suggested by Paul (Gal 2:7–8), but he was neither a bishop whether in Antioch or Rome; nor did he wear a papal tiara, all of which were later developments in the Christian tradition.[53]

Conclusions

The above review of the New Testament texts pertaining to Peter's role among the Twelve, in the early Church, and the subapostolic period leads to the following conclusions from this writer's standpoint:

1. Isolated texts in the Gospels (Matt 16:17–19; Luke 22:31–32; John 21:15–17) provide evidence of solemn logia of Jesus conferring distinct privileges of authority and leadership on the apostle Peter.

---

52. Raymond E. Brown and John P. Meier, op. cit., 164, where they note that, for example, Ignatius's letter to the Romans (ca. 110) is not addressed to a single reigning bishop, the pattern of Ignatius's letters.

53. Ibid., 215.

These privileges may be described as a particular Petrine ministry, or even primacy, in terms of both "function" and "status" insofar as these aspects cannot be separated from each other, nor from the person of Peter.

2. Jesus said that Peter was to be "the rock" on which Jesus would build his Church but did not say specifically how and to what extent (at least no words of Jesus have been preserved in this regard). Since the role of Peter remains in this respect undefined, the "primacy" of Peter must be critically assessed in terms of the larger contexts of the Gospels and the other New Testament writings. From this perspective, the privileges given to Peter, and the actual role of Peter in the early Church, must be seen in the closest possible association with the privileges and role of the Twelve and the other apostolic leaders who are equally granted divine commissions to preach and teach, to heal and serve, to pastor and discipline. Peter is a preeminent figure in the New Testament but not the only one. No single apostolic figure enjoys universal dominance or exclusive authority in the New Testament. In other words, the "primacy" of Peter is not power over other apostolic figures but an authorized leadership in the context of shared apostolic authority in the common life of the Church.

3. Further, the New Testament provides no decisive proof whether Peter's role is to be limited to his unique ministry fulfilled especially in the earliest Jerusalem church, a more likely option because of the lack of evidence to the contrary, or whether it also constitutes an intended permanent office of universal significance to be succeeded serially by single leaders. If the latter is argued, based on the principle that apostolic authority continues in the life of the Church and so must the Petrine ministry too, which is a theologically justifiable position, then the definition of the Petrine office in terms of specific forms and extent of power must be evaluated in the context of the developing tradition of Church order. In this respect, neither the logia of Jesus to Peter, nor the actual role of Peter, exercise any particular impact on the growing forms of leadership up to the institution of the monarchical episcopate in Ignatius. We have no evidence that the Christians of the first century viewed Peter as the universal leader of the Church. Indeed, within the New Testament period, one could speak of a Petrine ministry, a Pauline ministry, a

Jacobian ministry, and a Johannine ministry, according to the several great apostolic leaders and their respective impacts in the traditions of particular early Christian communities.[54]

4. The New Testament writings, in part because of numerous controversies within the early Christian communities, attest to an immense urgency toward unity.[55] The concept of God's messianic people, the powerful images of the Church as the body of Christ and the temple of the Holy Spirit, as well as the corporate significance of the acts of baptism and the Lord's supper, all express an intrinsic theological drive toward unity. In these ways, the New Testament bears witness to a rich ecclesiology of communion. Nevertheless, in spite of those powerful unitive factors, the New Testament gives evidence of no inkling whatever that the unity of the Church *requires* a single, universal leader other than Christ. At the critical point of the apostolic council, the governing voice was that of a plurality of leaders, as well as the community as a whole. Moreover, the New Testament writings tend to place the emphasis on the *quality* of participatory ministry for all believers (Rom 12:3–8, etc.), including those in leadership positions (Matt 20:20–28; John 13:7–17; Acts 20:18–35; 1 Tim 3:1–7; 1 Pet 5:1–4), rather than the specific developing *forms* of ministry, largely variegated and fluid. The critical factors behind the development of the monarchical episcopate (a trajectory already evident in the Pastorals) and much later the primacy of the bishop of Rome claiming universal powers, must be assessed according to their own historical and theological contexts. In such assessment one must not ignore the possibility that a historical reversal of emphasis occurred, or at least a tendency toward authoritarian forms of leadership, to the

54. Larry W. Hurtado, *Lord Jesus Christ: Devotion to Jesus in Earliest Christianity* (Grand Rapids: Eerdmans, 2003), 587, points out that the canonical collection of the fourfold gospel, allowing for a plurality of witness to the Jesus traditions, affirms reliance on the fullness of the apostolic tradition rather than on univocal claims centered on single figures or single Gospels. In addition, one should be mindful that the developing authority of the monarchical episcopate was balanced by the coleadership of presbyters and the participation of the people of God in the election of presbyters and bishops.

55. For example, Matt 18:15–20; John 10:16; 15:1–17; 17:20–23; Acts 15:1–29; Rom 15:7ff.; 1 Cor 12:12–13; Eph 2:14–20; 2:4–10; 4:1–6 and many other texts.

detriment of the fuller and more vital understanding of ministry in the Church.

5. The practical challenge of unity, as well as the theological urgency behind it, favor the value of a visible universal leader, just as they favor a visible local leader in the person of the bishop. Unity can hardly be maintained without certain patterns of worship, teaching, and order, including the embodiment of unity in specific persons and offices of leadership. In this respect, the New Testament can be said to support in part a Petrine ministry, upon which to define a historically developed and universally acknowledged Petrine office as an option, but one fully based on the principles of shared authority, love, and service, rather than on exclusive status, rights, and jurisdiction. It may be that, in the final analysis, Roman Catholic ecclesiology requires a universal leader, while Orthodox ecclesiology settled on the local bishop and the universal episcopate as signs and instruments of unity. In either case, the decisive factor remains the quality of servant leadership in truth and love in Christ's Church, which also provides the hope of future prospects of agreement and reconciliation of all concerned on the question of primacy.

Summary of Discussion

Several points of the morning discussion were taken up again, with a similar outcome.

From a Catholic perspective, Peter's ministry is clearly presented in the New Testament, not only in Matt 16 but also in John 21. Peter is seen as having an intermediate role between Paul and James; he is the only one to be called rock and shepherd; he is the one who drags the net—symbol of the Church—to the shore (John 21).

Though Orthodox theologians recognize that Peter played a representational role, he was not the only one to do so. They do not clearly discern a specific role for Peter, since he represents the gifts, the power, and the mandate that Jesus entrusted to the group of the twelve apostles, and to each one of them.

A basic question was raised from the Orthodox side: Is it possible to conceive a primacy of the bishop of Rome without reference to the ministry of Peter? Would that be acceptable and satisfactory to the Catholic Church? What are we concerned with: the definition and continuation of a specific Petrine ministry or the exercise of a ministry of unity in faith and love, on the universal level? This distinction may be helpful in the present discussion.

According to the Catholic tradition, the relation between the primacy of the bishop of Rome and the ministry of Peter is of fundamental importance. Tradition and Scripture should be kept together. The traditional link between the ministry of the bishop of Rome and the ministry of Peter, as supported by the Catholic Church, should be discussed in the light of the New Testament, by a common reading of the key references.

Part of the discussion was once more concerned with historical developments. The latter are not necessary, though all believe that they take place under the guidance of the Holy Spirit. History consequently is not entirely neutral. Starting from the New Testament, different developments were and are possible. It is in the light of the New Testament and the guidance of the Holy Spirit that we have to reflect on our different traditions.

The expression *primus inter pares* was used by several participants. There was a general agreement that its meaning can differ considerably according to the term that is emphasized more strongly: do we emphasize *primus* or *pares*? In order to avoid ambiguity, the meaning of this expression should be defined with greater accuracy.

PAPAL PRIMACY AND PATRIARCHAL PENTARCHY IN THE ORTHODOX TRADITION*

Vlassios Phidas

The canonical institution of papal primacy had been organically integrated in the common tradition of both Eastern and Western churches before, but also after, the Great Schism of 1054. But whereas, before the schism, it functioned in favor of the unity of the church, after the schism, for various reasons, it is accused of having caused not only the continuance of the schism but also the subsequent breach of ecclesial unity that occurred in Western Christianity in the Protestant Reformation, as underlined also in the recent encyclical *Ut unum sint.*

It is true that Orthodox and Roman Catholic theology each in its own way explains how papal primacy was understood differently in the first and second millenniums of the life of the Church. This emerges also from the relevant international literature. The difference could be ascribed to the fact that Roman Catholic and Orthodox theologians interpret differently the evidence provided by the sources of the first millennium. Whatever those interpretations may be, they are nevertheless subject to the absolute criterion of the ecclesial self-understanding and coherent practice of that time.

Yet the difference could also be due to the fact that after the schism of 1054, the theory of papal primacy underwent a substantial

---

* May 22, 2003 (morning session). Original text in French.

change. This transformation could explain the theological reactions observed in both East and West, particularly in the theology of the reforming currents from the fourteenth to the sixteenth centuries (the *via synodica*, the reforming councils, and the Protestant Reformation) and in the debates and the decisions taken on this matter (*De residentia episcoporum*) by the great Council of Trent (1545–1563). These reactions could be powerful arguments to sustain the affirmations of the Orthodox theologians.

1. Administrative Development and Conciliar Consciousness

In the common canonical tradition of the first millennium, ecclesial administration was indissolubly associated, on the one hand, with the synodal structure of an administrative jurisdiction and, on the other hand, with the canonical regulations regarding the allocation of the right of ordination (*jus ordinandi*), which includes also the right of judgment (*jus jurandi*) of the bishops. In fact, what is most important in ecclesial administration "is the ordination of bishops."[1] Thus the allocation of the right to ordain and to judge the bishops in clearly defined and well-delimitated territorial areas shaped the one administrative body of the local church, within which the conciliar consciousness of the universal church (provincial, major, patriarchal synods) expresses itself. This interpenetration of the administrative system and of the conciliar consciousness served to structure hierarchically the local conciliar bodies with a concrete administrative head (metropolitan, archbishop or exarch, patriarch) and concrete members, that is, the respective bodies of bishops or the metropolitans of the various administrative districts.

In this sense, the institution of the provincial synod is closely linked to the metropolitan system. The provincial synod chooses, ordains, and judges the metropolitan and the bishops of the province.[2] This is why the canons prohibit any ordination and judg-

---

1. Rhalli-Potli, *Syntagma*, 2:129.
2. Canons 4, 5, and 6 of the First Ecumenical Council; canons 13, 14, 15, 19, and 20 of the Council of Antioch, etc.

ment outside the limits of a concrete province, for "no bishop may dare pass from his province to another, and ordain there."[3] This typical form of administrative autonomy of a local church is the root of the canonical notion of the administrative autocephaly of the local church. This is what the patriarch of Antioch, Theodore Balsamon, appropriately underlines in his comment on canon 2 of the Second Ecumenical Council: "Note that it emerges from the present canon that in the past all diocesan metropolitans were autocephalous and that they were ordained by their own synods."[4]

Thus, the function of the provincial synod and its right to elect, ordain, and judge the metropolitan and the bishops of the province determine the administrative identity of the metropolitan system. The metropolitan of the province convenes the provincial synod, presides over it, and implements its decisions. All problems arising in his province must be solved by mobilizing the provincial synod. As chief of the administration, the metropolitan must obligatorily attend the synod, for, according to canon 16 of the Council of Antioch, "a plenary synod is only one which is attended by the metropolitan." For this reason, according to canon 19 of the same council, "a bishop cannot be elected without the synod and without the presence of the metropolitan; in addition to the indispensable presence of the latter, it would certainly be desirable that all coministers of the province be present, whom the metropolitan will have to convene by letter."

In this context, mention should be made of the significant comment made by the well-known Byzantine canonist Jean Zonaras about canon 6 of the First Ecumenical Council: "Nothing will be in due form without their opinion (that of the metropolitans) regarding the ecclesial administration, of which the consecration of bishops is the highest and most important part."[5] The general aim of the administrative system is rightly expressed in the thirty-fourth apostolic canon: "The bishops of each nation must recognize their primate and consider him as their head; they should not do too much without his advice, and each of them should take care only of what regards his diocese and the countryside attached to his diocese. But he too should do nothing

---

3. Canon 13 of the Council of Antioch, etc.
4. Rhalli-Potli, *Syntagma*, 2:171.
5. Ibid., 2:29.

without the advice of all; so will concord prevail and the Father and the Son and the Holy Spirit be glorified." In commenting on this canon, Jean Zonaras points out that "when the head does not take care of the health of the bodies, the bodies move in a faulty way or even become completely useless; similarly, the body of the Church, if its primate, he who has the function of head, does not benefit from the honor due him, will act in a disordered and faulty way."[6]

This canonical principle of administrative autocephaly of the local churches was weakened by the imprecise decrees of canons 2 and 6 of the Second Ecumenical Council. Besides, the arbitrary behavior of Arian partisans on the occasion of the election and trial of Orthodox bishops made it surely necessary to control the appropriateness of the decisions taken by the Eastern provincial synods to avoid the persecution of Orthodox bishops. This is why canon 14 of the Council of Antioch and canons 3, 4, and 5 of the Council of Sardica introduced—as we shall see later on—extraordinary and temporary procedures to control the decisions of the provincial synods.

Thus, in the way it operated, the metropolitan system no longer sufficed to meet the needs of the local church. The attempt of the Second Ecumenical Council to submit the metropolitans to a more extended authority, the major synod, failed (canons 2 and 6). Other canonical solutions had to be found. This led to the creation of the patriarchal system by subjecting all metropolitans to the five patriarchal sees: Rome, Constantinople, Alexandria, Antioch, and Jerusalem. Despite the appearance of certain currents aimed at imposing the suprametropolitan authority of these sees—which were endowed with canonically warranted honorary primacies (canons 6 and 7 of the First Ecumenical Council, canons 2 and 3 of the Second Ecumenical Council, canon 36 of the Quinisextum Council)—the metropolitans kept a certain administrative autonomy up until the Fourth Ecumenical Council. These currents, aimed at imposing a suprametropolitan authority regarding the right to ordain and judge the bishops, reduced and finally abolished the administrative autonomy of the metropolitans.

---

6. Ibid., 45.

Already from the end of the fourth century, sees with a considerable authority endeavored to extend their administrative jurisdiction to the detriment of metropolitan autonomy. The first half of the fifth century shows that the sees of Rome, Constantinople, Alexandria, Antioch, and Jerusalem often tried to make administrative claims that finally succeeded in abolishing the metropolitan autonomy and establishing the patriarchal system in ecclesial administration. Almost all metropolitan provinces were submitted to the suprametropolitan jurisdiction of the sees to which, by conciliar decision, a canonical honorary primacy was due. Except for the imprecision regarding the jurisdiction of the bishop of Rome in the West, the Fourth Ecumenical Council regulated the administrative boundaries of the canonical jurisdiction of the Eastern sees.[7]

Based on the "ancient custom," the appearance of the suprametropolitan authority of the five patriarchal sees vested with an honorary canonical primacy modified deeply and redistributed the right to ordain and judge the bishops within the universal Church. The introduction of the pentarchy of the patriarchs in the administration of the universal Church had serious consequences:

a) The metropolitans were deprived of their administrative autocephaly, but they kept their internal autonomy. Thus, although the ordination of the metropolitans rested with the respective patriarchal see, the election and the ordination of the bishops still remained within the canonical competence of the provincial synod.

b) The patriarch of each of the five patriarchal sees was recognized as the new autocephalous authority in the administration of the universal Church. Therefore, although he was himself elected and ordained by the patriarchal synod, he exercised directly the right to ordain the metropolitans and indirectly, through the latter, the bishops.

2. The Honorary Primacies and the Patriarchal Institution

The extraordinary authority of the pentarchy of patriarchs was based on two combined canonical principles: the extraordinary honor-

---

7. V. Phidas, *L'institution de la Pentarchie des patriarches*, I (Athens, 1969), 168–324.

ary primacies, on the one hand, and the suprametropolitan jurisdiction regarding the right to ordain and judge the bishops, on the other hand. This new institution relativized any other form of local administrative autocephaly. Indeed, never before had a local church acquired, on any account, all the privileges due a patriarchal see. Nor has any given local church ever been considered "equal in honor" to the patriarchal sees. It is true that each of these sees had been vested with an honorary primacy canonically warranted by an ecumenical council and that each had a suprametropolitan administrative function. The allocation of honorary primacies was not foreign to the ecclesial concern for the preservation of the communion in true faith and in charity among the local churches throughout the world. Through both the uninterrupted succession of the apostolic faith and the universal influence of their ecclesial life, these patriarchal sees acquired a great authority within the universal Church.

The jurisdictional division into territorial regions in no way abolished or reduced the exceptional function assigned to the privileged sees that had a canonical honorary primacy in the universal Church. On the contrary, this division confirmed the exceptional authority of those sees, exercised independently of any administrative regulation. Consequently, the "honorary primacies" and their order of precedence could not be ignored in the functioning of the pentarchy of the patriarchs, even when it was a question of solving administrative matters. Indeed, they were closely related to the structure and the canonical manifestation of conciliar consciousness in terms of both patriarchal jurisdiction and the universal fulfillment of the Church of God.

The right of appeal (ἔκκλητον) is a significant manifestation in the canonical tradition. Thus, the "first see" (prima sedes) had the canonical right to receive and judge in appeal any case beyond its own jurisdictional boundaries, that is, arising in the life of the universal Church. Every administrative system operated on this principle, that is, through the close link between the honorary primacy of the first see and the right of appeal. We know that canons 3, 4, and 5 of the Council of Sardica (343) indicate clearly such a conception concerning the competence of the bishop of Rome; independently of the interpretation given to this canonical trend.

The importance of the Council of Sardica would not have surpassed that of the other local councils assembled in the fourth century had not its canons been used as the main argumentation in favor of papal primacy and had they not exerted such influence on the relationships between Eastern and Western churches. Indeed, canons 3, 4, and 5 of the Council of Sardica are put forward from the beginning of the fifth century—together with canon 6 of the First Ecumenical Council—to provide a canonical basis for the ecclesial primacy claimed by the Roman See. During the Acacian schism (484–519) notably, Pope Gelasius I (492–496) integrated them organically in the theory of the Roman primacy. They are still alleged in the conflict between Rome and Constantinople to support canonically the supremacy of the old over the new Rome.

Therefore, it seems evident that the Council of Sardica has a particular importance for the West, especially on account of canons 3, 4, and 5, which are regulations interpreted by several canonists as a very clear legal foundation on which to base the prerogative of the papal see to judge in appeal all the bishops of the Church. This opinion is supported by a series of arguments in the present canonical literature, but there is also a series of solid arguments against it. They derive from the fact that canons 3, 4, and 5 of Sardica granted to the bishop of Rome not a right of appeal but merely a procedural competence meant to guarantee that the verdict of the local synod was not marred by any vice when judged on appeal.[8] Independently of the way the canonical content of these canons is interpreted, it appears clearly that it had a capital importance on the historical evolution not only of papal primacy but also of ecclesial relations between East and West.

In this connection, it must be underlined that the Council of Sardica did not recognize any preexistent canonical right in the See of Rome. Its members decided, through a conciliar procedure, to grant a canonical right to the bishop of Rome both to apply the right of appeal and to establish a procedure to guarantee the legitimacy of the local conciliar authority, called to judge on appeal the contested first sentence. Therefore, the proposal of Bishop Hosius of Córdoba was submitted to the council, which had the supreme right to accept or reject it. It is precisely for this reason that it was introduced with the consecrated formula "If you judge it sound, let us honor the memory

8. Ibid., 96–129.

of the apostle Peter." Thus, the council was called upon to appraise the question and to decide whether a canonical right should be given to the bishop of Rome. This is why it finally accepted the proposition of Hosius, with the usual formula: "What was said has been approved" (ταλεχθεντα ἥρεσαν).

The legates of the pope submitted the same claim to the Council of Carthage (419), with the request that the right of appeal to the papal see be acknowledged. To that effect, they relied on canons 3, 4, and 5 of the Council of Sardica by presenting them, deliberately or not, as canons elaborated by the First Ecumenical Council and thus alleging a right granted by a synod. The Council of Carthage first examined the authenticity of the relation between the said canons and those of the First Ecumenical Council. Then it rejected the request by a conciliar letter. The reason put forward was that the request was not based on a decision of the First Ecumenical Council. It is interesting to note that both the claim by the Roman See and its rejection by the Council of Carthage were based exclusively on the authority of the First Ecumenical Council, which demonstrates that the institution of the ecumenical council is the supreme authority in the Church.

The following is the decisive passage of the conciliar letter: "Your Holiness will also expel, as is fitting, those priests and lower clerics who shamelessly take refuge with you: for this has never been imposed on the church of Africa by any decision of the Fathers, and the decrees of the Council of Nicaea clearly refer both the clerics of a lower grade and even the bishops to the proper metropolitans. It was wisely and justly understood that all proceedings arising anywhere should be settled locally, knowing that the support of the Holy Spirit would not fail those involved, through which the justice of the pontiffs of Christ appears full of wisdom and without weaknesses; all the more so as anyone with doubts about the sentence of the investigators can appeal to the synods of his own province or even to the plenary synod. Unless there might be some who believe that our God could inspire a single man with his justice, whoever he might be, and deny it to the countless pontiffs gathered in synod....Concerning the sending of some attendants of Your Holiness, we do not find this to be authorized by any synod of the Fathers; for what was presented by Faustinus as a decision of the Council of Nicaea we did not find in the truthful copies of that council, made from the authentic texts.... Therefore, do not send commissioned clerics, nor give any to those who ask for it, so that we do not seem to be introducing the world's arrogance of domination into the Church of Christ."[9]

It is evident that the East considers with the same spirit the exceptional authority of the See of Constantinople, as shown in canons 9 and 17 of the Fourth Ecumenical Council, which recognize in this see the right of appeal outside its own administrative jurisdiction. The comments of the well-known Byzantine canonists Jean Zonaras and Theodore Balsamon highlight the relation of the right of appeal with the honorary primacy of that see.[10] Thus, the patriarch of Antioch, Theodore Balsamon, in commenting on canon 3 of the Council of Sardica, points out significantly: "What is defined for the pope must be so also for the patriarch of Constantinople, for the latter is honored in all things in the same manner as the pope through different decrees."[11]

3. The Two Different Concepts of Primacy

In the canonical institution of the pentarchy, there is a hierarchical order among the patriarchal sees, based on a later interpretation of canon 6 of the First Ecumenical Council (325). Thus, after the promulgation of canon 3 of the Second Ecumenical Council, the presidency of the council was passed to the archbishop of Constantinople, Gregory the Theologian, and, after his resignation, to his successor, Nectarius. This fact shows clearly the importance of the order of precedence in the honorary primacy for presiding at an ecumenical council. The criterion of equal authority in the honorary primacy, then, could not weaken the importance of the hierarchical order of precedence in the pentarchy. This is why canon 3 of the Second Ecumenical Council assigns to the bishop of Constantinople the honorary primacy "after the bishop of Rome," by which he is

---

9. Rhalli-Potli, *Syntagma*, 3:609–13.
10. Ibid., 2:237–40, 258–63.
11. Ibid., 3:237.

given the second place in the hierarchy of the sees honored with a similar primacy.

It is evident that the honorary primacy is not a purely honorary privilege, as it is associated with an exceptional authority (*singularis auctoritas*), which consists in guaranteeing the unity of the Church in the true faith and in the canonical discipline. Thus, in the order of precedence of the patriarchal sees, the *prima sedes* has a particular role in the manner in which the patriarchal pentarchy functions, for this privilege is associated with the presidency and with the function of the ecumenical councils. The bishop of the "first see" takes the presidency in the ecumenical council, and his authority is exercised in the life of the Church. In this sense, when commenting on canon 3 of the Second Ecumenical Council, Jean Zonaras defines clearly the exceptional authority due to the bishop of the first see. He specifies the canonical contents that the order of precedence must have in the functioning of the pentarchy: "It appears clearly that the preposition 'after' indicates a lower grade and a lessening. Otherwise, it would be impossible to keep the same level of honor for the two sees (that is, the old and the new Rome). It is necessary that when the names of the see holders are mentioned, one precedes and the other follows; this during the sessions when they assemble, and in the signatures, when these are needed. The explanation of the 'after,' implying that it is only a temporal preposition that does not indicate any lower grade, is forced, tortuous, and inappropriate."[12]

It is therefore commonly held that from the first centuries *the apostolicity* of the church of Rome was related to the coryphaei of the apostles Peter and Paul, whose deeds and martyrdom provided an extraordinary honor to the flourishing church of the capital city of the Roman Empire, leaving aside the subsequent differences in interpreting the evidence of the sources. The Eastern Church understood in their real dimensions neither the gradual elaboration of the theological theory that distinguishes the ministry of Peter (*officium Petri*) from that of the other apostles nor its discreet association, from the fifth century on, with papal primacy. In fact, they were systematically formulated only after the adoption of canon 28 by the Fourth

---

12. Ibid., 2:174.

74

Ecumenical Council (451), and they limited themselves to the antagonism opposing the old and the new Rome.

Of course, until the ninth century, the historical circumstances did not allow a straightforward exposition of the link between papal primacy and the theological elaboration concerning the particular ministry of Peter. Therefore, the *Libel* of the Council of Constantinople (869–870), favorable to the papal claims, took up almost integrally the *Formulary* of Pope Hormisdas (*Formula Hormisdae*), meant to eliminate the so-called schism of Acacius (519).[13] The two official documents have in common the fact that both refer to the antagonism between Rome and Constantinople on the "equal" or "higher" authority of the Roman See, within the pentarchy of the patriarchs, with regard to the See of Constantinople. The disagreement broke out concerning canon 28: it proclaims that the two sees have "the same" honorary precedence and describes the contents of the dialectical controversy opposing the East to the habitual claims of the papal see concerning its higher authority.

In fact, the Eastern Church situated the entire dialectic on papal primacy in the context of the canonical institution of the pentarchy of the patriarchs. It also refuted as unfounded, and even arrogant, the pope's claims, whatever they might be, without understanding, however, the parallel and latent evolution of the relation between papal primacy and the theory of the "ministry of Peter," of which no official mention was made in any document addressed to the East. In the understanding of the Eastern Church, the pope of Rome was the *patriarch of the West and the first among the five patriarchs.* From then on, until the schism of 1054, the disagreements of all kinds had as their sole purpose to verify the canonical foundations of the mainly administrative claims.

In this sense, the great disagreement between Rome and Constantinople during the patriarchate of Photius was settled through canon 17 of the Council of Constantinople (869–870), which integrated papal primacy into the function of the patriarchal pentarchy: "For this reason, this great and holy council decrees that the ancient custom must be kept in all things for the old and the new Rome as well as for the sees of Alexandria, of Antioch, and of

---

13. V. Phidas, *L'institution de la Pentarchie des patriarches, II* (Athens, 1970), 2:59f.

75

Jerusalem, so that their prelates may have authority on all metropolitans they shall elect and confirm in the dignity of bishop, either by imposing hands on them or by conferring them the pallium: that is to say, to convene them, in case of need, in synodal assembly or to act against them and correct them if ever there was a rumor of some deficit against them." In the same spirit, the Council of Constantinople (879–880) settled this divergence, with the agreement of the papal legates and on the canonical basis introduced by canon 1, concerning the total administrative independence of the Eastern and Western churches.

The Eastern ecclesial consciousness understood papal primacy within the context of the canonical institution of the pentarchy. In fact, it could not imagine the fermentation occurring in the West, which is not mentioned in any official document addressed to the Eastern Church. In addition, it could not accept the pope's claims of a higher authority with regard to the See of Constantinople; these claims were considered contrary to the canonical principle according to which the five patriarchs have equal authority. Thus, the consciousness of the Eastern Church, as manifested in the canonical tradition and in coherent ecclesiastical practice, recognizes at all times the pope of Rome as *primus inter pares* in the pentarchy of the patriarchs. For this reason, it rightly grants him always due honor in all manifestations of ecclesial life.

This is how the canonical tradition and Orthodox ecclesial experience conceive the true role of the "first see" and the authority it was given in the ecumenical council and in the canonical relations between the patriarchs of the universal Church. As a matter of fact, while recognizing in the papal see the exceptional authority due the *prima sedes* within the pentarchy, the Eastern Church maintains that the five patriarchs have equal authority in the celebration of ecumenical councils and in the life of the Church (*primus inter pares*). On the other hand, the Roman church interprets its precedence in the honorary primacies as a primacy of power within or outside the ecumenical council. These currents manifested themselves systematically after the Great Schism (1054). Scholastic theology and the canonical system (*Decretum Gratiani*) of the Western Church developed the idea that papal authority is higher than that of the ecumenical council. On the contrary, the Eastern Church stresses that, in conformity with the canonical tradition, the ecumenical council has an authority higher than that of the pope, and even of the five patriarchs of the universal Church. Thus the first interpretation submits the ecumenical council to the authority of the pope; the second interpretation, on the contrary, subjects the pope and the patriarchs to the authority of the ecumenical council.

Thus, while recognizing the exceptional canonical role due the *prima sedes*, the Eastern Church considers that this role, in terms of ecclesial administration, should only be exercised within the conciliar system. Therefore, it always interprets the relation "papal authority/ ecumenical council" in the canonical context of the relation "patriarchal pentarchy/ecumenical council." Indeed, on the basis of the criteria of canonical tradition and practice, the East insists on the canonical relation "pope/patriarchs" whereas the Western canonical currents redefine the canonical relation on the basis of "pope/episcopal body." In this spirit, the East considers that the pope has only the canonical prerogatives of the *prima sedes* in the system of the patriarchal pentarchy. On the other hand, the West interprets that same authority in the light of doctrine, introducing the theory of a special Petrine ministry to claim a direct relation between the bishop of Rome and the whole episcopal body of the universal Church.

4. Canonical Convergence

It is obvious that in the course of the first millennium and in spite of all sorts of episodic exacerbations, the purely *canonical basis* of primacy determined the relation of the pope of Rome with the Eastern patriarchs. Consequently, during that period, the papal primacy operated as an important institution to defend the unity of the Church in the communion of faith and the bond of charity. But after the schism of 1054, the theory of papal primacy *was dissociated from the canonical institution of the pentarchy of the patriarchs.* It claimed *direct reference to the whole body of bishops of the Church,* from now on associating papal primacy with the theological theory of a special Petrine ministry. Thus, to bring the Petrine ministry to the fore, the papal primacy was dissociated from its canonical foundation while, to bring to the fore its direct reference to the whole episcopal body of the Church, it was separated from the pentarchy of the patriarchs. These two facts clearly constitute changes introduced into the ecclesial tradition of the first millennium. They explain why this primacy was differently appreciated during the second millennium of the historical life of the Church.

The two currents opposed each other at the Council of Ferrara-Florence (1438–1442). Pope Eugene IV was compelled to accept the preliminary conditions set by the Eastern participants for the convocation and the work of the council, since the Eastern Church insisted on applying strictly the conciliar canonical tradition (patriarchal pentarchy). It insisted also on the necessity for the whole of the Western episcopal body to be canonically represented, since the Eastern Church considered that "it would be vain to discuss in the absence of the prelates who were present at the Council of Basle."[14] The four months time assigned to the prelates of Basle to appear at Ferrara-Florence expired, however, without their joining the council. Then Pope Eugene IV availed himself of the canonical criteria of the conciliar tradition to persuade the Eastern delegates to accept the official inauguration of the council: "The pope said: 'Where I am with the king and the patriarch [of Constantinople], there is the whole council of the Christians, all the more so as all the patriarchs and our cardinals are there too.'"[15]

This papal declaration referred, for sure, to the canonical criteria governing the canonical celebration of an ecumenical council. These criteria were clearly defined by the Seventh Ecumenical Council (787), and they concerned the need for the bishops of the old and the new Rome to act together (συνεργοι). They also concerned the need to have the agreement, prior or ulterior, of the other Eastern patriarchs, that is, of Alexandria, Antioch, and Jerusalem (συμφρονουντες). The criteria put forward by the pope could nonetheless also be interpreted according to Western canonical doctrine regarding the superiority of papal authority over that of the ecumenical council.

But when a letter of Pope Agathon was read, Cardinal Julian Cesarini seized the opportunity to expound the positions of the Western tradition: "It follows from this that whenever a disagreement

14. Mansi, 31:491.
15. Ibid., 494.

78

comes up about the faith, it is for the Roman primate to solve it; and once he has spoken, all councils and the whole Church have to conform to that truth."[16] Yet it is true that at the Council of Ferrara-Florence, the position of the Eastern Church, defending the superiority of the authority of the ecumenical council over the authority of the pope, received in principle a de facto approval by the very convocation of the council. The reaction of the metropolitan Bessarion of Nicaea is a very typical expression of the Eastern tradition. He stated that all bishops of the Church have the common function of teaching the peoples but that this expression of faith does not bind the Church, "for it belongs to anyone who respects the common dogmas to expound his own faith to the best of his ability and according to his will; that is, without intending to impose a common teaching or a common credo but by expounding his own faith. Thus, the right to state one's opinion belongs to everybody. In this way, there is a great need for the blessed Agathon—and even for the lesser of the bishops—to teach and counsel the peoples."[17]

In the same sense is to be understood the statement of Metropolitan Bessarion on the canonical relation between the pope and the ecumenical council: "We want you to know, Reverend, that it is not only to the Roman church that we contest the liberty it took [i.e., the addition to the Credo], but also to any church and to any council, even if ecumenical. For, although the Roman church has authority, it has less authority than the ecumenical council and the universal Church. Therefore, if we contest that right to the whole Church, all the more so to the Roman church. And we do not do so on our own initiative but because we believe that the prescriptions of the Fathers forbid it."[18]

Consequently, the Orthodox proposal can only be to reconnect this primacy with the governing criteria of the patristic tradition and ecclesial practice, valid during the first millennium. Those criteria serve the unity of the Church and extend the ecclesial authority of the papal see. The canonical criteria of *territoriality* of the ecclesial jurisdictions and of *conciliarity* in the functioning of the ecclesial body

---

16. Ibid., 600.
17. Ibid., 617.
18. Ibid., 624–25.

have always been the fundamental principles of the patristic tradition concerning the local church. Although they exclude a direct reference to the primacy of the pope with regard to the whole body of the bishops, these principles allow an indirect canonical reference to the whole body of the Church, in the pope's capacity of *first* among the administrative heads of all local churches.

In this context, patristic theology was consistent always with the canonical tradition regarding the way the conciliar system operates and with the ongoing ecclesial practice followed during the period of the ecumenical councils. It is the reason the Eastern Church, up to the schism of the eleventh century, attributed extraordinary honors to the bishop of Rome in his capacity as *patriarch of the West* and as the *first among the five patriarchs of the Church*. In his capacity as *patriarch of the West*, he has the same rights as the four other patriarchs. As the *first in the order of precedence in the pentarchy of the patriarchs*, however, he has the extraordinary function of coordinating his peers in order to face together the serious problems of faith or of canonical discipline threatening the unity of the Church in the communion of faith or in the bond of charity. It is for this reason that Rome reacts sharply when Constantinople contests the exclusivity of that canonical prerogative through the adoption of canon 28 of the Fourth Ecumenical Council.

Consequently, the Orthodox canonical tradition has always considered the papal primacy:

a) Within the framework of the eucharistic ecclesiology regarding the relation between the local church and the universal Church, since the one, holy, catholic, and apostolic Church is fully realized as the body of Christ everywhere and always and is not merely an addition of local churches;

b) Within the context of the extraordinary prerogatives due the *prima sedes* in the canonical institution of the patriarchal pentarchy, that is, within the framework of the Church's administrative system, since the canonical tradition rejects any direct relation of the pope with the episcopal body of the universal Church and considers that papal primacy can be exercised in the communion of faith and the bond of charity among the churches;

c) Within the framework of the operation of the conciliar institution, notably of the ecumenical council, which expresses perfectly the privileges of the first see in the canonical relation between the patriarchal pentarchy and the ecumenical council. Canonical tradition rejects, however, any problematics concerning the superiority of the authority of the pope or a patriarch over that of the ecumenical council.

d) The convergence of the canonical and conciliar criteria in force in the first millennium constitutes a reliable basis to engage in a constructive dialogue on the core of the "ministry of Peter" and on its function in the life of the Church. All that was not attested in the first millennium lacks the ecclesiological and canonical premises that are necessary to serve as a starting point for the dialogue.

Summary of Discussion

This presentation illustrated the historical developments that took place between the New Testament, the first Christian communities, and later constitutional features of the Church, in particular the pentarchy. It was generally accepted that external factors played an important role in the course of these developments.

The canons of the ecumenical councils should not be isolated from other documents and events surrounding the councils; they rather should be read and understood in their context. Canons should be separated neither from their historical nor from their theological setting.

It is important to recognize the historical dimension, the temporality of the life of the Church.

In this sense, it should be recognized that the pentarchy can no longer function as it once did, since historical circumstances have changed profoundly. The question remains, nevertheless, as to how the underlying vision of the Church as communion could be reinterpreted and reshaped today.

An Orthodox intervention stressed that "primacy of honor," an expression currently used in the Orthodox tradition, can never be understood as an "honorific primacy" only; such would be in line neither with the New Testament nor with the tradition of the Church. "Honor" was always related to a particular function or responsibility. "Primacy" encompassed duties and rights, at least the right of appeal.

Any kind of primacy, moreover, should be understood in the spirit of the thirty-fourth apostolic canon, which states that the first (prôtos) can do nothing without the others but similarly the others can do nothing without the first. This implies a real authority of the "first," who by his own presence and participation can and should determine the functioning of the assembled body.

Consequently, it seems difficult to say that ecumenical councils are above the first or primate, since no council can act validly without the "first."

Once more, it was pointed out that the Orthodox tradition is familiar with the concept of primacy, without making however any direct reference to the ministry of Peter. Is this reference to a Petrine ministry necessary for endowing the Church with real primacy? Apparently, the answer is yes for Catholics and no for Orthodox. How can we make these two positions meet?

Patristic Testimonies on Peter, Bishop of the Church of Rome: Aspects of a Historical-Theological Reading*

Vittorino Grossi

This brief survey on the primacy of Peter in the church fathers will attempt to identify some aspects of a question that has always been an underlying theme of patristic testimonies on Peter, that is to say, the extent of their significance, mainly in the Latin testimonies.

Naturally, it is not possible to respond exhaustively to such a challenging question. Yet after expressing my gratitude to His Eminence Cardinal Kasper, to the Pontifical Council for Promoting Christian Unity, and to those present for the invitation to discuss this issue, I would suggest that after presenting an outline of a possible, if incomplete, framework of the range of problems absorbing researchers of different backgrounds on the ancient testimonies we have at hand, we could seek to identify some aspects of the historical-theological approach. I am convinced that our pursuit is worthwhile, beyond the outcome of these words, as we have at stake a common Christian patrimony to be nonetheless received and transmitted.

---

* May 22, 2003 (afternoon session). Original text in Italian.

I. An Overview of the Possible Issues regarding Peter

Historical-theological research in this field runs along several channels:

1. the person of Peter that emerges from the New Testament, in particular from Matthew and John (Matt 16:16–19 and John 21:22–23);

2. the patristic Petrine testimonies, in particular Roman archaeological, literary, and juridical-curial sources, which, in turn, should be interpreted within different contexts:

   a) the role of the bishop/presbyter in ancient Christianity;

   b) the roles of presbyters and of the bishop/presbyter in the church of Rome, both as bishop of the *ecclesia principalis* of Latin Christianity and as a bishop/presbyter who occasionally intervened in non-Latin churches (to what extent and in what capacity?);

   c) the "presidency in agape" of the church of Rome (Ignatius of Antioch), its *potior/potentior principalitas* (Irenaeus), and *cathedra Petri–primatus Petri* (Cyprian) in the pre-Constantinian era;

   d) the *primatus* of the *sedes apostolica Romana* among the patriarchates in the post-Constantinian era (the *Decretum Gelasianum*).

Sources at Our Disposal

a) The Archaeological Sphere

If we turn to the archaeological evidence on Peter,[1] we find the *tropaia*, that is, the monuments or tombs of Peter and Paul in Rome,

---

1. The recent book on Peter (various authors, *Pietro: La storia, l'immagine, la memoria*) published and edited by the Fabbrica di San Pietro in the Vatican (1999, 247 pp.) gathers together the most recent data on the documentation on Peter, from the exegetical to, above all, the archaeological relating to monumental, iconographic, and epigraphic material. This text does not provide literary sources—indeed, the

attested to in the third century by the Roman presbyter Gaius as he extended an invitation to the Asian Proclus to visit them;[2] the graffiti in the memoria apostolorum on the Via Appia (the present Catacombs of Saint Sebastian) on the walls of the *triclia* (dining room), calling on the intercession of the apostles Peter and Paul;[3] and also the first iconography of Peter.[4]

The *tropaia* of Peter and Paul attest to the apostolic foundation of the church of Rome, and the graffiti to their cult; the first iconography of Peter readily identifies in him the new and legal representative of the heritage of the "true Israel."

b) Literary Evidence

From the point of view of the literary sources, including the Roman juridical-curial material relating to the apostle Peter, the various paths (by this I mean the different approaches adopted by the disciplines involved) have somewhat converged along the following

---

interest of the Fabbrica di San Pietro is primarily in the conservation of monuments—nor for the same reason does it attempt theological interpretation. The exegetical part offers a scriptural profile of Peter, edited by G. Ravasi, and a work on the messianic confession of Mark 8:27–33, by I. de La Potterie.

2. With regard to the veneration of their sepulchres—the basilicas constructed upon them date to a century after their deaths, approximately 165—we recall the words of the presbyter Gaius, at the beginning of the third century (199–217), to the Montanist Proclus of Asia Minor: "I can show you the *tropaia* [monuments or tombs] of the apostles. If indeed you should wish to take the royal road to the Vatican or the road to Ostia, you will find the *tropaia* of those who founded this church" (Eusebius of Caesarea, Hist. eccl. [= Historia ecclesiastica] 2.25.6–7); see also M. Guarducci, *Il primato della Chiesa di Roma: Documenti, riflessioni, conferme* (Milan, 1991).

3. This represents the first complex with notable traces of reverence for Peter and Paul, and constitutes the third site of veneration for Christians in Rome in memory of the two Roman apostle martyrs. The evidence consists of graffiti left by pilgrims on the plaster of the walls of the *triclia*, dating from the second half of the third and beginning of the fourth centuries (from 260 onwards) and asking for the intercession of the saints Peter and Paul. For example, "Peter and Paul intercede for Primus from Beneventum....Saints Paul and Peter, blessed martyrs, preserve us in the Lord." The *memoria* was a site of prayer not necessarily endowed with a tomb of the deceased.

4. See F. Bisconti, "All'origine dell'iconografia di Pietro e Paolo," in *Pietro e Paolo: Il loro rapporto con Roma nelle testimonianze antiche*, SEA 74 (Rome, 2001), 393–401.

lines: first, Peter as Simon son of Bar Jona/Jonas (i.e., the exegetical sphere with its relative *Sitz im Leben*); second, Peter from the time that Jesus confers this name on him, placing him in relationship with the Christian community, and identifying him, in the ancient tradition, with the name:

- Peter who receives the heritage of Israel;
- Peter martyr of the church of Rome;
- Peter apostle founder of the church of Rome;
- Peter *episcopus/papa* of the church of Rome: the *cathedra Petri*;
- Peter *episcopus* of the *ecclesia principalis* of the Latin churches and therefore their primate;
- Peter *episcopus* of the church of Rome, which, endowed with a presidency in the agape, "presides in charity" (Ignatius of Antioch), with a *potior principalitas* that underlines the "concordance" of the other churches with it (Irenaeus, *Adv. haer.* 3.3.2);
- Peter bishop of the church of Rome and the patriarchates of the post-Nicene period.

A reading of the texts of Ignatius of Antioch and of Irenaeus have always raised questions regarding the extent of a possible *ius* or primacy of the church of Rome and of its bishop with respect to the other churches and, when the historical record makes it possible, there has been an attempt to identify the means with which it was exercised.

Restricting ourselves to a *ius* within the religious sphere, our reading unfolds in a twofold manner or at least can be traced in two directions: either one pursues the New Testament references to Peter (the Petrine ministry), perhaps isolating the passages of Matt 16:16–19 and John 21:22–23 on the investiture of Peter, concentrating on his primacy (the extent of the exercise of the primacy),[5] or

---

5. The New Testament provides witness to the personal relationship of Peter with Jesus. He is called by the name Peter an appreciable 154 times, 27 times by the name Simon, 9 times by Cephas (rock). In the second letter of Peter (2 Pet 1:1) he is

otherwise one focuses on the historical institution of "the church of Rome,"[6] verifying its primacy within the ambit of the "region of the Romans" and with respect to the other churches.

The Christian churches seek clarification principally on this last point, making use of the available Petrine texts. Both exegesis and the history of exegesis and of our institutions (the historical churches)

---

called "Simon Peter, servant and apostle of Jesus Christ." Called to discipleship by the Sea of Galilee (Matt 4:8–20), overcome by the experience of the miraculous catch (Luke 5:8–11), he always appears in first place in the list of the apostles (Matt 10:2). Yet he is nonetheless called to take up his cross (Matt 16:24) and promises to die for his master (Matt 26:31–35) even though he is unable to keep awake with him one hour at the Mount of Olives (Matt 26:40). He intervenes against those who arrest Jesus, cutting off the ear of one of the guards (Matt 26:51 and John 18:10), only to disown him three times (Matt 26:74; John 18:15–16) even at the cost of bitter tears (Matt 26:75).

At the last supper—relates the evangelist Luke—Jesus prayed that "your faith may not fail, and you, when once you have turned back, strengthen your brothers" (Luke 22:31–32).

The evangelist John recalls furthermore that Peter, in the moment of crisis on the Eucharist, left no space for the disciples to abandon their master, "To whom can we go?" (John 6:67–69), and that he ran to the tomb with John on the morning of the resurrection (John 20:1–9), experienced the second miraculous catch (John 21:1–14; Luke 5:1–11), was warned that he would die in the same way as his master (John 21:18–19) and, lastly, received three times the command to feed the lambs and sheep of Jesus' flock (John 21:22–23).

Much of his work after the ascension of Jesus we know from the Acts of the Apostles (the first fifteen chapters are dedicated to Peter). Among other things, he replaced Judas with Matthias in the college of the apostles (Acts 1:15–26), acted as the representative of the new community before the Sanhedrin (Acts 3:11–26; 4:1–22; 5:21–42), and intervened with James and John at the assembly of Jerusalem on the observances for converted pagans (Acts 15:11). He also opened the series of addresses on the day of Pentecost (Acts 2), etc.

We know of his relations with Paul from Acts (from chapter 16 onwards dedicated to Paul) and from the Pauline epistles. In the letter to the Galatians (1:18) Paul states that he "did go up to Jerusalem to visit Cephas and stayed with him fifteen days," and that in Antioch he "opposed [Cephas] to his face" (Gal 2:11). Peter emerges in the Catholic Epistles as the guarantor of orthodoxy (1 and 2 Pet).

6. Cyrille Vogel, "Unité de l'Église et pluralité des formes historiques d'organisation ecclésiastique de III au V siècle," in *L'épiscopat et l'Église universelle,* Unam sanctam 39 (Paris, 1964), 591–636; idem, "Primatialité et synodalité dans l'église locale durant la période anténicéenne," in *Aspects de l'Orthodoxie* (Paris, 1981), 53–66.

offer a range of trends both in terms of historiographical data and interpretative keys that over the centuries have guided the churches.[7]

Historical methodology is well aware that historical evidence needs to be interpreted within an understanding of the issues to which they testify. The identification of such issues would in itself be a valuable starting point, although the difficulty seems to lie precisely

---

7. Bibliography: Eric Gaspar, *Geschichte des Papstums von der Anfängen bis zur Höhe der Weltherrschaft*, vol. 1, *Römische Kirche und Imperium Romanum* (Tübingen, 1930); A. V. Seumois, *La papauté et les missions au cours des six premiers siècles* (Louvain, 1951); L. Hertling, *Communio: Chiesa e papato nell'antichità cristiana* (Rome, 1961); M. Maccarrone, "Apostolicità, episcopato, e primato di Pietro," *Lateranum* 42 (1976): 220–27; J. Rigal, *L'ecclésiologie de communion: Son évolution historique et ses fondements* (Paris, 1997); J. M. R. Tillard, "Tre trattati sulla Chiesa come comunione nella linea teologica ad es. Carne de la Iglesia, carne de Cristo," in *Las fuentes de la eclesiologia de comunion* (Salamanca, 1994); J. R. Villar, *Eclesiología y ecumenismo: Comunión, iglesia local, Pedro* (Pamplona: Eunsa, 1999).

For studies on communion, from the identification Christ-Church to the Petrine ministry: C. Colombo, "Episcopato e primato pontificio nella vita della Chiesa," *La scuola cattolica* 88 (1960): 401–34; S. L. Greenslade, "Sede vacante: Procedure in the Early Church," *JThS* 12 (1961): 210–26; A. Demoustier, "Épiscopat et union à Rome selon saint Cyprien," *Recherche de science religieuse* 52 (1964): 337–69; J. A. Fischer, "Die Konzilien zu Karthago und Rom im Jahre 251," *Annuarium historiae conciliorum* 11 (1979): 263–65. On the Augustinian literature: A.-M. La Bonnardière, "Tu es Petrus: La péricope Mt 16,13–23 dans l'œuvre de s. A.," *Irenikon* 34 (1961): 451–99; K. Baus, "Wesen und Funktion der apostolischen Sukzession in der Sicht des hl. Augustinus," in *Ekklesia* (Festschrift Matthias Wehr) (Trier, 1962), 137–48; Agostino Trapè, "La 'sedes Petri' in S. Agostino," *Lateranum* NS 30 (1964): 57–75 (Miscellanea A. Piolanti II); J. Pintard, "Notes sur 'sedes apostolica' selon s. Augustin," *Studia patristica* 16 (1985): 551–56; Robert B. Eno, "Forma Petri-Petrus, figura ecclesiae: The Uses of Peter," *Augustiniana* 41 (1991): 659–76. On relations of Rome with Africa: Paul Zmire, "Recherches sur la collégialité épiscopale dans l'église d'Afrique," *Recherches augustiniennes* 7 (1971): 3–72; Werner Marschall, *Karthago und Rom: Die Stellung der nordafrikanischen Kirche zum Apostolichen Stuhl in Rom* (Stuttgart, 1971); V. Saxer, "Autonomie africaine et primauté romaine de Tertullien à Augustin," in *Il primato del vescovo di Roma nel primo millennio*, ed. M. Maccarone (Vatican City, 1991); Ch. Munier, "La question des appels à Rome d'après la Lettre 20* d'Augustin," in *Les lettres de s. A. découvertes par J. Divjak* (Paris, 1983), 287–99; Jane Merdinger, "The Politics of Persuasion: Augustine's Tactics towards the Papacy in Letters 22*, 23*, and 23*A," in *Congresso internazionale su S. Agostino nel XVI centenario della conversione*, SEA 25 (Rome, 1987), 531–40; various authors, *Pietro e Paolo: Il loro rapporto con Roma nelle testimonianze antiche*, SEA 74 (Rome, 2001).

in their identification. The patristic period is no different, and one proceeds with working hypotheses.

II. Some Historical-Theological Aspects of Peter and the Church of Rome

1. Peter as Legal Representative of the "New Israel"

The importance of the figure of Peter, delineated in the Roman tradition in line with chapter 16 of Matthew, gained consistency against the background of the controversy between Christians and Jews on the "true Israel" when the former began to differentiate themselves from the latter.

The question that arose between Jews and the nascent Christians about the true Israel was of a juridical nature in addition to its spiritual significance and was keenly felt in the first decades of the Christian era, much more than in the following centuries, when much was taken for granted and when focus was placed not so much on the matrix of one's Christianity as on the aspect of how one becomes faithful to Christ.

Christians very quickly presented themselves vis-à-vis Judaism as the heirs of the promises of God. In view of his investiture as head of the new community (Matt 16:16–19; John 21:22–23), Peter was considered to be the official guarantor of this inheritance, the person with whom Jesus had stipulated the deed of passage of the promises of God from the synagogue to the church.[8] It is not a mere coincidence that in the ancient iconographical tradition, Peter is often placed next to Moses, who, by giving the Jewish people the tablets of the law, was considered the founder of Judaism. Peter, like Moses, assumed the role of legal representative of the new religious reality of the Christians, indeed the role of true founder for the churches. In this same perspective, when the iconography presents Moses opposite Jesus to indicate the two founders, Peter either sits or stands at the right of Jesus, in the role of his representative.

---

8. See in this regard Ernst Bammel, *L'eredità di Gesù: Le tradizioni neotestamentarie* (Rome: Borla, 1994) (German edition: *Iesu Nachfolger* [Heidelberg, 1988]).

The words of Pope Siricius (384–399), dating to the end of the fourth century, provide an excellent commentary in this context:

We bear the burdens of all who are oppressed, or rather the blessed apostle Peter, who in all things protects and preserves us, the heirs, as we trust, of his administration, bears them in us.[9]

2. Peter, Martyr of the Church of Rome

The Petrine evidence, taken as a whole, identifies Peter and Paul as the apostolic founders of the church, by virtue of their primary position in the church of Rome and their martyrdom.[10] In this perspective, some would also bring to bear the words of Irenaeus regarding the *potior principalitas* of the church of Rome.[11]

And perhaps the witness of martyrdom was not so foreign as to impede the Christian community of Rome from being considered even by non-Romans as worthy of admiration and reverence, as one that "presides to charity" (Ignatius of Antioch), as one that, among the apostolic churches, "enjoys particular sovereignty; all the other churches are called to agree with her" (Irenaeus, *Adv. haer.* 3.3.2). With regard to the martyrdom of Peter and Paul, the church of Rome was not parsimonious in reserving particular honors to the two apostles, and particularly to Peter.

---

9. The Latin text is (Siricius, *Directa ad decessorem* 1; PL 13:1133): "Portamus onera omnium qui gravantur: quinimmo haec portat in nobis beatus apostolus Petrus, qui nos in omnibus, ut confidimus, administrationis suae protegit et tuetur haeredes."

10. Clement of Rome writes in his letter to the Corinthians (1 Cor 5:1–7) that with their martyrdom Peter and Paul, together with the other martyrs of the Neronian persecution, left the Romans a "magnificent example."

11. For example, M. Simonetti, "Presbiteri e vescovi nella Chiesa del I e II secolo," *Vetera Christianorum* 33 (1996): 119–21; L. Padovese, "Roma e la sua sollecitudine delle chiese: Espressioni di comunione ecclesiale nei primi due secoli," in *La comunità cristiana di Roma: La sua vita e la sua cultura dalle origini all'Alto Medioevo* (Rome, 2000), 65–82; F. A. Sullivan, *From Apostles to Bishops: The Development of the Episcopacy in the Early Church* (New York, 2001).

3. *Peter, Apostolic Founder of the Church of Rome*

The intraecclesial controversy on orthodoxy, the ascertainment of which, from the end of the last decade of the second century and into the third century, was based on the proof of the apostolicity of a church (Tertullian, *De praescriptione;* Irenaeus, *Adv. haer.* 3), produced a focus on the role of the founder apostles of a church. Though fruit of the trunk of the Christian tree, heresy was not a doctrine to be pursued, as it did not derive from the apostolic furrow (Tertullian, *Praescr.* 32.8). This argument increased the need to guarantee the development of the seeds of doctrine received by Christ, and transmitted by the apostles to the churches, through the apostolic succession, from one bishop/presbyter to another. The heretics, argued Tertullian, cannot offer such a proof (*Praescr.* 32.5, 7–8). Peter (together with Paul in Irenaeus) was the apostle recognized as the founder of the church of Rome, to whom Clement was linked, as was likewise Polycarp to John for the church of Smyrna. Tertullian wrote in *De praescriptione* (32.2), "Hoc enim modo ecclesiae apostolicae census suos deferunt, sicut Smyrnaeorum ecclesia Polycarpum ab Iohanne collocatum referet, sicut Romanorum Clementem a Petro ordinatum est." Making the same case, Irenaeus also mentions Linus and Anacletus as bishops/presbyters prior to Clement, whereas Peter and Paul are apostles (*Adv. haer.* 3.3.3: "Fundantes igitur et instruentes beati apostoli Ecclesiam, Lino episcopatum administrandae Ecclesiae tradiderunt....Succedit autem ei Anacletus. Post eum tertio loco ab apostolis episcopatum sortitur Clemens, qui et vidit apostolos ipsos"; the text is preserved also in Eusebius (*Hist. eccl.* 5.6.1). There has not yet been a satisfactory explanation for the different traditions regarding the episcopal lists of Tertullian and Irenaeus,[12] yet the concept is quite clear: with Peter the apostle and Clement the bishop, the church of Rome could guarantee its apostolic origin and was therefore endowed with apostolic authority. This aspect—as we can see—

---

12. G. D. Dunn, "Clement of Rome and the Question on Roman Primacy," *Augustinianum* 43 (2003): 5–24. Perhaps Tertullian's source is not Irenaeus but the *Epistola ad Iacobum* of the *Pseudo-Clementine* (in *Augustinianum* 43 [2003]: 25–39). On the name Anacletus, or, more properly, Anenkletos (J. Bernardi, in *Augustinianum* 41 [2001]: 287–90).

does not strengthen so much the primacy of the bishop of Rome as it does the *sanitas* of the doctrine of the church of Rome in view of its apostolic origin, compared with that of the heretics who emerged later.

In the context of the historical identification of the Church of Christ through the apostolic succession, Irenaeus cites the example of the church of Rome in these terms: "As it would be too lengthy in this work to list all the successions of all the churches, we will take the greatest and oldest church known to all, the church founded and established in Rome by the two most glorious apostles Peter and Paul." The text in Latin continues: "Ad hanc enim ecclesiam propter potentiorem principalitatem necesse est omnem convenire ecclesiam, hoc est eos qui sunt undique fideles, in qua semper ab his qui sunt undique conservata est ea quae est ab apostolis traditio" (*Adv. haer.* 3.3.2–3).

The "in qua" can be understood as the Roman church (most likely) or the universal one, constituted "ab his qui sunt undique" and, referring to *Adv. haer.* 4.26.2 and 4.32.1 with its expression "ab his qui sunt undique presbyteri," and in the translation proposed by E. Cattaneo as: "In fact, due to its most excellent origin, it is with this church that every church must necessarily be in agreement, that is, believers dispersed everywhere, because in it has been conserved, by its presbyters, the tradition that comes from the apostles."[13] The bishops, by virtue of being elders (presbyters), were considered to be the custodians of the tradition entrusted to them by the apostles.

Although Irenaeus, like Tertullian, recognizes this doctrinal *sanitas* or *integritas* in all the churches founded by the apostles, he nonetheless recognizes in the church of Rome a *potior/potentior principalitas* that offers a guarantee to the other churches in ascertaining their own orthodoxy; indeed it is the very reason agreement is neces-

---

13 For an overview of this much-debated text, see SCh 210 (Paris, 1974), 3:223–36; Emmanuel Lanne, "L'église de Rome 'a gloriosissimis duobus apostolis Petro et Paulo Romae fundatae et constitutae ecclesiae' (*Adv. haer.* 3.3.2)," *Irenikon* 49 (1976): 275–322; E. Cattaneo, "'Ab his qui sunt undique': Una nuova proposta su Ireneo *Adv.haer.* 3, 3,2b," *Augustinianum* 40 (2000): 399–405. The likely Greek original, *dynatōterē hegemonía*, of *principalitas* would lead to the analogy that later (at least by the fourth century) equated the empire and its *princeps* with the Church and its princes, Peter and Paul.

sary. Perhaps in the text of Irenaeus we could note that it is not so much a need in the juridical sense as it is a question of the evidence of the apostolic origin of the Roman church, upon which it is impossible not to agree. It is fundamentally the same argument that Tertullian made for the churches in *De praescriptione*—that is, there is not a first, second, or third church, but all are first because of their common apostolic origin, and all shape the unity of the vine that is propagated by propagation.

4. Peter, episcopus/papa *of the Church of Rome: the* cathedra Petri *(the Development of the Theology of Primacy)*

In the period between the *De praescriptione* (end of the second century) of Tertullian and the era of Cyprian (†258), a whole vocabulary developed on the role of Peter and his chair as bishop of Rome, a vocabulary that was not available before this time but was to become widely known thereafter.

In *De praescriptione*, Tertullian makes reference to the authority of the keys given by Jesus to Peter (Matt 16:18–19) and by the latter to the church: "Petro et per eum ecclesiae" (*Praescr.* 22.4; *Scorpiace* 10.8; *Monogamia* 8.4). Yet in *De pudicitia* (21.14–16), in opposing the conception of the church founded on the bishop—which was customary—to that of the church/bishop–Spirit, he restricts to Peter alone the authority of the keys, limiting it to the pardon of *crimina* classified by him as *remissibilia* and *irremissibilia*. In thus extricating Peter from the *ecclesia*, he explains that such authority was the personal privilege of Peter as apostle and was not therefore transmitted to his successor in the church of Rome. Such a distinction became a temptation that often re-emerged in postpatristic Christianity, above all in the field of exegesis.

Cyprian of Carthage, within the framework of the African church, which identified in Rome the *ecclesia principalis*, strengthens the relationship between the bishops themselves and consequently their point of convergence.

The Church is founded on the bishops ("ecclesia super episcopos constituatur et omnis actus ecclesiae per eosdem praepositos gubernetur," *Ep.* 33.1.1), who by succession receive their authority from the mandate of Jesus to Peter, and of the latter to all the others. In this understanding of succession, the apostles are considered to be the first bishops ("Inde [Matt 16:18–19] per temporum et successionum vices episcoporum ordinatio et ecclesiae ratio decurrit," *Ep.* 33.1.1 and 3.3.1). Yet, while many, the bishops constitute the one Church founded by Peter ("cum sit a Christo una ecclesia per totum mundum…item episcopatus unus," *Ep.* 55.24.2; 59.7.3; 66.8.3). In Cyprian's *De ecclesiae catholicae unitate,* these elements find, let us say, their official yet popular expression based on the *primatus* of Peter, "primatus Petro datur," as symbol of the one Church. Peter is symbol of the one Church: "exordium ab unitate proficiscitur" (*De unitate* 4). Cyprian continues: "ad Petri cathedram atque ad ecclesiam principalem unde unitas sacerdotalis [= episcopalis] exorta est" (*Ep.* 59.14.1).

Beyond the well-known difficulty with regard to the *textus primatus* and the *textus receptus* of chapter 4 of *De unitate ecclesiae,* the question these texts raise concerns their significance with regard to the primacy of Peter. Three points should be considered:

1. the underlying question in these texts is not so much the primacy of Peter as the deeper understanding of the relationship of a bishop with his church and of the bishops with the whole Church;

2. Cyprian refers to the church of Rome as the *ecclesia principalis* of the Latin churches and therefore refers directly to the African church;

3. the fuller understanding of the relationship of the bishops among themselves, who upon Peter form a single Church, gave rise to a deeper theological study on the text of Matt 16:16–18 on the authority of the keys given to Peter. In other words, the bishops derive their episcopacy from Peter, symbol of the unity of the Church.

If one raises the question in concrete terms regarding the relationship of the apostle Peter with his successors in the church of

Rome, and of the latter with the bishops of the other churches, one could well say that perhaps this question was not raised at the universal level as much as within the ambit of the *ecclesia principalis*. We would do well to say "perhaps" because in the controversy between Pope Stephen and Cyprian regarding rebaptism, accusations were made by both Cyprian and Firmilian of Cappadocia (*Ep.* 75.6.1–2 and 17.1) against Pope Stephen that he had claimed for himself the right to authority and—with insolence—had claimed this right by virtue of being the successor of Peter. That is, Cyprian, who seems not to have denied the right but only to have noted the insolence—"nec Petrus quem primum dominus elegit et super eum aedificavit ecclesiam suam...vindicavit sibi aliquid insolenter" (Ep. 71.3.1)—seems not to have stressed the primacy of the bishop of Rome as the principal church with respect to the African church. The suspicion in some way persists that in this controversy the bishops of Rome intended such primacy even beyond the *ecclesia principalis*.

Moreover, before Pope Stephen (254–257) we have Pope Victor (180), who, going beyond the confines of the Latin churches, had threatened the Asians with excommunication—with similar insolence—over the issue of the date of Easter (Eusebius, *Hist. eccl.* 5.24.8). The suspicion is further reinforced by the fact that after the Council of Chalcedon there was an attempt to disparage the *De unitate ecclesiae* of Cyprian, inserting it among the apocrypha, perhaps precisely because of the *primatus Petri* contained in the text.[14] Furthermore, the ecclesiological formulation of Cyprian did not arrive at considering each bishop, simply by virtue of originating from Peter, as *cathedra Petri*.[15]

---

14. Pope Gelasius, Ep. 165. In *Decretum Gelasianum* 5 Cyprian also heads the list of heretics and their apocryphal texts (opuscula Thascii Cypriani, apocrypha).

15. This expression of Cyprian of Carthage (*De ecclesiae unitate* 4, CCL 3/1:252; Ep. 55.8.1, CCL 3B:265) later became customary in the Latin Church to distinguish the church of Rome from the other churches. Optatus of Milevi, for example, affirmed that Christ gave Peter "the keys and the chair" and that he was the first to occupy the chair of the church of Rome, later passed on to his successors (2.3; CSEL 26:37), see Pierre Batifol, *"Cathedra Petri": Études d'histoire ancienne de l'Église* (Paris, 1938).

5. *Peter,* episcopus *of the* ecclesia principalis *of the Latin Churches*

Within the ambit of the Latin churches, the community of Rome was considered to be the *ecclesia principalis,* with the right to pronounce final decisions regarding measures taken by bishops and local churches (that is, Africa, Gaul, the Iberian Peninsula, and the other Italian churches).

Tertullian wrote: "Si autem Italiae adiaces, habes Romam unde nobis quoque auctoritas praesto est" (*Praescr.* 36.2), that is, in Africa as elsewhere, Rome was the *ecclesia principalis.* If the attribution is correct, Ambrose reiterated this in *De sacramentis:* "In all I wish to follow the Roman church" (3.1.5). Two centuries later, Augustine repeated it: "From the church of Rome, in which the authority of the *principalitas* of the Apostolic See has always abided, the gospel arrived also in Africa" (*Ep.* 43.7);[16] Paulus Diaconus in the eighth century summarized the close relationship between the center (Rome) and the periphery (the Latin world), identifying Peter as the one who, upon arriving in Rome, had sent disciples to evangelize the major cities of the West ("Tunc denique Apollinarem Ravennam, Leucium Brundisium, Anatolium Mediolanum misit. Marcum vero, qui praecipuum inter eius discipulos habebatur, Aquileiam destinavit, quibus cum Hermagoram, suum comitem, Marcus praefecisset, ad beatum Petrum reversus, ab eo nihilominus Alexandriam missus est," *MGH [= Monumenta Germaniae historica],* Scriptores 2:261).

These and other similar texts on the close relationship between the church of Rome and the other Latin churches should therefore be interpreted in the light of an understanding of the then existing rela-

---

16. In the same context, Augustine states that the authority of the Christian faith had reached Africa even though the gospel had arrived there from the root of the Oriental churches. (*Ep.* 52.2–3), and for that reason invoked the authority of the church of Rome with regard to the Donatists (*Ep.* 43.3.8–9; 44.2.3). The procedure was normal; in one of its sentences the Apostolic See, for example, had excluded two bishops from Mauritania (*Ep.* 129.7). The role of the primacy of the bishop of Rome was also placed in the context of the internal order of bishop primates of some churches. Augustine states that a council should deal with the regular succession within the primacy (*Ep.* 59.1), as the provinces of Mauritania had their own primates (*Ep.* 59.1).

tionships between the evangelizing church and the evangelized churches. Mission and the dissemination of Christianity found in the great cities of antiquity (Antioch, Jerusalem, Rome, Alexandria, Constantinople) a point of convergence, mirroring the civilian dimension. The mission of the Church was given an impulse by these great centers, with the evangelizing church becoming the *ecclesia principalis* with respect to the others, that is, the point of reference in terms of doctrine and liturgical and disciplinary regulations for the new communities. This order contributed to creating doctrinal and liturgical homogeneity over vast areas, for the most part similar among themselves in cultural terms. This led to the formation of the ancient Christian traditions, later leading to the great liturgical families. This relationship did not underrate either local or aggregate features of the other churches, for example, Africa, Lyon, or Milan, for, although they may have been evangelized from Rome, they were also—principally through commercial exchanges—influenced by Eastern Christian traditions.

For their part, the bishops of Rome affirmed due respect for this principle, with the tradition of the principal church followed whenever circumstances called for a new order. I recall in this context the famous words of Pope Stephen regarding the readmission of heretics into the ecclesial community, resolved by the bishops of Africa with a new baptism. He asserted that the tradition of the church of Rome (*ecclesia principalis*) held that readmission was undertaken by the imposition of hands and not by rebaptism, and that consequently the decisions of the Council of Carthage holding otherwise were to be considered invalid. "No innovations!" wrote Cyprian. "Hold to what has been handed down. If heretics come to you, impose your hands that they may be received in penitence."[17]

This course of action had a particular application to the liturgical traditions of the Latin Church, in particular in the periods of general reorganization during the fifth century. Innocent I, for example, replied to Decentius of Gubbio to follow "what has been handed down, not what to them may seem,...given that in all Italy, in Gaul, in Spain, in Africa, in Sicily and the nearby islands, no one founded

---

17. *Ep.* 74.1 (CSEL 3/2:799): "Nihil innovetur nisi quod traditum est."

these churches apart from those whom Peter and his successors had constituted as bishops" (PL 20:550). At the close of the sixth century, Gregory the Great reaffirmed the same position with the young church of England. "Choose quickly," he wrote to Augustine of Canterbury, "from the church of Rome, from that of Gaul, or from whatever other church, all that you have found in them that would please Almighty God, and all that from the many churches you have put together, infuse into the church of the Angles, which is still young in its faith and in its principal institutions" (*MGH*, E 2:334).

6. The Church of Rome in the Post-Nicene Period—the Patriarchates

The post-Nicene Church was called to measure itself against a new order, both internally and in relation to the imperial institutions with which it had come into agreement. For example, the primacy of the bishop of Rome over the church of Carthage had been in the pre-Nicene period only a religious relationship—given that Carthage at the time was not a province of Rome—but after the Constantinian agreement, the public reorganization of the Christian religion, now the religion of the empire, was carried out according to the civil parameters of the new territorial divisions of Constantine and his successors. The origin of the five patriarchates of the historical churches—Rome, Alexandria, Antioch, Constantinople, and Jerusalem—date back to this period. The territorial jurisdictions of the patriarchates replaced the ancient "principal churches," while the patriarchal church of the imperial city (Constantinople) asserted its rights as a second Rome (the sense of canon 28 of the Council of Chalcedon). That the change was fundamental can be inferred from the fact that the election of the patriarchates required the confirmation of the emperor whereas the latter was elected directly. The election of a bishop of a patriarchal church without the behest of the emperor resulted, in the West, in the rupture between the bishop of Rome and the Eastern emperor (fifth century). Ours is not the context to delineate the history of the papacy but rather to delineate the historical development of the exercise of its primacy in the patristic era, offering possible insights into its underlying theological rationale.

The emerging questions on orthodox Christianity, initially of an ecclesiological, trinitarian-christological nature and later, in the West, of an anthropological nature (the Pelagian controversy) were resolved through local synods, plenary councils (e.g., of the African church), and "ecumenical" councils convened and organized under the direct coordination and presidency of the emperor. It was common practice for a conciliar or synodal decision to be undersigned by the bishops of the particular primacy; in the case of an "ecumenical" decision, five copies of the proceedings were issued and forwarded to the respective patriarchates for signing, with the request for the signature of the episcopate concerned. Refusal incurred penalties determined by the religious legislation of the council, which was acknowledged as imperial law by the civil authorities.

The three historical patriarchal sees that directly referred to Peter's authority (Rome, Alexandria, Antioch) were the most important in terms of decision making, and when mutual rivalries permitted, they even worked in positive collaboration—for example, the church of Rome at the councils of Ephesus and Chalcedon.

The role of the bishop at the time,[18] inferred from the words of Saint Augustine, could be described along the following lines. In terms of the duties of his office,[19] a bishop was responsible for the care of his own church (*Ep.* 34.5); thus, he could respond to the request of another bishop but could not spontaneously write to the faithful of another diocese (*Ep.* 64.2). Each catholic bishop was nonetheless considered to be a colleague of all the other bishops (*Ep.* 85.1), who were listed in order of episcopal seniority whenever an *epistola tractoria* (circular letter) was distributed (*Ep.* 59.1). The Council of Nicaea prohibited the ordination of a suffragan bishop (*Ep.* 213.4), and the *consuetudo* dictated that a bishop could not be transferred to another see (*Ep.* 209.7) and also that a bishop demoted by a plenary council could not be honored by the faithful, which, on the contrary, had occurred in Vegesile, a city of Numidia west of Theveste (*Ep.* 64.3–4).

Furthermore, a bishop was obliged to chastise those fellow bishops favorably disposed towards heretics (*Ep.* 228); indeed, Augustine

---

18. For an overview, see various authors, *Vescovi e pastori in epoca teodosiana: XXV Incontro di studiosi dell'antichità cristiana (Roma, 8–11 maggio 1996)*, 2 vols., SEA 58 (Rome, 1997).

19. The origin of the title of bishop and of bishops' authority is outlined by Augustine in two epistles (*Ep.* 181.1; 182.2).

himself broke ecclesial communion with a bishop deemed to be unworthy (*Ep.* 85.1). The relationship with bishops in favor of heresy became a real problem after the condemnation of Pelagianism (Carthage 418), when some bishops of northern Italy, together with Bishop Julian of Aeclanum (then within Beneventum and currently within the Diocese of Avellino), refused to undersign the condemnation after receiving the *epistola tractoria* of Pope Zosimus. The vicissitudes of Julian and Pope Zosimus were brought to a resolution on the juridical level with the bishop's exile from the *ecclesia aeclanensis,* while on the doctrinal level they became the source of debate until the death of Augustine of Hippo. From our point of view, we can discern in this debate aspects of the trends developing in the church of Rome in relation to the other churches after the Council of Nicaea.

Our reading of Augustine enables us to identify two of these trends in particular: (1) the bishops of East and West were in agreement against the "Pelagian" position of Julian (*Contra Iulianum* 3.17.32); (2) the position of the Roman Apostolic See was binding as the last resort. "You [Julian]," retorts Augustine, "seek an examination already undertaken by the Apostolic See" (*Opus imperfectum contra Iulianum* 2.103).

While the second aspect may yet have fallen within the primacy of the bishop of Rome as bishop of the *ecclesia principalis* of the Latin churches, the first most certainly extended beyond the ambit of the Latin Church, extending to the universality of the Christian Church, then under the government of the emperor although merely from an administrative point of view and not in matters of doctrine. It is the second aspect, understood as communion with the Apostolic See through adherence to its decision, that nonetheless emerged as the normative doctrinal criterion. It was increasingly appealed to by the bishop of Rome in disputes and remained the fundamental criterion of the Apostolic See in relation to the other churches.

Cyril of Alexandria, for example, approached Bishop Celestine for support on his position towards Nestorius, patriarch of Constantinople, whom he brought to the Council of Ephesus in 431; to give another textual reference, on May 13, 449, Leo the Great wrote to the Second Ephesian Synod, convened by Theodosius II, in the following terms: "The zeal for the faith of our most clement emperor...has rendered homage to divine law by requesting this apostolic see to confirm his imperial decree [the convocation of the Council of Ephesus]." After citing Matt 16:13–18, he concludes: "Whosoever does not embrace the confession of Peter and contradicts the gospel is therefore completely beyond this structure" (*Ep.* 33; PL 54:797ff.).

In other words, communion with the church of Rome was expressed by the extent of one's orthodoxy in thought and expression in relation to positions adopted by the church of Rome. While the emerging issues of the post-Constantinian Church were evaluated together whenever these arose in the course of synods and plenary and ecumenical councils, the judgment of the bishop of Rome remained binding. Assent was an obligation, and the penalty incurred was the rupture of communion.[20] The principle of communion, in other words, was the bond of catholicity although in the post-Nicene Church this was regulated, if there was need, by the approval of the bishop of Rome. During the Roman council of 378 the emperor was informed of Pope Damasus thus: "ut auctore (Ursino) damnat...de reliquis ecclesiarum sacerdotibus episcopus Romanus haberet examen";[21] that is, metropolitans judged other bishops but they themselves must submit to the judgment of the bishop of Rome.

An overall survey of the relations of the churches with the Roman Apostolic See and of the regulation of the exercise of its magisterium was outlined in the so-called *Decretum Gelasianum*.

7. The Decretum Gelasianum, *a Roman Document (End of Fifth Century to Beginning of Sixth Century)*

The main difficulties the decree presents are related to the text itself (sources and content), to its paternity and therefore to its dating, and to its authority. Our discussion aims principally to place into

---

20. R. E. Brown, *Antioch e Roma: Chiese madri della cattolicità antica* (Assisi, 1987), 135–39 (English original, 1983). The struggles of the post-Chalcedonian christological question is informative in this regard; see V. Grossi, "L'auctoritas di Agostino d'Ippona nelle questioni cristologiche postcalcedonesi (secoli V–VII)," in *Gesù Cristo, speranza del mondo* (miscellanea in honor of Marcello Bordoni), ed. Ignazio Sanna (Rome: PUL, 2000), 89–110.

21. Damasus, *Ep.* 6; Coustant, 254.

context both its authoritative elements within the development of ecclesiastical legislation at the time and its use of terminology denoting the authority of the bishop of Rome that later came into common usage.[22]

In the manuscripts themselves the decree is attributed, all or in part, to popes Damasus (366–384), Gelasius I (492–496), and Hormisdas (514–523),[23] and so it is a Roman document dating not beyond the first two decades of the sixth century. Either Damasus or Gelasius reorganized the third chapter into five sections:

1. *De Spiritu sancto et de nominibus Christi* (1, the partite spirit; 2, the different names for Christ; the dual procession of the Holy Spirit taken from Augustine, *In Evangelium Johannis* 9.7)

2. *De canone sacrae Scripturae*

3. *De primatu Romano et de sedibus patriarchalibus*

---

22. There have been two main studies to date on the *Decretum Gelasianum*: the first a critical work on the text, by Dobschütz (TU 38/4 [Leipzig, 1912], 3ff.); the second, on its sources, by D. J. Chapman ("On the 'Decretum Gelasianum de libris recipiendis et non recipiendis,'" [*Revue bénédictine* 30 1913]:187–208 [examining chapters 4 and 5 attributed to Pope Gelasius] and 315–33). The text is in PL 59:157–80; critical edition by Dobschütz in TU 38/4:3–13, with detailed study, pp. 184–94 and 283–312; with corrections proposed by Chapman in *Revue bénédictine* 30 (1913): 162, 187, 197, 315. See the recently published proceedings of the international study conference "Il Papato di San Simmaco (498–514)," held at Oristano, 19–21 November 1999 (Cagliari, 2000). Ad essi rimandiamo per gli studi: Salvatore Vacca, "Il principio 'Prima sedes a nemine iudicatur': Genesi e sviluppo fino a papa Simmaco," 153–90; Alessandro Fadda, "'Prima sedes a nemine iudicatur': Rilevanze e conseguenze giuridiche di un principio ecclesiologico," 337–49; Vittorino Grossi, "L'autorità magisteriale della Sede Romana al tempo di papa Simmaco (498–514)," 421–42; idem, "Il Decretum Gelasianum: Nota in margine all'autorità della chiesa di Roma alla fine del sec. V," *Augustinianum* 41 (2001): 231–55.

23. The *incipit* reads: "Incipit concilium urbis Romae sub Damasus papa de explanatione fidei." The attribution to Damasus—reconstructed by Dobschütz (TU 38/4, [Leipzig, 1912], 3ff.) with the councils of Ephesus (431) and Chalcedon (451) and the succeeding bishops of Alexandria and Antioch (Proterius, Petrus Monus, Petrus Fullo, and Acacius of Constantinople [471–489]) and therefore during the schism of Acacius and shortly after his death—was not received by Chapman (in *Revue bénédictine* [1913]: 188, n. 1).

4. *De synodis oecumenicis suscipiendis, de scriptis…recipiendis,* known also as *Epistula decretalis de libris recipiendis et non recipiendis,* that is, regarding the doctrinal sources of the church of Rome (three synods, twelve Fathers, *Tomus Leonis papae ad Flavianum…*)

5. *De libris non recipiendis,* designated by the generic term "apocrypha."

Attribution to Pope Damasus (366–384)

The attribution to Damasus is related to the insistence, in the third chapter of the decree, on the hierarchy of the three principal sees of the ancient Christian world, namely Rome, Alexandria, and Antioch, which were all of Petrine origin.

A number of facts converge in throwing light upon this insistence and upon the attribution to Damasus. In 422 Pope Boniface faced the opposition of a number of Eastern bishops regarding his legate Rufus, archbishop of Thessalonica. These bishops attempted to withdraw Rufus from the jurisdiction of the bishop of Rome and to place him under that of Constantinople. In response, Pope Boniface wrote three letters in which he made reference to the Roman council under Damasus of 382. One was addressed to the bishops of Thessalonica (*Ep.* 14), another to the legate Rufus (*Ep.* 15), and the last, outlining the relevant canonical sanctions, to all three sees.[24]

Coustant would hold that this amounts to an appeal by Pope Boniface to canon 6 of Nicaea as opposed to canon 28 of Chalcedon. The reference to Damasus can be explained by the fact that the decree literally states: "Est ergo prima Petri apostoli sedes Romana ecclesia…secunda autem sedes apud Alexandrinam…tertia vero sedes apud Antiochenam."

---

24. In Petrus Coustant, *Epistolae Romanorum pontificum* (Paris, 1721), 1042: "Quoniam locus exigit, si placet recensere canonum sanctiones, reperietis quae sit post Ecclesiam Romanam secunda sedes, quaeve tertia. A quibus ideo ita rerum videtur ordo distinctus, ut se ecclesiarum pontifices ceterarum, sub uno tamen eodemque sacerdotio, habere cosgnoscant quibus caritate servata propter ecclesiasticam disciplinam debeant esse subiecti…Alexandrina et Antiochena…servant, inquam statuta maiorum."

At the council of 382, which was attended by Paulinus of Antioch,[25] Pope Damasus was sensitive to the report about a canon of a council in 381 (held in Constantinople) at which Constantinople was spoken of as the new Rome, so that it assumed second place after Rome. The canon was rejected by the bishop of Rome, as it seems that the proceedings of the council were never sent to Rome. This period also saw the development of the concept of the "new or second Rome" as being due not so much to its status as the capital of the empire as to its possession of apostolic relics after those conserved in Rome.[26]

In his reflection on the succession to the chair of Peter, Siricius (384–399), the successor of Pope Damasus, developed the argument that the inheritance of Peter was entrusted to the bishop of Rome.[27] The succession of the bishop of Rome in the ministry of Peter was delineated by this pope with the expression "cum in unum plurimi fratres convenissemus ad sancti apostoli Petri reliquias, per quem 'et apostolatus et episcopatus in Christo coepit exordium'" (synodal letter *Cum in unum;* CCL 149, p. 59), in which Peter is the first of the apostles and of the bishops of Rome.

According to Chapman, however, the writings of Pope Gelasius are among those that speak most often of *prima, secunda, tertia sedes* against the claims of Constantinople (e.g., *Ep.* 10.5; Thiel, p. 344), proffering as the source of Roman jurisdiction the fact that Christ promised to Peter the keys to his Church. Indeed, Gelasius cites the nine Fathers referred to by Leo the Great in 458 (Ilarius, Athanasius, Ambrose, Augustine, John Chrysostom, Theophilus, Gregory of Nazianzus, Basil, Cyril of Alexandria), with the addition of Cyprian,

---

25. See C. H. Turner, "The Roman Council under Damasus A.D. 382," *Journal of Theological Studies* 1 (1900): 554–60. Mention is also made at this council of the martyrdom of Paul in association with that of Peter in order to assert the preeminence of the church of Rome.

26. Paulinus of Nola gave Nola the same title, *Carmen* 13.26–30: "O Nola...you have received the title of second city after Rome itself"; see Barbara Agosti, "Appunti su Paolino di Nola: Il nome di s. Paolino e Nola 'secunda Roma,'" *Rendiconti dell'Istituto Lomabrdo di Scienze e Lettere* 123 (1989): 279–89.

27. This is an application of the controversy with Judaism on the "true Israel"; see above, n. 9; see also J. Fellermayr, *Tradition und Sukzession im Lichte des römisch-antiken Erbdenkens.*

placed first in the list *(beati Caecilii Cypriani opuscula)*,[28] and Jerome and Prosper of Aquitaine at the end.

The *auctoritas* and *auctoritates* of the *Decretum Gelasianum*

Two questions arise regarding the authoritativeness of the *Decretum Gelasianum;* one concerns its authority, that is to say, its authoritative source; the other, the doctrinal authorities recognized as such in the decree.

The *auctoritas* of *Gelasianum*

The text of the *Decretum Gelasianum* is an authoritative document. It belongs to the class of Roman jurisdiction known as a decree, that is, an authoritative judgment issued by the imperial curia and by magistrates responsible for legitimately resolving controversial issues. In the Church of the sixth century, a decree was issued as a papal letter containing an authoritative response (= decree) to a request and was known as a "decretal" (= of a decree, and hence also *decretalis pagina*).[29]

The *auctoritas* of the Roman See regarding the decisions taken by Pope Gelasius (the *Decretum Gelasianum*) was justified by the primacy conceded to it by Christ through the apostle Peter. To him was accrued the *societas* of the apostle Paul, whose death, according to the decree, occurred on the same day as that of Peter.[30] This authority was therefore clarified in relation to the other patriarchal sees.

---

28. *Ep.* 165. As mentioned earlier, in *Decretum* 5 Cyprian also heads the list of heretics and their apocryphal texts *(opuscula Thascii Cypriani, apocrypha)*. The motive for such disparagement has yet to be clarified.

29. Pope Gelasius, for example, decreed in the Roman synod of 494: "Item Decretales Epistolae quas beatissimi Papae pro diversorum Patrum consultatione dederunt, venerabiliter suscipiendae sunt." The first surviving "decretal letter" is that of Pope Siricius (384–399) "ad Himerium," bishop of Tarragona, transmitted to us as the *Decretale ad episcopos Galliae* of Pope Damasus (= Siricius, *Ep.* 10; see E. Babut, *La plus ancienne décrétale* [Paris, 1904], 69–87). The other decretal letters attributed to Pope Siricius by Isidore in the ninth century are spurious (see P. Coustant in the preface to vol. 1 of *Epistolae Romanorum pontificum*, nn. 153 ff.). It should also be noted that letters to the clergy and faithful sent by the metropolitan for the consecration of a designated bishop were also known as "decrees."

30. *Decretum Gelasianum* 3.1: "Incipit decretale de recipiendis et non recipiendis libris qui scriptus est a Gelasio papa cum septuaginta....2. Addita est etiam societas beatissimi Pauli apostoli...uno tempore uno eodemque die gloriosa morte cum Petro in urbe Roma sub Caesare Nerone."

The primacy conceded to the Roman See through the apostle Peter was spoken of in these terms: "Sancta tamen Romana ecclesia…ceteris ecclesiis praelata est, sed evangelica voce domini et salvatoris nostri primatum obtinuit: 'Tu es Petrus' inquiens [Matt 16:18–19]" (*Decretum* 3.1).[31]

The conclusion to be drawn regarding the relationships between the Roman See and the other patriarchal sees is this: the first see is that of Rome, the second that of Alexandria, followed thirdly by Antioch although all three trace their origins to Peter. The decree states: "Est ergo prima Petri apostoli sedes Romana ecclesia…secunda autem apud Alexandriam beati Petri nomine a Marco…consecrata. Tertia vero sedes apud Antiochiam beatissimi apostoli Petri habetur" (*Decretum* 3.3).

The *auctoritates* of the Roman See

Chapters 4 and 5 identify the doctrinal authorities together with the related texts that guide the Church in its defense of orthodoxy; these chapters also list proscribed works.

Chapter 4 specifies the recognized authorities: synods, received authors, and written texts.

The synods correspond to the first ecumenical councils (4.1), with mention being made of the role, in the councils of Ephesus and Chalcedon, of the bishops of Rome, who condemned Nestorius through Cyril, and Eutyches through the bishops of Alexandria.[32]

The written texts are those of Cyprian, Gregory of Nazianzus, Basil, Athanasius, John of Constantinople (John Chrysostom), Theophilus of Alexandria, Cyril of Alexandria, Hilary of Poitiers, Ambrose, Augustine of Hippo, Jerome, Prosper (4.2), the epistle of Leo to Flavianius (*Tomus ad Flavianum*), together with the writings of all the orthodox Fathers who had never deviated from communion with the church of Rome, the *litterae decretales* of the popes (4.3), the official

---

31. The passage from the *Decretum Gelasianum* finds confirmation in the Roman council of 378, already cited above (n. 29).

32. *Decretum* 4.1: "[the Council of Ephesus] in qua Nestorius damnatus est consensu beatissimi Coelestini papae mediante Cyrillo Alaxandrinae sedis antistite et Arcadio episcopo ab Italia destinato; sanctam synodum Calcedonensem mediante Mariano Augusto et Anatolio costantinopolitano episcopo."

deeds of the martyrs venerated by the church of Rome, the lives of
the hermits by Jerome, the Acts of *St. Sylvester,* the texts relating to the
finding of the cross (4.4), the writings of Rufus with the annotations
of Jerome, the writings of Origen not repudiated by Jerome, the
Chronicle of Eusebius, Orosius, the text on Easter by Sedulius, and
Juvencus (4.5).

The patristic section is presented in positive and negative parts.
In its positive component, the *Regula Benedicti* (9.1) is cited whenever
there is reference to the reading of the Fathers, *orthodoxi, sancti, catholici
Patres,* who had never deviated from communion with the church of
Rome. Conformity to this underlying principle of communion char-
acterizes the list of persons and works constituting the doctrinal *auctoritates* of the catholic Church.[33]

The Primacy of the Bishop of Rome (*Decretum Gelasianum* 3)

There are two particular aspects that converge to give weight to
the authority of the *Decretum Gelasianum:* the juridical context and
some, let us say technical expressions used to designate the primacy
of the bishop of Rome, namely, *papa* and *ecclesia Romana.*

The text of chapter 3, which deals with this primacy and is held
to be the most ancient part of the decree (382, the pontificate of
Damasus), states: "Sancta tamen Romana ecclesia nullis synodicis
vocibus ceteris ecclesiis praelata est, sed evangelica voce Domini et
Salvatoris nostri primatum obtinuit, 'tu es Petrus' inquiens." It continues, expressing the purity of the faith conserved by the church of
Rome, "Est ergo prima Petri apostoli sedes Romana ecclesia 'non
habens maculam nec rugam nec aliquid eiusmodi' [Eph 5:27]."

The *Decretum Gelasianum,* which places the magisterial function of
the Roman See in an authoritative juridical perspective, should be
understood in a threefold context: the *auctoritates,* the heresiological

---

33. *Decretum* 4.2: "item opuscula beati Caecilii Cypriani...Gregorii
Nazianzeni...Basilii...Athanasii...Iohannis Constantinopolitani...Theophili Alexandrini...Cyrilli Alexandrini...Hilarii Pictaviensis...Ambrosii...Augustini Hipponer-
egiensis episcopi...Hieronimi presbyteri...Prosperi"; 4.3: "epistolam beati papae
Leonis ad Flavianum...ita opuscula atque tractatus omnium patrum orthodoxorum,
qui in nullo a sanctae Romanae ecclesiae consortio deviarunt."

current, and the new juridical line, a symbiosis of the ecclesiastical and the imperial, that developed from the period of the Constantinian peace onwards in the *Libelli confessionis* defining orthodoxy and ultimately in the *Decretum de libris recipiendis et non recipiendis*, more simply known as the *Decretum Gelasianum*, whose full title is *Incipit decretale de recipiendis et non recipiendis libris qui scriptus est a Gelasio papa cum septuaginta viris eruditissimis episcopis in sede apostolica urbis Romae*.

Not just concerning themselves with identifying heresies, the latter documents seek to mark the boundaries of the catholic *campus*, or territory, beyond which the heretic was located. This territory was that of orthodoxy, and in turn it coincided with the ambit of the catholic Church, which, in the juridical terminology of the time, was expressed as *catholica lex*.[34]

Dissident groups were known as "sects" or *conventicula* with respect to the Great or "catholic" Church.[35]

In this way a *Corpus canonum* developed, becoming known in the fifth century as the *christiana lex* or the *catholica lex*.[36] The first of these found its reference point, for the most part, in the *episcopalis audientia* (introduced by Constantine in 318, in *CTh* [= *Codex Theodosianus*] 1.27.1); the second, in the councils.

There is with Theodosius I a gradual decline of interference in the internal order of the Church on the part of the empire. In fact, there is in imperial legislation a shift to the adoption of ecclesiastical norms, appropriating them as its own together with their respective penalties. In this way, a juridical *ratio* was grafted onto imperial legal provisions, preventive and repressive, issued in support of the religious politics of the catholic Church.

---

34. See, for example, *Codex Theodosianus* 16.11: "Iam pridem sanximus ut catholicae legis antistes et clerici…minime devincentur." For a more extensive survey, see Elio Dovere, "CTh. 16,11: Sistematica compilatoria e 'catholica lex,'" *Vetera Christianorum* 31 (1994): 53–77.

35. For general information, see F. Winkelmann, "Grosskirche und Haeresien in der Spätantike," *Forschungen und Fortschritte* 41 (1967): 245ff.

36. The first was the Eastern *Corpus canonum*, known in the West from the *Corpus canonum Africanum* (ca. 420), see A. M. Stickler, *Historia iuris canonici Latini, Historia fontium* (Turin, 1950), vol. 1; with modern revision by B. E. Ferme, *Introduzione alla storia delle fonti e della scienza del diritoo canonico* (Rome, 1998), 31–32.

Dissent of the faithful/subjects from the *lex sacra*—that upheld by one's bishop—was, in definitive terms, deemed inadmissible for the *imperium*.[37] This led to the creation of the imperial *ius ecclesiasticum*, which, if moderated in the *Codex Theodosianus* by laws in force, assumed the value of a general norm in the code instituted by Justin. In this regard, it is worth recalling that in the Basilian codification, priority listing was given to entries relating to questions of faith (*De summa Trinitate et fide catholica et ut nemo de ea publice contendere audeat* B.1.1), followed by sources and by other norms.[38]

In the East, imperial ecclesiastical legislation was at first appended to the codes of canon law and was incorporated only later; on the contrary, in the West we find independent compilations of solely Roman law for ecclesiastical use.[39]

This brief overview serves to illustrate the independence, in the West, of ecclesiastical law from civil authority, which, in turn, recognized that law as its own. This was a natural development within the ambit of what was later juridically recognized with respect to the five patriarchates.[40] For the latter, the coincidence of the reorganization of the territorial divisions of the empire with its ecclesiastical constituents

---

37. See G. Puglisi, "Giustizia criminale e persecuzioni antieretiche: Priscilliano e Ursino, Ambrogio e Damaso," *SicGymn* 43 (1990): 91ff.

38. G. L. Falchi, "Osservazioni sul fondamento ideologico della collocazione della materia ecclesiastica nel Codice di Giustiniano e nei Basilici," in *Atti del V Colloquio Romanistico Canonistico (8–10 marzo 1984)* (Rome, 1985), 379f.

39. Pope Gelasius expressed the Roman ecclesiastical position to Emperor Anastasius in the epistle *De ecclesiastica et civili potestate* (494). For the divergencies in the placement of ecclesiastical material in the Theodosian, Justinian, and Basilian codifications, see C. Capizzi, "Potere e ideologia imperiale da Zenone a Giustiniano (474–527)," in various authors, *L'imperatore Giustiniano: Storia e mito* (Milan, 1978), 3ff.; for the continuity of Theodosian legislation in the Justinian codification, see Gian Luigi Falchi, "La tradizione giustinianea del materiale teodosiano (CTh. XVI)," *Studia et documenta historiae et iuris* 57 (1991): 1–123.

40. The "Petrine triarchy" was a constant feature until Gregory the Great (F. Cocchini, "Gregorio Magno e le sedi petrine," in *Atti del VI Simposio di Tarso su S. Paolo apostolo.* ed. L. Padovese [Rome, 2000], 253–62); five as the number of patriarchates is mentioned for the first time in a juridical document in the *Novellae* of Justinian 123.3, with Jerusalem listed last (F. Sollazzo, "I patriarchi nel diritto canonico orientale e occidentale," in *Atti del Congresso internazionale tra i canoni d'Oriente e d'Occidente* [Bari, 1994], 239ff.).

(the patriarchates) was not an indifferent occurrence, with its consequent loss of the original distinction between imperial and canonical
laws. This reality, which emerged after the Council of Chalcedon,
was to have its development in the sixth century. The patriarchs, in
other words, began to act as institutional representatives of their
communities. I believe that this was also the fundamental significance
of the subsequent synthesis of the Symmachian position expressed in
the rule "Prima sedes a nemine iudicatur."[41]

If in Symmachus's predecessor, Anastasius II (496–498), we
identify an attempt at reconciliation with the East, in Symmachus we
discern the very opposite tendency. At stake were the issues relating
to the question of the election of the bishop of Rome and to his
authority in the alienation or otherwise of ecclesiastical property,
which had been until then the prerogative of the presbyters as the
holders of tituli.[42]

The authority over presybterial tituli, conceded to Pope
Symmachus by King Theodoric, was most certainly an anti-imperial

---

41. Pope Symmachus (Ep. 16; Thiel, p. 729) received the Libellum petitorium from
Caesarius of Arles in 514: "Apostolica sedes sibimet vindicat principatum, et syn-
odalibus decretis firmior eius praecellit auctoritas...a se concessa debent inconcussa
servari"; that is, conciliar decrees confirmed the sovereignty of Roman authority; see
F. De Marini Avonzo, "I vescovi nella 'Variae' di Cassiodoro," in Atti dell'Accademia
Romanistica Costantiniana (VIII Convegno internazionale) (Rome, 1990), 249ff.
42. The presbyterial tituli, initiated in the third century, were twenty-five in
number by the time of Pope Innocent I (401–417) with the foundation of the titulus
of San Vitale. It was not until the sixth century that each had a patron saint and was
used as a statio with the role of strengthening the communion of the local community.
Due to their progressive evolution, they were not always distributed according to the
ecclesiastical division of Rome into seven regions, and even less according to the
fourteen civil regions of Augustus (see A. Chavasse, "L'organisation stationnale du
carême romain avant le VIII siècle," Revue de sciences religieuses 56 [1982]: 17–32;
Federico Guidobaldi, "L'organizzazione dei 'tituli' nello spazio urbano," in Letizia
Pani Ermini, "Christiana loca": Lo spazio cristiano nella Roma del primo millennio [Rome, 2000],
123–29). The election of the bishop of Rome was by means of his nomination by his
predecessor, in the absence of which the new pope was elected by the presbyters. If
agreement was impossible, two popes could even be elected, as in the case of
Laurentius and Symmachus (the Laurentian schism). For further updated reading on
the sociopolitical activity of Symmachus, see Teresa Sardella, Società, Chiesa, e stato nel-
l'età di Teoderico: Papa Simmaco e lo scisma laurenziano (Armarium 7) (Soveria Mannelli:
Rubettino, 1996).

political reality, but it also expressed the authoritative new order of the Roman church, rendered famous by the words uttered at the Council of Rome in 502: "Prima sedes a nemine iudicatur." That is, being the first see, the Roman Christian See (the other two mentioned in the decree are, in order, Alexandria and Antioch) cannot be judged by anyone.[43] The fact that priests were forbidden by King Theodoric to alienate their *tituli*, and the transferal of this authority to the pope brought about within the Church itself an affirmation and an awareness of the *potestas* of the bishop of Rome that had never been known before.

Undoubtedly the Symmachian affirmation "Prima sedes a nemine iudicatur" was intended, from the juridical point of view, to confirm that Rome, on equal terms with the other metropolitan sees (Alexandria, Antioch, Jerusalem, and Constantinople, although the last two are not mentioned in the *Decretum Gelasianum*), was not subject to external judgment. It also represented an authoritative self-realization on the part of the Church of Rome, that only some years before in the *Decretum Gelasianum* had already specified the sources of its authority, the first of which was the authority of the apostles Peter and Paul.

The advent of Emperor Justin (518–527) marked an important stage in the East for the orthodox movement. With the dimming of previous anti-Chalcedonian tendencies, there came about a return to the schism of Acacius and an embracing of the guiding principles of the Christology of the *Libellus Hormisdae*.[44] The orthodoxy of the empire coincided in the East with that of the Church and vice versa. In the East, the *societas christiana* was based on the indissoluble dyad

---

43. This text is first attested in *Ep.* 10.5 (*Commonitorium ad Faustum*) of Pope Gelasius in 493: "primam sedem...de tota ecclesia iudicare, ipsam ad nullius commeare iudicium nec de eius unquam praeceperunt iudicio iudicari [referring to canons 3–5 of the Council of Sardica, 342/343]" (ed. Thiel, I, 344; see Albert Michael Königer, "Prima sedes a nemine iudicatur," in *Festgabe A. Ehrhard*, ed. A. M. Königer (Bonn, 1922), 273–300; Hans Christof Brennecke, "Rom und der dritte Kanon von Serdika (342)," *Zeitschrift für Religions- und Geistesgeschichte KA* 100 (1983): 15–45; see also *MGH, Auctores antiquissimi* 12:395–455, in Augustine Fliche—Victor Martin 4:341–52; Klaus Martin Girardet, "Gericht über den Bischof von Rom," *Historische Zeitschrift* 229 (1998): 1–38.

44. This refers to the *libellus Fides Hormisdae papae*, in *Collectio Avellana*: CSEL 35:800.

empire-Church, which was definitively consecrated by Justianian law, but in the West developments took quite a different course, with the *Decretum Gelasianum* representing the official document of the Roman See marking its orientation and distinctiveness.

8. The Triad: Bishop of Rome (= Pope)—Roman Church— the Apostle Peter

The designation "pope," from the honorary title for Latin bishops in the fourth to sixth centuries, became the standard title identifying only the bishop of Rome *(episcopus ecclesiae Romanae)* as successor to the apostle Peter. The *Decretum Gelasianum* clearly acknowledges this shift.[45]

"Bishop of Rome (= pope)—Roman church—the apostle Peter" constitutes a tripartite expression delineating a single entity. The bishop of Rome thereby emerges as the minister of the catholic and apostolic faith,[46] and it is in line with this understanding that he orients his role. Moreover, one century earlier—more precisely in 380— Emperor Theodosius had already defined as a "catholic Christian" only one who professed "the religion that the divine apostle Peter gave to the Romans," recognizing "Damasus as his successor and Peter, bishop of Alexandria, as a man of apostolic holiness."

---

45. In the conservative councils in Latin, from that of Ilarius in 465 to that of Symmachus, mention is made of *papa* and *ecclesia Romana* ("Caelius Symmachus episcopus ecclesiae Romanae"); in that of Gelasius ("sanctae romanae ecclesiae"); in the *libellus* of the deacon John presented to Symmachus in 506, he is called "Caelius Joannes, diaconus ecclesiae Romanae" (Thiel, p. 697). The term *papa* was used as an abbreviated form in the synods; Liberatus of Carthage (560–566), for example, uses this term only for the bishop of Rome ("papa Leo," "papa Simplicius," "papa Felix," "papa Joannes," "Silverius papa," or "papa Romanus"). In an inscription from the catacombs of Saint Callistus (in the crypt of the martyrs Calocerus and Partendus and the double cubiculum of Severus), dating not beyond the year 304, the bishop of Rome, Marcellinus, is called *papa*, and this is perhaps the first such inscription. On the development of the authoritative terminology of the church of Rome, see also Pierre Batifol, "Papa, sedes apostolica, apostolatus," *RAC* 2 (1925); idem, *"Cathedra Petri": Études d'histoire ancienne de l'Église* (Paris, 1938).

46. The expression *catholica et apostolica fides communioque* is that of Gelasius; see *Ep.* 3.9 (Thiel, p. 317); *Ep.* 12 (Thiel, p. 355).

The bishop of Rome could not embrace within his communion any person who was an enemy of the catholic and apostolic faith and of its communion, as this person would necessarily be a heretic. This is the light cast, for example, on the heresy of Eutyches and his followers and sympathizers in the *Libellus* of Misenus presented at Gelasius's council in 495, which could be considered to be the basis of chapter 5 of the *Decretum Gelasianum*.[47]

The Designation *(sancta) Romana ecclesia*

The Roman See is identified in the *Decretum Gelasianum* by the designation *(sancta) Romana ecclesia*. This term does not denote what would have been the equivalent of the papal chancery, which did not then exist as we know it today, but the popes themselves as such.[48] Indeed, mention is made of famous popes, such as Pope Gelasius. This passage marks the identification of the bishop of Rome with the church of Rome and the genesis of the understanding of the pope himself as an authoritative person.

---

47. See *Libellus:* "me omnes quidem haereses et quidquid inimicum est catholicae et apostolicae fidei communionique sincerae, prona mente refutare; tum praecipue Eutychianam haeresim cum suo scilicet auctore Eutychete et eius sectatore Dioscuro, vel successoribus eius atque communicatoribus Timotheo Aeluro, Petro Alexandrino, Acacio Costantinopolitano, Petro Antiocheno, cunctisque eorum complicibus et communicatoribus respuere, damnare et anthematizare perpetuo, omnesque istos et huiusmodi horribiliter execrari; nec unquam me cum talibus ullum quolibet modo profiteor habiturum esse consortium, sed ab his omnibus futurum prorsus alienum...sub conspectu Dei et beati Petri apostoli eiusque vicarii ac totius ecclesiae, mea (sicut dixi) professione voceque condemno, detestor, exhorreo, in sola me fide communioneque catholica et apostolica semper duraturum esse confirmans" (Thiel, pp. 439–40); this is repeated nearly verbatim in the *Decretum Gelasianum* (5.9): "Dioscorus, Eutyches, Petrus et alius Petrus, e quibus unus Alexandriam, alius Antiochiam maculavit, Acacius Costantinopolitanus cum consortibus suis necnon et omnes haeresei hereseorumque discipuli sive schismatici docuerunt vel conscripserunt, quorum nomina minime retinuimus, non solum repudiata, verum ab omni Romana catholica et apostolica ecclesia eliminata, atque cum suis auctoribus auctorumque sequacibus sub anathematis insolubili vinculo in aeternum confitemur esse damnata."

48. For further information and documentation on much of this data, see Edith Pásztor, *Onus Apostolicae Sedis: Curia romana e cardinalato nei secoli XI–XV* (Rome, 1999).

From the fifth and sixth centuries on, the *sancta Romana ecclesia* became in papal letters simply *Romana ecclesia*.[49]

Nonetheless, in writing to the bishops of Syria, Gelasius makes an innovative and unique statement: "Dominis meis religiosissimis et sanctissimis episcopis...Gelasius miseratione divina *minister catholicae et apostolicae fidei*."[50] That is, the bishop of Rome presents himself as the minister of the catholic and apostolic faith and, in this perspective, orients his role for the defense of orthodoxy.

In order to express the purity of the faith conserved by the church of Rome, chapter 3 of the *Decretum Gelasianum* states: "Est ergo prima Petri apostoli sedes Romana ecclesia 'non habens maculam nec rugam nec aliquid eiusmodi' [Eph 5:27]." The same concept is reiterated later in *Ep.* 7 of Hormisdas in 515: "quia in sede apostolica immaculata est semper catholica servata religio" (Thiel, p. 755).

In his long letter written against Acacius in 488–489 (*Ep.* 1; Thiel, pp. 287–311), Gelasius reprimands him that as he had not conserved the catholic faith and the communion, he no longer had the right to communion with the Apostolic See, identified expressly as *communio mea* or *nostra, catholica fides* and *catholica communio*. There is at this point no mention of *catholica et apostolica*—which was done intentionally from 492 onwards[51]—with its emphasis on confirming the primacy of the Roman See given its relationship with Peter. In fact, the *Decretum Gelasianum* states: "Sancta tamen Romana ecclesia nullis synodicis vocibus ceteris ecclesiis praelata est, sed evangelica voce Domini et Salvatoris nostri primatum obtinuit, 'tu es Petrus' inquiens" (3.1).

The sovereignty of the Roman church over all the churches of the empire had already become state law in 382, and it was now confirmed by the Roman See itself as the conscience of the universal Church.[52]

---

49. See, for example, Pope John I in 523 or 526 (in *Mansi* 8:603).

50. *Ep.* 43 (Thiel, pp. 471–72; Mai, *Patrum nova bibl.* 2:654).

51. *Ep.* 3 *ad Euphemium:* (Thiel, p. 313) "quibus una catholica apostolicaque communio"; (p. 314) "ecclesiae catholicae atque apostolicae dispositio"; etc. The question depended on Euphemius, who in not wanting to condemn Acacius could not be in communion with Rome (Gelasius, *Ep.* 9 [Thiel, p. 340]; *Ep.* 10).

52. A certain opposition to the decree is testified to by the prologue at the beginning of some martyrologies at the end of the fifth and beginning of the sixth centuries (B. De Gaiffier, "Un prologue hagiographique hostile au Décret de Gélase?" *Analecta bollandiana* 82 [1964]: 341–53).

Conclusion

Four historical-theological periods can be identified in the development of the primacy of the bishop of Rome, each presenting its own distinctive aspects:

1. The Pre-Nicene Period

The Roman church was described as she who "presides to the agape" in the region of the Romans (Ignatius of Antioch). The sense of this expression is understood in the context of the service undertaken by the church of Rome in this territory in the same measure as that undertaken with regard to the other churches, for example, that of Corinth (the *Epistle to the Corinthians* of Clement of Rome), that is, a presidency of coordination and intervention in favor of the Christian *domus* in Rome and of the churches recognized by them. This was the period of the *domus ecclesiae* and of the "presbyters" during the second century.

Its proven apostolic origin conferred upon it a *potior/potentior principalitas* that brought to the fore the need for the other churches to "agree with the church of Rome."

The bishops of the Latin Church developed their coepiscopality with the *cathedra Petri* as the focal point, identifying in Peter the genesis of the episcopacy (Cyprian, the *primatus textus* of *De ecclesiae unitate* 4). This understanding led to extending the understanding of the primacy of the church of Rome beyond its primacy as *ecclesia principalis*.

2. The Post-Nicene Period

The post-Nicene period is linked to the reorganization of the churches into patriarchates, the latter functioning and interacting in unison with the Roman emperor. Conciliar decisions emanating from an ecumenical council were sent to the patriarchs of the five patriarchates, with the request for their signature and their commitment to ensure the signature of their respective episcopates. These decisions were received as imperial law or, better, as *lex catholica,* with accompanying sanctions for defaulters or those condemned as schismatics or heretics according to imperial laws. In this way, the effective consensus of the churches of the East and West was obtained, and the extent of possible controversy was contained. The consensus, for example, of the bishops of the East and West, observed Augustine, was against the "Pelagian" position of Julian (*Contra Iulianum* 3.17.32).

At the same time and within the same context arose the development of the authoritativeness—we could say prejudicial—of the stance of the Apostolic See on doctrinal questions. "You [Julian]," retorts Augustine, "seek an examination already undertaken by the Holy See" (*Opus imperfectum contra Iulianum* 2.103). If this last aspect could in some way still find a place within an understanding of the primacy of the bishop of Rome as primate of the *ecclesia principalis* of the Latin churches, there was nonetheless at the same time an affirmation of the principle of the absolute authoritativeness of the church of Rome in questions relating to orthodoxy and of the necessarily consequent communion with the Apostolic See. The criterion of consensus with the church of Rome increasingly focused more directly on its bishop, leading to the subsequent development of the personal primacy of the bishop of Rome. Cyril of Alexandria, for example, approached the bishop of Rome, Celestine I, for support on his position against Nestorius, whom he brought to the Council of Ephesus in 431; in this same context, Leo the Great, on May 13, 449, wrote to the Second Ephesian Synod, convened by Theodosius II, as follows: "The zeal for the faith of our most clement emperor...has rendered homage to divine law by requesting this apostolic see to confirm his imperial decree [the convocation of the Council of Ephesus]." And after citing Matt 16:13–18, he concludes: "Whosoever does not embrace the confession of Peter and contradicts the gospel is therefore completely beyond this structure" (*Ep.* 33; PL 54:797ff.).

There are two facets related to the post-Constantinian development of the doctrine of the primacy, and both can be inferred from the letter of Pope Gelasius against Acacius in 488–489 (*Ep.* 1; Thiel, pp. 287–311), in which the pope reprimands Acacius for not having conserved the catholic faith and communion with the Roman Apostolic See and informs him that by so doing he has lost his right to communion with him. The two principles of the integrity of the catholic faith and communion with the Apostolic See were delineated in the *Decretum Gelasianum* (end of the fifth and beginning of the sixth centuries) in two ideas later to become characteristic of the primacy of the bishop of Rome: first, the designation pope, from its original meaning derived from the honorary title for Latin bishops in the fourth to sixth centuries, comes to denote the standard title identifying only the bishop of Rome *(episcopus ecclesiae Romanae)* as successor to the apostle Peter; and second, the designation *(sancta) Romana ecclesia* denotes not the equivalent of the papal chancery but the very popes themselves, endowed with authority deriving from the apostle Peter. This development and practice led the church of Rome to identify itself with its bishop and emerged as the criterion of orthodoxy of the Christian churches. Lack of conformity, that is, the rupture of the principle of communion with the Church founded by Peter, would see a bishop and his church confined to the realm of schism or heresy. In the *Decretum Gelasianum* the overall authority of the pope was upheld, as always, by reference to the text of Matthew (16:18–19): "You are Peter....I will give you the keys of the kingdom of heaven." It is clear that from this point onwards the bishop of Rome carried more weight in terms of self-determination, and in practice a consciousness of his "primacy" began to spread.

As the *Decretum Gelasianum* leads one to conclude, however, this primacy was exercised in line with tradition as it was officially recognized. This aspect is currently the object of the greater part of research on the exercise of the Petrine primacy by the bishop of Rome. The exercise of this primacy can be discerned along the channels that constituted, let us say, the protocol.

The first channel was the pope's consciousness of being in possession of an authoritative interpretation of fidelity to Jesus Christ, as this was transmitted in the Sacred Scriptures and in the ecclesiastical customs often introduced and confirmed in the holy synods. In this perspective, the constant reference to the 318 Fathers of the holy synod of Nicaea remained emblematic. The second channel relates to the range of action of the Roman Apostolic See within the boundaries of the tradition of the Church, which is conserved and transmitted through its doctors and their recognized works. Thus, the *Decretum Gelasianum* speaks of *auctoritas* and of *auctoritates*, that is, of the authoritative source and of the doctrinal authorities recognized by the Roman See and within which it exercises its magisterium. Regarding the primacy conceded to the Roman See through the apostle Peter, the text says, in the sense of confirming, "Sancta tamen Romana ecclesia...ceteris ecclesiis praelata est, sed evangelica voce domini et salvatoris nostri primatum obtinuit: 'Tu es Petrus' inquiens [Matt 16:18–19]" (Decretum 3.1).

Regarding the auctoritates, chapters 4 and 5 identify the texts that guide the Church in its defense of orthodoxy and also list proscribed works. The Petrine primacy was thus understood in the sense that the bishop of Rome would act with authority to safeguard the correct reading of the gospel, not so much and not principally as an individual called also to pass judgment on that tradition.

3. Medieval Period

The Middle Ages stalled at the understanding of having acquired the knowledge of the universality of the authority of the bishop of Rome, expressed, on the social level, in the authority of the two keys and, on the doctrinal level, in the authority of infallibility, was considered during the Middle Ages as an indisputable fact.[53] Innocent III developed this idea in De sacro altaris mysterio 1.8: De primatu Romani pontificis (PL 217). The work of Pietro Giovanni Olivi, a Franciscan friar, has yielded the questiones on the potestas of the pope in spiritualibus (dispensation from vows) and in temporalibus from the text Quaestiones de Romano pontifice (ed. M. Bartoli [Grottaferrata, 2002]), containing the quaestiones quodlibetales (no. 17) De universalissima potestate papae, (no. 19) De proelio ex mandato papae, (no. 20) De solutione debitorum pro excommunicatis, and an appendix, De perfectionibus summi pastoris. No

---

53. On the universality of the papacy: J. Leclercq, "L'argument de deux glaives (Lk 22,38) dans le controverses politiques du Moyen Age," Recherches de science religieuse 21 (1931): 299–329; A. Paravicini Bagliani, Il trono di Pietro: L'universalità del papato da Alessandro III a Bonifacio VIII (Rome, 1996); on infallibility: B. Tierney, Origins of Papal Infallibility, 1150–1350: A Study on the Concepts of Infallibility—Sovereignity and Tradition in the Middle Ages (Leiden, 1972); J. Heft, "John XII and Papal Infallibility: Brian Tierney Thesis Reconsidered," Journal of Ecumenical Studies 19 (1982): 759–80; R. Baumer, "An die Anfänge der päpstlichen Unfehlbarkeitslehre," Theologische Revue 69 (1973):

doubt was cast in the Middle Ages on the universality of the pope, although discussion may have arisen in connection with concrete cases (dispensation from vows, considered to be an interpersonal relationship; the defense of material possessions by means of arms, which is against the gospel). The age of humanism confronted the same issues with the addition of the question concerning infallibility in relation to a council (see also, e.g., Mario Zanchin, *Il primato del romano pontefice in un'opera inedita di Pietro del Monte del sec. XV* [Pisa, 1997]).

4. Modern Era

The last aspect of the Roman primacy emerged with Vatican I and concerned papal infallibility, both personal and with respect to a council, and the universality of the exercise of its authority.[54]

After the Council of Trent, the balance in the exercise of the Petrine ministry tended to shift towards the very person of the bishop of Rome. Moreover, some criteria serving as a guarantee of the orthodox tradition, for example, its doctors, such as Jerome and Augustine, were themselves also subjected to the judgment of the pope.

As an example that may be useful in casting light on what may have been a new phase in the understanding of the exercise of the magisterium of the bishop of Rome, we could bear in mind the

---

441–50; A. M. Stickler, "Sulle origini dell'infallibilità papale," *Rivista storica della Chiesa in Italia* 28 (1974): 583–94; D. L. D'Auvray, "The Idea of Innocent III and Idea of Infallibility," *Catholic Historical Review* 66 (1980): 417–21; M. Maccarrone, *Romana ecclesia–cathedra Petri*, 2 vols. (Rome, 1991); R. Manselli, "Il caso del papa eretico nelle correnti spirituali del sec. XIV," in *Archivio di filosofia* (Rome, 1970), 113–29; M. Bartoli, "Pietro di Giovanni Olivi nella recente storiografia sul tema dell'infallibilità pontificia," *Bollettino dell'Istituto Storico per il Medio Evo—archivio muratoriano* 99 (1994): 149–200.

54. The principal passages read: "ex hac Petri cathedra...salutarem Christi doctrinam profiteri et declarare constituimus" (constitutio *Dei Filius de fide catholica*, proemium); constitutio *Pastor aeternus de Ecclesia Christi* (session 4, July 18, 1870), ch.1, "De apostolici primatus in beato Petro institutione"; ch. 2, "De perpetuitate primatus beati Petri in Romanis pontificibus": "Quicumque in hac cathedra Petro succedit, is secundum Christi ipsius institutionem primatum Petri in universam Ecclesiam obtinet," canon "Si quis ergo dixerit, non esse ex ipsius Christi Domini institutione seu iure divino, ut beatus Petrus in primatu super universam Ecclesiam habeat perpetuos successores: aut Romanum Pontificem non esse beati Petri in eodem primatu successorem:

intervention of two popes regarding Saint Augustine. Writing to the bishops of Gaul in 431 regarding questions concerning the orthodoxy of the bishop of Hippo, Pope Celestine I wrote: "Augustine is among the supreme teachers holding authority in the catholic Church, beyond the difficult questions at issue" (the beginning of *Indiculus Coelestini*).[55]

At the end of the seventeenth century, Alexander VIII, in approving the decree of the Holy Office (December 7, 1690) regarding the errors of the Jansenists (in Denzinger-Schönmetzer 2301–2330), also condemned the affirmation that a given doctrinal stance of Augustine could be held and taught without consideration for any given papal bull.[56] This attitude presumes that a bull of the pope could affirm something contrary to the doctrine of Saint Augustine. We therefore confront a possibility that before the Council of Trent would certainly have been difficult to imagine.

As you will appreciate, our overview has covered some of the historical questions regarding the Petrine primacy that are still the

---

anathem sit." The exposition is given in chapter 3 ("De vi et ratione primatus Romani pontificis"), while chapter 4 ("De Romani pontificis infallibili magisterio") ends with the canon "Si quis autem huic nostrae definitioni contradicere, quod Deus avertat, praesumpserit: anathema sit"; see U. Hirst, *Papst–Konzil–Unfehlbarkeit: Die Ekkesiologie der Summenkommentare von Cajetan bis Billuart* (Mainz, 1978).

55. Celestine I, *Ep.* 21 (PL 50:528–537; at col. 530A, c. 2, 3 the eulogy of Augustine) of 431: "Augustinum sanctae recordationis virum pro vita sua atque meritis in nostra communione semper habuimus, nec unquam hunc sinistrae suspicionis saltem rumor adspersit: quem tantae scientiae olim fuisse meminimus, ut inter magistros optimos etiam ante a meis semper praedecessoribus haberetur." The *Indiculus* or the *Capitula Coelestini* has always been appended to *Ep.* 21 (in PL 51:205–212).

Celestine had received correspondence from Augustine while still a deacon (*Ep.* 192 of the Augustine letters) and, as bishop of Rome (*Ep.* 209, in which Augustine congratulates him on his peaceful election to the papacy [the year 423] and requests also the confirmation of the discharge of Bishop Antoninus from the See of Fussala). Referring to his predecessors, Celestine alludes to the letters of Innocent I at the councils of Carthage (*Ep.* 181) and of Milevum (*Ep.* 182) regarding the condemnation of the Pelagian heresy, and perhaps also to *Ep.* 183–184, in which he shows his solidarity with Augustine and friends (Alipius, Aurelius, Evodius, Possidius).

56. In *DS* 2330: "Ubi quis invenerit doctrinam in Augustino clare fundatam, illam absolute potest tenere et docere, non respiciendo ad ullam Pontificis Bullam."

object of research and that, furthermore, require the capacities of more than one individual in order to arrive at an overall evaluation.

Summary of Discussion

Some Orthodox expressed their astonishment at the developments that took place between the New Testament and the epoch of the church fathers, when a constantly growing power was claimed for one person, the bishop of Rome. They also questioned the Catholic thesis that the church of Rome was founded by the apostles Peter and Paul. In their view, the New Testament offers no sufficient basis for such conclusions.

In the Catholic view, however, the New Testament references to a possible presence of Peter and Paul in Rome should not be neglected.

When it comes to examining how the notion of pentarchy could be adapted or revived today, it may be useful to reflect on the distinctions between, and the order of, the various titles given to the bishop of Rome, even in official publications like the *Annuario Pontificio*: Bishop of Rome, Vicar of Jesus Christ, Successor of the Prince of the Apostles, Supreme Pontiff of the Universal Church, Patriarch of the West, Primate of Italy, Archbishop and Metropolitan of the Roman Province. It is indeed a historical fact that the authority of the bishop of Rome was different or was differently exercised in relation to the West, on the one hand, and to the East, on the other. The role of the emperor in the East and the absence of an emperor in the West certainly played a considerable part in this difference.

Regarding the pentarchy, the question was raised whether its establishment was based on theological grounds or was the result of concrete historical developments only.

According to one intervention, Catholics and Orthodox agree that different developments took place in the East and the West as a result of different historical circumstances in both parts of the empire. On the other hand, they also agree that throughout history the Church is guided by the Holy Spirit. As a consequence, would it be possible to consider these different developments as the work of the Holy Spirit, at least to some extent? Would it then be possible to consider them not as contradictory but as complementary to each other, as correcting each other? Would this vision not deserve careful consideration?

THE ROLE OF THE BISHOP OF ROME IN THE ECUMENICAL COUNCILS*

Vittorio Peri

The term and the concept of *primacy*, in its specific ecclesiological meaning of Roman primacy, papal or Petrine, are today commonly understood and used, to the extent that they constitute the theme of our symposium and that for over a century they have occurred frequently in modern theological, historical, and ecumenical bibliographies, and not only Catholic ones. Notwithstanding this observation, those involved in the three meetings of the Joint International Commission for Dialogue between the Roman Catholic Church and the Byzantine Orthodox Churches, from 1980 to 2000, from Rhodes to Emmitsburg (Baltimore), will well remember the cultural and methodological psychological difficulties arising from the simple attempt to use the term and concept of primacy, even if only cited to introduce the envisaged theme of the canonical structure of the Church in the joint texts. The meeting room would suddenly transform itself from a tranquil and dignified site of the New Pentecost into a riotous Babylonian marketplace besieged by linguistic confusion!

My own academic background and personal experience in the theological preparation of many members of the Commission, both Orthodox and Catholic, has always led me to hesitate in sharing the view that these difficulties have arisen mostly from an insufficient mutual knowledge or understanding of the other's position, from

---

* May 23, 2003 (morning session). Original text in Italian.

confessional prejudices, or from polemical and cultural obduracy due to formulas and expressions of the past. For if that were to be the case, a verbal exercise in forgetting, avoiding or going around, or substituting could have favored agreement in a creative way or even automatically. In the *Plan to Set Underway the Theological Dialogue between the Roman Catholic Church and the Orthodox Church*, the word *primacy* does not appear among the themes to be confronted in the first phase of the dialogue, which had nonetheless proposed for itself the declared aim of reestablishing full communion between the two churches. As well, the phenomenon of uniatism—the direct outcome of an Eastern theological conception and of an exercise of papal primacy affirmed in an official and systematic way after the Council of Trent, in 1595— is mentioned as a practical example of the many "situations désagréables" to be usefully reconsidered in parallel with the dialogue itself, confronting the historical phenomenon, dealt with individually by nation, in smaller subcommissions informed by sound moral principles and the political realities of the nations concerned. Imposed by the hierarchical authorities of both churches, this pragmatic approach, embarked upon by the Theological Dialogue at Freising, led to an unprecedented stalemate.

The great ecumenical insight of our era traces the historical and communitarian profile of the Church back to the original dialogue in truth and in charity. This remains the evangelical approach to maintaining and developing *visible* communion in unity and concord. This idea was reintroduced with new spiritual and cultural force in the encyclical *Ecclesiam suam* of Paul VI in 1963, following gestures of authentic friendship and Christian concord jointly expressed by pontiffs (true architects of sacred bridges) such as John XXIII and Athenagoras I of Constantinople. Joint theological discussion, however, seems possible only within the eucharistic *communio* of the Church. The recent encyclical of John Paul II on the Eucharist strongly affirms this conviction of faith.

This premise, which perfectly conforms to the unchanging tradition of the Church, entails the exclusion of two methods. It does not admit, for the sake of admission, that its historians may in some way be able to adequately represent or describe the very phenomenology at work in the Church by considering it simply as one of the many existing collective entities, *etsi Spiritus non daretur* or as if the mysteries of the Incarnation and the Resurrection had no impact on historical reality, since these can be known, at least inchoately, by every human being. That is, it is methodologically incomplete to represent or imagine the Church *only* as an external institution, constituted or adopted by the community of believers over the centuries, after first having responded to the gospel and organizing together its religious life, either due to personal motives, or to circumstances, or to the desire to follow the teaching of the Master. Nonetheless, it is in this perspective that a historiography has developed, confining itself to the sociological, administrative, political, cultural, and institutional aspects of the concrete and historical churches.

Regarding another formal approach to the recognizable truth of the Church, the same modern ecumenical insight should discourage theologians from conceptually defining ecclesiology as a sort of "transcendent hypostasis actually preexisting the work of Christ in the world" (de Lubac).[1] Concrete and historical institutions such as councils, patriarchates, the pentarchy, and the Roman primacy itself guarantee the function of the ecclesial structures of the pilgrim Church visible in history and in time, but they cannot be considered from an Aristotelian viewpoint as such, as entities of reason, unchanging and definable in absolute terms, independently of the recognizable and variable forms of their exercise in diverse eras or historical contexts, and even less so can they be identified in the sort of atemporal and abstract speculative and theological principles, ultimately Platonizing,

---

1. H. de Lubac, *Cattolicismo: Gli aspetti sociali del dogma* (Rome: Studium, 1948), 46, 48, cites the Protestant theologian K. Barth affirming, "if we seek to resolve the question of the unity of the Church by appealing to an invisible Church, we make Platonic speculations rather than listen to Christ." Cf. M. D. Chenu, *La parole de Dieu*, vol. 2, *L'évangile dans le temps* (Paris, 1964), 666–67: " L'histoire entre dans le tissu du Royaume de Dieu, l'Église en marche vers son accomplissement dans le Christ resuscité. La philosophie des essences et des *vérités éternelles* ne fournit pas les médiations conceptuelles appropriées à la perception de la foi dans l'économie chrétienne. Amère déception pour les hommes, si l'Évangile n'est que un idéalisme....Disons, en reprenant les catégories des Docteurs Orientaux, que n'a pas su conserver le juridisme statique del Latins, que la *théologie*, science de Dieu, n'est concevable que par et dans une économie, c'est-à-dire par une venue de Dieu dans le temps, préparée dans le peuple élu, consommée dans le Christ, réalisée deshormais dans l'Église....L'histoire du salut entre dans la construction de la théologie. Elle entre dans le tissu même de la *vérité*, substance de la foi dans le croyant: verité *de salut.*"

that characterize the formal definitions of faith about the Trinity by speculative or classical theology.

Nonetheless, reference to the role of the bishop of Rome, rather than to papal primacy as such, in order to seek to identify in concrete terms its development and popular consciousness in the historical and cultural context of the ancient ecumenical councils celebrated and recognized by both churches, is not intended to be a superfluous semantic *escamotage*, the latest of many, a sort of polite ecumenical euphemism alluding in essence to the currently widespread Catholic understanding of the term and theological concept of papal primacy. An encouraging sign in this direction is *Ut unum sint*, 94 and 95, where the pope declares that the mission of the bishop of Rome consists of assuring in every age, as provided by his primacy, the unity and visible communion of all the churches. The encyclical, however, also specifies that this primacy is exercised at various levels and in conformity with the forms of exercise associated with the historical evolution of the Church, these forms being alterable and improvable as well as, naturally, being subject to wear and deterioration. He ultimately invokes the Holy Spirit to shine his light upon all the pastors and theologians of our churches, "that we may seek—*together, of course*—the forms in which this ministry may accomplish a service of love recognized by all concerned."

The apostolic letter *Novo millennio ineunte*, 48, confirms the teaching that had developed after the Second Vatican Council on the more vivid understanding of the Church as a mystery of unity. The faith in the *one* Church "has *its ultimate foundation in Christ, in whom the Church is undivided* (cf. 1 Cor 1:11–13). As his Body, in the unity which is the gift of the Spirit, she is indivisible"; the mysterious supernatural communion in faith will not fail, nor will it ever fail. In this perspective, one can coherently speak in the same way of the undivided Church in the first, as in the second and third millenniums. "The reality of division among the Church's children appears at the level of history, as the result of human weakness in the way we accept the gift which flows endlessly from Christ the Head to his Mystical Body." These words echo the innovative and fundamental concrete and historical form of ecclesiology of Paul VI, who as Archbishop Montini as far back as January 1963 spoke in these terms to a group of ordinands in Milan: "The Church cannot understand itself properly if not in relation to the world, and not to the abstract world, but to a concrete, historical world." The background to this can be traced to the memorable opening address of John XXIII on October 11, 1962, at the commencement of the council: "The Christian, Catholic, and apostolic spirit of the whole world expects a step forward toward a doctrinal penetration and a formation of consciousness in faith and perfect conformity to the authentic doctrine, which, however, should be studied and expounded through the methods of research and through the literary forms of modern thought. The substance of the ancient doctrine of the deposit of faith is one thing, and the way in which it is presented is another. And it is the latter that must be taken into great consideration, with patience if necessary." In this vital innovation of faith, that which unites is not only a memory of the distant past but this memory relived in the modern Christian experience. The prophetic and wise role played in the modern Church by John XXIII and Athenagoras I, together with the other great pioneers of modern ecumenism, begins now to emerge more clearly, a role that bears similarities to that of the "homo paterfamilias qui profert de thesauro suo nova et vetera" (Matt 13:52).

The living and vital tradition of the Church, *unitary* and *normative* in the relevance of its ecclesial critical and historical consciousness, *pluralist* in its development in the various churches, now returns to the forefront, a position it had always enjoyed in the ancient Church. Today, however, it emerges in a new way, ceasing to be an ancillary function—simply pragmatic, apologetic, and polemical—of speculative theology. Moreover, the history of the Church cannot be conceived and used in fact as a database, a memory box full of documentary tools, or a static museum piece of "objective" (because material and documentary) information to which one resorts in order to obtain abstract dogmatic and juridical concepts. This would all be well if such concepts were to be held as fixed—independently of their semantic, cultural, and historical development—in definitions holding atemporal and definitive value to the word and to the letter, despite being able to trace their development to mental, cultural, and historical contexts that are quite different and therefore necessarily subject to historical development.

Tackling the theme of primacy as a study of the *role of the bishop of Rome in the ancient councils*—in the custom and developing understanding of the popes and council fathers as expressed in their practices and declarations—seems thus a feasible and advantageous historical-ecumenical approach, indeed I would say in our times an almost obligatory one, in order to pursue the dialogue between the churches. In this way, the new (and original) experience of ecclesial life is a development of the common and universal tradition of the Church. If for no other reason, such an approach rids the ecumenical scene of hypotheses that have revealed themselves to be rhetorical and far-fetched, even if they have been promoted and accepted over the last decades by reputable Catholic theologians. There is a ring of this, for example, in the desire of some for the Church to return to its profile in the first millennium, combining a reunified organizational entity with the auspicated pontifical concession of a dual canonical regime of the universal papal jurisdiction for the two restored parts of the one Church. This outlook betrays an understanding of reality and a conception of history (including the history—or "economy"—of salvation) that are rather extrinsic or, to say the least, idealistic, rationalist, or fanciful. It suffices to recall in this context the modesty and sense of self-criticism with which—on June 10, 1969, to the World Council of Churches in Geneva,[2] but already previously in 1963 in his programmatic encyclical *Ecclesiam suam*, 114,[3] and again on February 10, 1975,[4] to priests of the Diocese of Rome—Paul VI had reiterated the indispensable and inalienable character of the Petrine ministry for the safeguard of visible unity and communion among the churches. It is up to the believers—including exegetes, dogmatists, canonists, Church historians, and ecumenists—to perceive and to observe the tradition of the Church in their own time, which simply coincides with the current historical consciousness of the faith professed and

---

2. *Insegnamenti di Paolo VI*, 7 (1969) (Vatican City, 1970), 395–96.

3. "Are there not those who say that unity between the separated Churches and the Catholic Church would be more easily achieved if the primacy of the Roman pontiff were done away with? We beg our separated brothers to consider the groundlessness of this opinion. Take away the sovereign Pontiff and the Catholic Church would no longer be catholic. Moreover, without the supreme, effective, and authoritative pastoral office of Peter the unity of Christ's Church would collapse. It would be vain to look for other principles of unity in place of the true one established by Christ Himself. As St. Jerome rightly observed: 'There would be as many schisms in the Church as there are priests' [*Dialog. contra Luciferianos*, PL 23:173]" (*Ecclesiam suam*, 1971).

4. *Insegnamenti di Paolo VI*, 13 (1975) (Vatican City, 1976), 133–35.

lived in common by the Christian churches from era to era: reformulations, hypotheses, and combinations of formulaic expressions emerging in this process may appear as formal, rhetorical, and semantic rather than as re-proposals of the revealed truth.

Nor is another proposed hypothesis more feasible, namely, to reestablish unity by distinguishing bilaterally between "nontheological" and theological factors in the past at the origin of ecclesial and political historical facts—such as schisms, scissions and excommunications, persecutions, wars. Such phenomena, which may well in concrete terms comprise a religious, or rather ecclesial, component, are in fact inevitably subject to the inextricable confluence of all these factors due to their collective and social nature itself. Moreover, the assumption that division has been due to mere "theological factors," explained abstractly in theory, is manifestly dualistic, as if orthodoxy and orthopraxy were not connected and indispensable conditions for the very unity of the Church. At least since the eve of its second world conference in Edinburgh in 1937, and more assiduously after the Lund Conference (1952), the ecumenical movement "Faith and Order" has dedicated itself to the "increasing awareness that divisions have been created and are maintained by many factors other than those of difference in theological convictions and their expression. Theological differences have always been related to a context of historical, social, economic, racial, and other forces, which have sometimes played a greater part in precipitating division than the purely theological factors."[5] The timely ecumenical reemergence of this obvious and ancient insight, widely understood in traditional ecclesiology, should, on the one hand, dissuade theologians and canonists from treating concrete and datable events, situations, and institutions of ecclesial history as metaphysical principles and, on the other hand, should remind historians of their inadequacy in absolute terms either to morally condemn or to acclaim, in the absence or in the stead of Christ the Judge, the moral intentions or responsibilities of distant and long-dead protagonists in the historical development of the Church. The communitarian plea for forgiveness for collective infidelity, error, contradiction, procrastination, capitulation, acts contrary

---

5. *A History of the Ecumenical Movement*, 1517–1948, ed. R. Rouse and S. C. Neill (Geneva: World Council of Churches, 1986), 2:440.

to witness, and scandal of the historical Church in understanding and following the gospel, as the saints of the time recognized, is a sacred act of historical purification of memory and a sign of the defeat of our long-standing ancient prejudices; but it could never transform itself into some sort of idealistic chest beating of *mea culpa* on the part of past individuals, who have already in truth been judged by God on the basis of an intention and will that we cannot now know.[6] *The reality of division generates itself in the domain of history*, in the relationships between the children of the Church, and it is in the same *domain of history and contemporary thought* that, without disregard for tradition, we can begin to reconstruct the dissent, incomprehension, and recurring schisms in the uninterrupted dialogue of charity and truth between the children of the Church, for whose unity in the Spirit Christ invoked the Father.

1. Novelty and Innovations (KAINOTOMIAI, "Traditions of Men") in the Living Tradition of the Church

I have had the opportunity on various occasions to comment and write on the ministry and ecclesial role of the bishop of Rome in the common doctrine of the churches and on the diversification of its form of exercise: at a colloquium held in Gazzada in 1973, "Le sens de la primauté romaine pour les églises d'Orient entre Chalcedoine et Photius"; at the convention in Trent in 1982, "Papato e istanze ecumeniche"; at the historical-theological symposium in Rome in 1989, "Il primato del Vescovo di Roma nel primo millenio"; at the international colloquium in Salamanca in 1991, "Chiese locali e cattolicità

---

6. I have contributed a reflection on the purification of memory and the plea for forgiveness by the Church to God and to humanity for its historical responsibilities and shortcomings, in the article "Incoerenze della Chiesa nel passato, tentazioni della Chiesa nel presente," *Studium* 96, no. 1 (January–February 2000): 19–40. Similar reflections have appeared as an introduction to the volume: V. Peri, "La communione visibile tra le Chiese: Esigenze evangeliche e torti storici," in *"Orientalis varietas": Roma e le Chiese d'Oriente—storia e diritto canonico* (Rome: Pontificio Istituto Orientale, 1994), 11–50.

nel primo millennio"; at a colloquium in Milan in 1999, "Il ministero del Papa in prospettiva ecumenica," to cite those relevant in our present context.[7] I will limit my discussion to briefly recalling the fruits of philological and historical research on the constancy, in the ecclesial consciousness, of a role of the church of Rome in the maintenance of visible communion and the public profession of faith between the churches, as well as on the various historical models of its exercise. This role, exercised *pro tempore* in the person of its bishops, over time gained greater definition in terms of expression and scope in doctrinal and canonical recognition and was undertaken by degrees in forms compatible with the societies, civil institutions, cultures, and mentalities within the framework of which the ministry consciously undertook its role in the contemporary concrete and historical Church. Up until the dogmatic constitutions *Pastor aeternus* of Vatican I and *Lumen gentium* (23) of Vatican II, the bishop of Rome and the bishops of the other local churches had been traditionally proposed as the *visible* principle and foundation of unity by the bishops, the individual churches, and the greater part of the faithful. In order to remain concrete and historical and yet in permanent renewal, their mutual relations emerged as a visible hierarchical and universal communion.

---

7. The issues discussed were "Pro amore et cautela orthodoxae fidei": Note sul ministero ecclesiale del Vescovo di Roma nella dottrina comune tra l'VIII e il IX secolo," *Rivista di storia e letteratura religiosa* 12 (1976): 341–63; "Sul ruolo ecclesiale del Vescovo di Roma: Il problema attuale alla luce del passato unitario," in G. Ghiberti, V. Peri, H. J. Pottmayer, and D. Valentini, *Papato e istanze ecumeniche*, "Scienze religiose": Pubblicazioni dell'Istituto di Scienze Religiose di Trento 6 (Bologna, 1984), 61–118; "La Chiesa di Roma e le missioni "ad gentes" (secc. VII–IX)," in *Il primato del Vescovo di Roma nel primo millennio: Ricerche e testimonianze*, ed. M. Maccarrone, Pontificio Comitato di Scienze Storiche: Atti e documenti 4 (Vatican City, 1991), 567–642; "Chiese locali e cattolicità nel primo millenniodella tradizione romana," in *Lo scambio fraterno tra le Chiese: Componenti storiche della comunione* Storia e attualità 13 (Vatican City: Libreria Editrice Vaticana, 1993), 321–48 (this text was also published in the proceedings of the colloquium in Spanish, English, and Italian); "Sinodi, patriarcati, e primato romano dal primo al terzo millennio," in *Il ministero del papa in prospettiva ecumenica: Atti del Colloquio, Milano, 16–18 aprile 1998*, ed. A. Acerbi (Milan: Vita e Pensiero, 1999), 51–97. It is worth citing in this context the article entitled "La synergie entre le pape et le concile oecuménique," *Irénikon* 56, no. 2 (1983): 163–93, which takes up in French part of the second text.

The communitarian life of the churches, which embraced and disseminated the proclamation of the universal and salvific lordship of the risen Christ, was from the outset internally familiar with the continuity of a hierarchy possessing moral and organizational authority. This authority presented itself traditionally as a succession, a concrete and historical transfer of the public and social custody and transmittal of the faith authoritatively handed over by the "apostolic" fathers to men by them chosen and ordained by sacred rite in order to take their place with a specific sacred authority in the mission of guiding the consenting community. All the individual churches, mirroring their catholic whole, thus considered themselves to be apostolic, well before some principal sees, by virtue of a particular historical or exegetical reason, reserved for themselves the title of apostolic see, or apostolic throne. In the publicly proclaimed unity of faith, all the Church of Christ, all the churches of Christ, in line with the most ancient symbols of the faith, are historically apostolic.

"The primitive idea of the Church finds continuity in the Jewish idea of the *qahal*, a word that the Septuagint rendered precisely with the Greek *ekklêsia*. The *qahal* is not a restricted group or a purely empirical assembly, but the totality of the people of God, a concrete...visible reality."[8] In the Jewish mentality, this idea also found continuity with the institutional experience jointly and severally encountered in various political situations and at diverse levels. The organized body of Israel, its religious assembly, was according to the prophets summoned by Yahweh himself, and it always felt itself to be constituted as a group, irrespective of size, of individuals convoked together for religious, civil, or political reasons together with its ordained sacred hierarchy (although in this case the Septuagint preferred to render *qahal* with the Greek *synagogê*) in accordance with its laws and traditional customs: whether in exile, in Palestine, or in the Diaspora.

There is no doubt that the very first Christian apostolic communities, in Jerusalem as well as in the most ancient Jewish communities of the great Hellenistic cities (Rome, Alexandria, Antioch, the

---

8. H. de Lubac, *Cattolicismo: Gli aspetti sociali del dogma*, 46–47.

three megalopolises of the empire, and later Corinth, Thessalonica, Ephesus, Philippi, Colossae), were aligned in terms both of mentality and custom with the Jewish synagogical and ecclesiastical system, only distinguishing themselves more definitively between the second and third centuries. It is precisely in the first decades of the second century that the revolt of Bar Kobba and the persecution of Adrian (132–135) provoked significant changes in this system: first with the prohibition of Jewish ordination by the liturgical ritual of personal transmission by the imposition of hands, as Moses had done with Joshua; and subsequently with the nomination, execution, and confirmation of all ordinations—which had previously been entrusted to individual teachers or local sanhedrins—reserved to the Jewish Patriarch of Babylon, legally recognized by the Roman state as the ethnarch or national representative of the Jews of all the empire. This new universal and hierarchical system, which was introduced in order to bring about and convalidate, with the personal authority of the patriarch in agreement with his college, all the Jewish ordinations of the empire, led to the abolition of the previous autonomous and local practice for selecting and consecrating priests.

As far back as 1905, under the entry "Ordination" in *The Jewish Encyclopedia*, J. Z. Lauterbach outlined this change in a way evocative of the history of the primitive Christian hierarchy: "Another cause may have contributed to the abolition of the custom: the dedication of disciples as independent officiants by means of the laying on of hands, and the transference of the office of teacher by this ceremony had been adopted by Christianity;"[9] the apostles laid their hands, while praying, upon the seven disciples elected by the congregation of Jerusalem (Acts 6:6; cf. 13:3).[10] As an act dedicating the candidate as a teacher of the Law and recipient of the divine grace the cere-

---

9. We could say it otherwise—namely, that it was abandoned by the Jewish community and preserved instead by the primitive Jewish-Christian community at a time when the latter was increasingly differentiating itself from the former through the developing thrust of its polyethnic proselytism among followers of the religious and spiritualistic cults and philosophies of the Hellenistic-Latin society.

10. Other New Testament passages could also be cited, for example, Acts 4:23 concerning consecration through the laying on of hands by Paul and Barnabus at Lystra, Iconium, and Antioch.

mony is mentioned three times in the two Epistles to Timothy (1 Tim 5:22; 2 Tim 1:6). The custom, therefore, had become a Christian institution by the middle of the second century, and this fact may have induced the Palestinian Jews to abandon it."[11] The *vexata quaestio* much debated by modern theologians of the primitive Church regarding the effective "apostolic" and unitary continuity of a personal and hierarchical ministry, ordained in the Holy Spirit in the midst of each local ecclesial assembly by means of the imposition of hands (usually by three ordinants), and of a personal and authoritative control (*episkopê*) of the transmission of the correct doctrine in the midst of the community, seems to find a rather unexpected historical and critical response by a historian of Judaism whose reading and interpretation of Christian sources cannot certainly be suspected of ecclesiastical and post-Tridentine apologetic ideology.

The visible communion and public transmission of the Christian faith took place from the outset in a composite and stable structure of liaison and coordination among bordering local churches in terms of urban and regional organization (within the Roman Empire) and in terms of ethnic, linguistic, or social affinities outside the empire (e.g., in the Persian, Armenian, Georgian, Ethiopian, and Gothic kingdoms) well before the official passage of these kingdoms towards Christianity. Before this, a similar relationship of contact by religious, hierarchical, and ethnic osmosis had been experienced by the Jewish communities, both from Palestine and from the Babylonian Diaspora.

After the second century and up until the Theodosian Code, the Roman authorities legally recognized, with specific prerogatives of civil and religious jurisdiction, the patriarch or *ethnarchês* for the Jews throughout the empire and the *archisynagôgoi* under his supervision. The system naturally gave rise to controversy between Christians and Jews in writers such as Origen, Cyril of Jerusalem, and Theodoret of Cyrrhus, who denied that the Jewish patriarchs had been the visible guarantors of the survival of the true Davidic kingdom promised in Scripture. The system was abolished by Theodosius II only in 429. Before the edict of religious tolerance in 313, Christianity, unlike Judaism, which had been legalized and regulated by legislation, was

---

11. J. Z. Lauterbach, "Ordination," in *The Jewish Encyclopedia* (New York, London, 1905), 9:428–30.

prohibited and persecuted in the empire. The growing controversial divergence between Jews and Christians was accentuated by the difference in attitude of their respective clergies with respect to the political and legal system of the pagan empire. Nonetheless, the parallel evolution of a Christian clerical class, distinguishable from its Jewish counterpart and likewise spread among the new People of God throughout the known world, cannot obscure the historical fact that in both cases a sacred hierarchy based on a recognized structure of primatial authority was a constant feature in both instances in line with their own respective mentalities and traditional rites.

This primatial structure can be discerned in activities and acts recorded in the sources during the first three centuries, well before certain terms taken from secular speech, such as *prôtos, prôteion, principalitas, principatus, and primatus,* had become part of the Christian Greek-Latin canonical and theological vocabulary and had been used specifically to identify an ecclesiastical responsibility or office that was already existing and functioning with the approval of the community. The initial reluctance to adopt these terms in canonical and conciliar norms, in those cases where the New Testament did not expressly use them, finds an analogy in the hesitation that accompanied the inclusion of terms unknown in Scripture *(homoousios, Theotokos, trias/trinitas)* in the professions of faith. Yet at a certain point these terms did assert themselves, in response to changing cultural and social needs, with the very aim of preserving unaltered in the Spirit and in a more intelligible way the proclaimed faith itself.

In the case of social institutions and behavior, which are inherently alterable and changeable, one cannot be satisfied with a facile or ingenious historical concurrence, merely imagining such institutions as definitive and immutable per se, forcing oneself to discern total permanence and continuity simply on the basis of semantic similarity and historical appearance. One could be led to assert, as has certainly not been unfamiliar to theologians in the past, that the urban episcopacy, the Roman primacy, and the ecumenical patriarchates all constitute ecclesial realities existing ideally from time immemorial (perhaps in an unutterable and indescribable celestial hierarchy), even though they have at the same time all been culturally and conceptually defined over time with increasing precision, thanks to an authorized interpretation of certain Gospel passages that would infuse them once and for all with the same contingent characteristics. Yet, in the final analysis, this would also be a pretension to understanding historical facts and concrete realities quite outside the lived spiritual and collective experience, which is instead the very essence of the unitary and living tradition of the Church.

A more methodologically specific approach to the historical phenomenon of the birth of the Church of Christ set in the context of the society, scriptural understanding, and religious life of the Jewish community in Palestine and the Diaspora[12] enables one to identify from the very outset the evolution of an ecclesial community into a sacred organization of visible communion characterized by a communitarian, polycentric, and hierarchical system based avowedly on the authority of the "apostles" and on the spiritual consent of the faithful. While imbuing a new Spirit, this new order drew upon and reflected that of the *qahal* and thus its mentality and its institutional and organizational practices in full development in the first decades of the second century.

It is insightful to read the much-quoted canon 34 "of the Apostles," documented as far back as the end of the third century, in the light of a passage of the Palestinian Talmud (*Sanhedrin* 1.3, 19a): "Initially each personally conferred ordination on his own disciples. Later, direct ordination was renounced and it was stated: if a tribunal ordains without the knowledge of the patriarch, that ordination is against regulations; yet if a patriarch ordains without the knowledge of the tribunal, that ordination is valid. Subsequently it was established that the *Sanhedrin* could ordain only with the consent of the patriarch and that the patriarch could ordain only with the consent of the *Sanhedrin*." The nasi for the Jews denoted the then highest sacred institutional responsibility and was recognized as such by Roman imperial laws (until the Theodosian Code), like *patriarcha* in Latin and *patriarchês* in Greek. For this reason, no bishop or metropolitan of the

---

12. Some comments and notes on the sociological and cultural development of the first Christian community in Jerusalem are outlined in V. Peri, "La visita religiosa dei luoghi santi prima dell'età costantiniana," in Pontificio Comitato di Scienze Storiche, *L'idea di Gerusalemme nella spiritualità cristiana del medioevo: Atti del Convegno internazionale (Gerusalemme, Notre Dame of Jerusalem Center, 31 agosto–6 sett. 1999)*, Atti e documenti 12 (Vatican City: Libreria Editrice Vaticana, 2003), 7–19.

catholic Church, at least from the time of legalization, would have dreamed of using the title for any member of its hierarchy, as Saint Jerome recalled in *Epistle* 41 to Marcella in 385. However, such a use of the ecclesiastical term cannot detract from interpreting canon 34 of the Apostles as an ancient normative description of the internal Christian hierarchical structure when it states: "The bishops of each people must know which of them is the chief one *[prôtos]* and consider him as head *[kephalê]* and not do anything of particular importance without his opinion *[gnômê]*; each individual [bishop] must limit himself to all those activities that concern his own parish [today: diocese] and the territories subject to it. But neither should they [i.e., the primates] do anything without the opinions of all. In this way there will be unanimity *[homonoia]* and glory given to the Father, the Son, and the Holy Spirit."

Likewise, a hierarchical and collegial exercise of sacred authority in the guidance of the Church was already traditional by the time that such authority was defined as a positive canonical norm in canon 9 of Antioch, canons 3, 4, 5, and 14 of Sardica, canons 4 and 6 of Nicaea, canon 8 of Ephesus, and canon 280 of Chalcedon. Leo the Great declared to the emperor Marcian that the "privilegia Ecclesiarium, sanctorum Patrum canonibus instituta, et venerabilis Nicaenae synodi fixa decretis, nulla possunt improbitate convelli, nulla novitate mutari." Indeed, for him the *stabilis constructio* of the universal Church is founded on "paternarum regulae sanctionum, quae in synodo Nicaena, ad totius Ecclesiae regimen, Spiritu Sancto instruente, sunt conditae."[13] This conception, which the churches still maintain together, does not exclude but rather implies that the change had involved—Spiritu Sancto instruente—development, formulation, alteration, comprehension, and application that the canonical norms themselves would have demanded in the various ages and situations. No matter what was presumed by the modeling of political theology and the ancient conception of canonical law on Roman law, no ecumenical conciliar decree could remain unaltered in eternity, a presumption made also in ancient imperial ideology for imperial decrees, subject as they were to amendment, in fact and in

---

13. Leo Magnus, *Epistola CX ad Marcianum Augustum* 3 (PL 54:995 AB).

law, by a subsequent ecumenical council or a new imperial decision respectively.

John Meyendorff, one of the most important thinkers on contemporary Orthodox history and ecclesiology, in 1989 wrote: "But Tradition, which involves historical change, must also show at least some degree of consistency and continuity especially with the period of the ecumenical councils, when, in spite of problems and tensions, Rome and the East were able to find common criteria to solve the difficulties which stood between them. The study of Church history would be meaningless if it did not include a search for consistent and permanent ecclesiological principles, enshrined in Holy Tradition, but frequently hidden by the 'traditions of men.' In this sense, Church history[14] is the indispensable tool of any legitimate search for a theology of Christian unity."[15]

2. Synodal and Hierarchical "Ecumenical" Authority in Its Historical Manifestations

The traditional continuity of the unitary constitution of the Church was a constant feature in the outlook and experience of all the Christian communities in their cultural practices, their public profession of faith (even if for a long time unwritten), and their consent to the pastoral and magisterial directives of a unitary sacred authority regarding their social behavior. The professed basis of such consent had as its reference point the bond of concord, solidarity, and mutual charity intended to unite—also in practice, through the reciprocal exchange, where possible, of ideas and gifts, of support and respec-

---

14. V. Peri, "Le storie della Chiesa e il recupero della prospettiva ecumenica," *Orientalia christiana periodica* 57 (1991): 11–25; reprinted in V. Peri, *Lo scambio fraterno tra le Chiese: Componenti storiche della comunione*, Storia e attualità 13 (Vatican City: Libreria Editrice Vaticana, 1993), 29–42.

15. J. Meyendorff, *Imperial Unity and Christian Divisions*, Church in History 2 (Crestwood, NY: St. Vladimir's Seminary Press, 1989), 379–80. This author places his impressive ecclesiological research in continuity with the renewal of the historical and theological method developed in the heart of Russian Orthodoxy by the work of authors such as V. V. Bolotov and V. S. Solov'ëv (1853–1900).

tive capabilities—all individual Christians and the diverse churches with territorial or cultural affinities.

Synodal decisions were reached by an established "order" (*taxis* in Greek) and a *religiosa disciplina*. The system presumed a customary and consensual endorsement of the participants to the conclusions and decisions of a unitary moral and hierarchical authority developed, recognized, and effective in a pyramidal structure of "primates" within the network of the established catholic churches: urban, regional, and in more general areas and spheres of geographical influence, similar to the civil and administrative units of the Roman Empire, as in the *pars Occidentis* and the *pars Orientis*. This perception and vision of the Church of the first millennium can be reconstructed from contemporary documentary sources.

From the very first centuries, the communitarian entity for ecclesiastical institutional consultation and dialogue assumed a specifically Christian terminology (*synodos/synodus, concilium, conventus*). Against a background of a diverse range of historical situations, its encounters were motivated by the need to harmonize and to settle disputes in behavior and public teaching arising between communities and bishops of territorially adjacent churches and, at most, between the wider groups and families of the existing catholic churches.

The possibility of convening a council among the representatives of all the churches throughout the civilized world (corresponding to the cultural and political conception of the Greek-Roman ecumene) could not be fully realized until the catholic Church had obtained, between the second and third decade of the fourth century, legal recognition in the Roman Empire and, together with this status, had attained the economical and logistical means afforded by state support with which to convoke a general synodal meeting and to enforce its deliberations among Christians and local churches. The preceding established synodal tradition, which was consolidated in customary procedures for debate and decision making, had already become canonically normative and continued to operate, although inevitably it worked in coordination with the cultural and juridical structures of the imperial civil system and in part conformed to them.

One needs only to recall the way in which the new attitude towards the proclamation of the gospel—extended to all men of good will and throughout the world to its very ends in line with the Jewish vision—was psychologically woven into classical philosophical universalism and political anthropology, preserved even by an empire that had officially become Christian and based on the sociological discrimination between "Roman" citizens and barbarians, between free agents and slaves. Or to recall the means of enforcement of public order that the state, consolidating the sacredness attributed to the personal and absolute power of the emperor (now a Christian), now superimposed on the merely moral and consensual respect upon which ecclesiastical directives could rely in the past.

In the same way, the churches that had been established in the apostolic age in the principal centers of the empire—among them that of the sole capital Rome, where the martyrial *trōpaia* of Peter and Paul were venerated before Constantine created the new and second capital on the banks of the Bosphorus—saw their (traditional) ecclesial authoritativeness recognized in the First Ecumenical Council, a recognition stemming from their dissemination and unitary preservation of the "revealed deposit" and their spontaneous placement at the peak of an ecclesial hierarchy that had already found affirmation among the principal and most important sees; but beginning with the Second Ecumenical Council they also saw this authoritativeness brought into line with the subsequent public role that the state expressly assigned to the titulars of the principal ecclesiastical sees. The ecclesial oversight was extended to include the civil responsibility of ensuring unanimously for all the churches of the empire the public unity of the professed faith and of social behavior before the Christian emperor. The Theodosian Code formalized this role with precise provisions of law in which the rank of the first, old Rome was formally recognized.

In order to transmit unaltered in history the immutable divine word and promise, tradition could not but reject any unilateral or arbitrary human formulation deviating from the whole truth as accepted by faith, or any inconsistency blatantly clashing with Christian morality. Yet, it could not do so by taking refuge in magic formulas or in abstract and atemporal ideologies, but just as the Master himself, it was called to bear witness to the true faith with congruent actions and to express this faith *multifarie* in languages and cultures accessible to humans. The synods traditionally and concretely represented the most qualified ecclesial venue to present the permanent and unalterable evangelical message in contemporary and accessible forms in various ages and diverse Christian societies. Inevitable adaptations nonetheless required justification—citing the testimony of Scripture or antecedent customs—as a sign of fidelity to that which "always, everywhere, and by all" was required by faith to be believed and lived in keeping with the Fathers.

The constant innovation in the development and in the social and cultural relationships of the Christian communities brought them to confront the dilemma of deciding which of the differences in individual local traditions were compatible and homogeneous in the unity of the one faith professed and lived in a communion that was also visible, and which, instead, were to be rejected as deviations from this common faith. One calls to mind the resistance and opposition of the Jewish communities to the growing differentiation of the Christian groups from their own tradition, and also Gnosticism, Manicheism, and other early deviations emerging not only as currents of thought but above all as parallel and alternative religious organizations.

Each church and each family of churches, with the authority of their bishops and their doctors, witnesses and custodians of the authentic doctrine and of the common profession of the one faith transmitted by their apostolic Fathers, felt obliged to defend themselves through consultation and debate in a communitarian system, the *synodal* aspect of which could be traced to the apostles themselves. From the very outset, the rule of unanimity was to inspire this rule of faith, which was in turn to be guaranteed by the hierarchical authority of the principal participants. Conscious of being "workers" of God, as Paul wrote (1 Cor 3:9), the bishops and "elders" made decisions and together imparted directives that, to be precise, were based on judgments that, in faith and in their shared religious sentiment, could be traced back to themselves and together back to the Holy Spirit.

In this perspective, the councils, and in particular the "ecumenical" ones, were customarily seen as the ecclesial venue in which the highest sacred and binding authority of the entire Church ("catholic" in accordance with the symbol of faith) was historically expressed.[16]

---

16. As the representative of the Pontifical Committee for Historical Sciences of the Vatican at the 17th International Byzantine Congress, held in Washington in 1986, I presented a major paper, "I concili ecumenici come struttura portante della

Yet a deeper and more specific theological reflection on the nature, divine (and thus metahistorical) prerogatives, and holders of such sacred authority, whether personal (e.g., the pope of Rome, the titulars of principal sees) or collective (the ecumenical council), was not developed before the fifteenth century, at which time the attempt to once again retrace the traditional conciliar path—in order to bridge the growing division in visible communion between the Latin Western Church and its counterpart in the Byzantine-Slavic East and to reestablish canonical unity between the two—brought to light, in both Constance and Florence, the impracticable nature of the venture due to the changes over four centuries in the historical life, culture, and internal organization of the two churches.

There was a tendency, especially in the West, from Nicholas of Cusa to Juan de Torquemada, to identify the positive criteria and the rank of participants that would confer upon the conclusions of an ecumenical council the legitimacy and authority for the universal Church that the common tradition had always upheld for them. The question arose, in scholastic terms, of which requisites the *ratio universalitatis* of a council could be drawn from and, after the Council of Trent, whether this ecumenical characteristic did not depend preeminently or even exclusively on the convocation, participation, and approval of the Roman pontiff.

In the controversy with the Western heretics of the time, Robert Bellarmine affirmed and dialectically maintained the latter thesis and ecclesiological criterion. His theological conclusions inspired the official consolidation, in a single list, of the ancient Greek-Latin ecumenical councils and the Western general councils, including Florence. The proceedings of these appeared in the four volumes of the *Editio Romana* of the councils published between 1604 and 1608 by the Tipografia Vaticana following the lengthy preparatory work of a Congregatio pro Editione Conciliorum Generalium. The contemporary theological view on the role of the pope of Rome in conferring rank and ecumenical validity on a council and the ordinal number

gerarchia ecclesiastica" (The ecumenical councils as structuring the ecclesiastical hierarchy), published in Italian in *The 17th International Byzantine Congress: Major Papers, Dumbarton Oaks/Georgetown University, Washington D.C., August 3–8, 1986* (New Rochelle, NY: Aristide D. Caratzas, 1986), 59–81.

twenty-one itself, attributed to Vatican II, depend on these modern Western theological developments.

In a shared ecumenical search, the divergence in the number of ecumenical councils celebrated and received by the Roman church and the Byzantine church in their liturgy and doctrine should not reduce itself to identifying the undeniable differences in the theological and ecclesiastical development of the two churches, influenced in large measure by the factors that have profoundly marked the historical evolution of the second millennium. From the time of the Council of Nicaea and its deliberations, whether dogmatic (the repudiation of the Arian positions) or practical (the standardization of the date of Easter), the decisions of the councils met with reaction and contention throughout vast sectors of the episcopacy; this was soon manifested at the councils of Rimini, Seleucia, and Constantinople, between 359 and 360, with the support of the Christian emperor and his power. In the face of this new situation, the Second Ecumenical Council dedicated itself to decreeing that the literal formulas approved by an ecumenical council could not be altered by anyone, whether an individual or a local church, by either adding, altering, or omitting even one iota of the texts emanating from it. The Council of Ephesus, itself at issue with the *conciliabulum* held for ecumenical purposes in the same city, confirmed the prohibition, which manifested clear dependences on the conception of the material and literal inspiration of the revealed biblical text. In fact, the norm did not exclude the verbal and conceptual extensions of the intangible *horos* of the professed faith, which both the Council of Constantinople (with its inclusion of versicles on the Holy Spirit) and the Council of Ephesus (with those on the mother of God) had introduced. The peremptory prohibition obviously did not extend itself to the liberty of the Fathers gathered in a legitimate ecumenical council to expound the faith in expressions of greater clarity for the mentality and culture of the age, in this case the predominant Greek-Latin culture.

The bishops gathered in an ecumenical council would later reach agreement also on abrogating unanimously a council that had been celebrated as ecumenical but had either detracted from, or been in opposition to, traditional conceptions and regulations. The most sensational case was the Constantinopolitan council of Hieria in 754, which sought to affirm as traditional, in the worship and doctrine of the entire Church, the heresy of the iconoclasts. The ecumenical authority of the council celebrated in 867 under Michael III and that of 867/70 under Basil I was also annulled.

The history of the Church reveals that the seven councils acknowledged and unanimously numbered as ecumenical from the fourth to the ninth centuries underwent not only a chronological process of development but also a qualitative and conceptual evolution in terms of celebration and effective reception in the life of the churches. Their unitary list thus remained open against a background of the changing sociological, cultural, and political events in which the assemblies took place. The period marking the reception and definitive convalidation by the churches became increasingly more critical for their acceptance and integration into ecclesial life. Citing traditional requisites and criteria, many churches chose to assume, sometimes over long periods of time, differentiated positions before accepting definitively as valid and binding for worship, for the public profession of faith, and for canonical practice the definitions and norms of a given ecumenical council. There have been cases of deferred or selective reception of the deliberations of a council.

The Roman church, for example, did not in substance raise objection to the canons considering the role of the pentarchy (a law of the Christian state always respected by Rome in the ecumenical councils and in ecclesiastical practice in the following centuries), not even when Constantinople was assigned second place in that pentarchy; but Rome polemically refused to accept the formulation with which the canon justified this ecclesial placement of Constantinople on the profane basis of the status of the city in the empire. Thus the reception of the canons of the "in Trullo" council of 692 as of ecumenical value was concurred in by the two churches only at Nicomedia in 711, with the exclusion of those conciliar decrees concerning the so-called anti-Roman canons. Likewise, the dogmatic reception of the Seventh Ecumenical Council was undertaken by Rome with a reservation regarding the unfulfilled restoration of its patriarchal jurisdiction over the dioceses of southern Italy and Sicily, although full adherence to that ecumenical council was formally declared in the Council of Santa Sofia in 879/880. Similar cases could be cited for other councils and other churches. Their existence attests to the fact that even in the first millennium, the effective ecclesial "ecumenicity" of a council was traditionally accomplished by means of a historical and dynamic process of assimilation and implementation in the public profession of faith and in canonical practice. Indeed, its concern was the developing growth of visible communion between the churches, to which the ecumenical movement today aspires with new impulse.

To consider the reception of councils—that is, of events occurring in the life of the Church—simply as a theological concept or a juridical obligation, thus abstract and atemporal, leads to the possible hazard, unfortunately often arising, of the churches and their theologians limiting themselves to referring to one or other of the previous stages attained in the process of reception (or of repudiated reception) of a council almost as if these were conclusive and irreversible phenomena. This extremist handling of misunderstanding or controversy in the past had led to the acceptance of the ineluctable and definitive permanence of schisms and divisions among the churches. Such a position strays not only from the gospel's call but from the very tradition of the Church. Certainly it had been foretold that schisms and scandals would come, but always with the hope and exhortation that they be settled in time in unity, concord, and peace. Phrases such as "The Catholics (or Orthodox or Anglicans or Protestants) would never accept it," while commonly touted, do not betray in the Christians and ecclesiastics who utter them the steadfastness of their dogmatic convictions but rather mental stubbornness and hearts of stone.

3. The Hierarchical Exercise of Synodality until the Ninth Century: Ecumenical "Synergy," "Consensus," "Symphony"

The conception and common practice of the conciliar assemblies in the concord of faith preceded, in the life of the Church, the later and tardy ecclesiological description or theological and canonical definition of the ecclesiastical phenomenon itself: in much the same way as a conception of the family or a reflection on its origins, nature, values, and rights can only come after the personal experience of love that the fortunate child comes into contact with. Historical circumstances have contributed to modeling such a conception, practice, and understanding of the councils and the exercise of a sacred authority extended to all the churches, in particular those councils of the Christian Roman Empire, from the beginning of the fourth century, that were by common consensus defined as "ecumenical."[17]

These councils retained the custom, procedure, Christian vocabulary, and shared mentality of the bishops and communities that had participated in synodal assemblies from the very beginning. Each age, however, required a new and specific classification of the typology of the synods (urban, local, regional, provincial, and "diocesan" for the larger civil administrative units so named; "general" for the East and West; and "ecumenical" for the entire empire and the ambit of its direct political influence). Parallelly, difficulties and disputes arising from opposing theories presented and liberally debated in a given council led increasingly to the need to define the conditions for the participation, celebration, and hierarchical responsibility of the council fathers, based on the status of the sees and churches they guided and represented. This was achieved in part on some points but never in a systematic theoretical form, much less in the formulation of conciliar treatises with a pretense to organic unity. In any case, the interventions and clarifications were such as could be raised by pastoral and canonical practice—for example, the literal text of the public profession of faith, which the council fathers "updated" and extended with new formulas, always with the conviction of maintaining it in this way absolutely identical in the substance of its revealed content and even in its literal and verbal expression.

The long and painful crisis fomented and endorsed by the emperors, by privilege the "most orthodox" but in reality iconoclasts, dealt a blow to the catholic Church at the very heart of the ecumenical synodal system with the celebration of a council that promoted itself as orthodox and "ecumenical" according to the traditional regulations and

---

17. Twenty–four essays and research papers on philological and historical ecclesiology, mainly on the ecumenical councils, previously included in various publications between 1963 and 2001, have been collected in V. Peri, *Da Oriente e da Occidente: Le Chiese cristiane dall'Impero romano all'Europa moderna*, Medioevo e umanesimo 107–8 (Rome, Padua: Editrice Antenore, 2002).

procedures without being so in effect. The reaction to this, when it finally could be expressed in the Council of Nicaea in 787, obliged the Fathers to list all the requisites and conditions whose absence in the pseudo-synod of 754 had forced them to repudiate it and to abrogate it as unlawful and self-styled. Despite its negative configuration, for it was a question of their absence at the assembly of Hieria, the repudiation gave rise to the first specific and complete list of criteria and canonical regulations that the churches had until then only traditionally abided by or referred to in celebrating, recognizing, receiving, and confirming as universally binding, both in doctrine and in life, the dogmatic statements and canonical norms of a council, which would then be unanimously accepted, classified, and officially numbered as ecumenical.

The unanimous approval of the assembly after the public reading of the denunciation[18] represents the first and, to our knowledge, the only text of conciliar authority attesting to the ancient tradition pertaining to the ecumenical councils that had remained alive and

---

18. "How can [a council] be considered great and ecumenical that has not embraced or unanimously admitted those presiding over [*hoi proedroi*] the remaining churches, and who condemned [it] with anathema? [A council] that has not had as cooperator the pope of the Romans then in office [*ton tênikauta tês Romaiôn papa*], and the ecclesiastics surrounding him [*tous peri auton hiereis*], or persons representing him or an encyclical letter, as is canonically required for councils [*kathôs nomos esti tais synodois*]? [A council] that has not obtained the consent [*symphronountas autê*] of the patriarchs of the East, of Alexandria, of Antioch, and of the Holy City [Jerusalem], respectively prelates and highest members of the ecclesiastical hierarchy, who are themselves united? True smoke full of haze, obscuring the eyes of the foolish, is their speech [i.e., the speech of the participants of that council], and not a lantern on a candelabrum illuminating all those within: because it is locally [*topikôs*] as if in hiding that it issued its conclusions and not at the peak of the mount of orthodoxy. Nor in the manner of the apostles [*apostolikôs*] was their sound diffused or did their words reach the ends of the earth [*ta perata tês oikoumenês*] like the six holy ecumenical councils! How could it in turn be the seventh if it does not agree [*hê mê symphônêsasa*] with the six preceding holy and ecumenical councils? In order to be collocated in seventh place, things should follow each other coherently with the scheme of preceding things: as that which has nothing in common with what has been counted before cannot be inserted in the same scheme. Likewise if someone added a bronze coin to a series of six gold coins, he could not designate it as the seventh because of to the diverse nature of its material [*hylê*], as gold is a precious and valuable [metal], and bronze is vile and disparaged; so this council, having nothing

---

commonly held in the ecclesiological consciousness and canonical practice of the first millennium. Its historical value is quite evident.

Among the conditions determining whether a council could be received, and thus liturgically celebrated by all the churches as ecumenical, both requisites in fact and in law and dogmatic criteria of doctrine were canonically provided for. Regarding our context, the customary and canonical norms stipulated that the pope of the church of Rome, whether in attendance or represented by a personal delegate or encyclical letter, participate as a "collaborator" (*synergos, cooperarius, coadiutor*) of the overall proceedings of the council, "as is law for the synods." The council, however, seems to have been considered as a collective unitary subject composed of all the bishops of all the churches, clearly including that presided by the bishop of Rome, although the latter seems to have been called to a special relationship of collaboration by virtue of his status as head of the Roman See. The deliberations of the council also needed to attain the collegial consensus (*symphronountas autê*) of the patriarchs of the principal sees, duly listed by their ancient internal order, which order the Council of Nicaea had already received in its canons even before the emergence of a pentarchical formation. The churches of this directorate, including the Roman See at its vertex, participated also as individual members of the council, whose conclusions nonetheless required collective consensus. Also, to be considered "great and ecumenical," a council needed also to count upon reception and acceptance by all the other churches of the ecumene, including those which had not directly participated. On the other hand, ecumenicity required the concordance (*symphonia*) of the conciliar definitions and decrees with the dogmatic doctrine defined in the series of previous councils in their numeric order, the equal importance of the topic under consideration, and the dissemination and application of the

---

golden or substantial in its dogmatic theses [*en dogmasin*], being practically bronze and false, impregnated with lethal poison, was not worthy of being counted among the six holy councils reflecting the golden words of the [Holy] Spirit": J. D. Mansi, *Sacrorum conciliorum nova et amplissima collectio* (Florence, 1767), vol. 13, col. 208–9. The Greek text, found in the four best manuscripts, can also be read in V. Peri, *I concili e le Chiese: Ricerca storica sulla tradizione d'universalità dei sinodi ecumenici* (Rome: Studium, 1965), 24, n. 17.

emanating decrees not only at the local and individual level but also universally *(apostolica)*. As the detailed insistence on the concurrence and specific roles of the episcopal hierarchy denotes their importance for the ultimate ecumenicity of a council, all the requisites are presented as essential for the final outcome and for its acceptance and reception in the life of all the Church. It is only much later, when it became impossible to respect all these parameters, that a distinction was made between factors that are indispensable to the *esse* of the ecumenical council and other functional characteristics pertaining only to its *bene esse:* but this distinction introduces a theoretical dimension to the preceding traditional and pragmatic description of this type of council.

A number of simple observations and a question arise from an understanding and consideration of this text, which reflects the common position that both parts of the "imperial" Church, West and East, shared as traditional in the last of the seven councils consensually celebrated and received as ecumenical up to today. The first observation is that the Fathers of the Second Council of Constantinople have been held to be traditionally aware of concerning themselves with a specific historical type of council, identifiable through established terminology such as "holy and great" and an official ordinal sequence updated definitively upon the celebration of the succeeding council of the same type and "ecumenical" value. They do not, however, offer an express description or canonical or ecclesiological definition, which they nonetheless imply as subsisting and shared by living tradition in all the churches of the Christian empire. They limit themselves to identifying the requisites in fact and the practical conditions that, in their judgment, may sanction the execution and recognition of such a council and guarantee the definitive validity of its doctrinal and canonical conclusions for all the catholic Church. In other words, a universal, consensual, and free assembly of the churches of the one Christian empire seems to have felt the impact of the concrete historical and environmental circumstances in which the one shared faith and discipline are unanimously reaffirmed and reproposed together by the regional and local churches in the face of change and diversity occurring in the society and culture in which they live.

The utmost attention is focused on the continuity and preservation of the "deposit" handed down by the Fathers, while the adaptation or "updating" of ancient regulations in line with new circumstances are felt to be simple practical measures. For example, it is invariably reaffirmed that a certain type of council, namely "ecumenical," inscribes itself with perfect and homogenous organic unity in the ancient synodal tradition aimed at establishing or rediscovering through dialogue the free consensus of the churches in the public profession of faith and in visible communion, should these have been subject to diversification or damage in the plurality of historical situations. Less frequently is a parallel fact raised: until the Constantinian peace, this type of council was historically unfeasible, and the historical model it presents cannot be considered eternal and definitive in every historical aspect in each individual pragmatic component and decision recorded until the eighth century.

One could today ask why among the questions put to the Fathers by John of Constantinople at the Seventh Council the following was not raised: "How can a council in which the orthodox emperor, with his sacred authority, imposes on the gathered bishops the proclamation of heterodoxy as a binding doctrine for the entire Church be considered holy and great?" While perfectly justifiable given the inadmissible conduct of the Christian emperors during the crisis and the iconoclast council of Hieria—and likewise for the conventicles of Rimini, Seleucia, and later Ephesus—such a question was nonetheless never raised in front of the assembly. Indeed, it would not have cast doubt, as other questions might, on the legitimacy and authority of the claim for recognition of the so-called Seventh Ecumenical Council, but it would have galvanized discussion about the political theology of the Church at that time regarding the Christian sacredness of imperial power as such: autocratic, "ecumenical," and eternal by direct divine investiture.[19] With the advent of Christianity, the Roman Empire, ruled by a monarch with power and stewardship "imitating that of God" in all the civilized world, that is,

---

19. In the last fifty years Byzantine research has amply demonstrated the Roman-Byzantine conception of the Christian sacred and autocratic empire and the "ecumenical" political theology that it legitimized in the doctrine and practice of the Greek-Latin catholic episcopacy. Suffice it to recall F. Dvornik, *Early Christian and Byzantine Political Philosophy*, Dumbarton Oaks Studies (Washington, DC: Dumbarton Oaks Center for Byzantine Studies, 1966); S. Runcimann, *The Byzantine Theocracy*

the ecumene, could feel the effects, in a contingent way, of the private moral lapses of an individual "wayward" emperor, but it could never deviate from its sovereign and permanent mission of guaranteeing the ordered social system of its exclusively Christian subjects and of the churches spiritually guiding them, for their earthly happiness. If the empire was destined to endure to the ends of the earth and to close only with the second coming of Christ at the end of all time, an ecumenical council celebrated outside the empire or without the empire could not even be conceived. Deprived of the ordered and hierarchical collaboration of all its churches, it would not have been a council.

This political theology, which incorporated the ancient ideology of relations between the state and the Church, survived in the two churches until modern times under the guise of theoretical ideology and abstract juridical convention. The actual system that such a political theology idealized had nonetheless already commenced

---

(Cambridge, London, New York, Melbourne: Cambridge University Press, 1977); shortly we will have access to the most important Byzantine treatise on the subject, written in 532/533 by the patrician Mena, prefect of Constantinople and later of the praetorium under Justin, discovered by Angelo Mai in a Vatican palimpsest that has now been deciphered, critically annotated, and translated into Italian: *Menae patricii cum Thoma referendario De scientia politica dialogus: Iteratis curis quae extant in codice Vaticano palimpsesto*, ed. C. M. Mazzucchi (Milan: Vita e Pensiero, 2002). As an unfortunate result of the focus, over the centuries, on the scholastic and canonical issues relating to the nature, origin, and extent of papal authority, theologians continue to define these issues outside their historical context, which would enable a clarification, at least in part, of the origin and the differentiation of the recent doctrine and practice of an absolute sacred authority. Yet even fragmentary excerpts from the fifth book of the ancient writing present us with the ancient conception of political authority and its exercise in a civil and juridical constitution avowedly inspired by Christian values. In considering the state in absolute terms—as moderate and optimal (that is, as a concrete and historical ideal)—and not any given one in particular, such as the Roman model of Cicero, this writer of the sixth century thought of the Christian ecumenical empire as destined to perpetuate itself until the end of time. "Imperial authority is the imitation of God among men: it should be established in the state assigned by God to the emperors, although it should also be instituted according to human justice and with a public law"; "Imperial authority should concern itself with the State, have as its aim the well-being of this according to justice and as its fulfilment the accomplishment of this, with the benefit that necessarily

to undergo profound historical changes: from the ninth century on with the birth of the two sacred Roman empires, the Western and Eastern; later with the disappearance of one of them in the fifteenth century and the proliferation in the other of national monarchies and sovereign states; and finally with a new conception, introduced by the French Revolution, of the origin of power and its expression in institutional entities. In real terms, these developments shaped the definition and management of new relations, which the churches subsequently undertook with representatives of public authorities and modern secular societies at the level of civil law and social doctrine.

Throughout the long period that can be more or less defined as the second millennium of historical European Christianity, the two great churches have sought repeatedly through bilateral contact and "ecumenical" conciliar dialogue to overcome the growing decline of visible communion as it had been traditionally conceived, promoting several times the celebration of an ecumenical council. From the

---

ensues, that is, the salvation of men"; "By legality I mean that no citizen may appropriate power by his own initiative against the will and knowledge of the others, or seize it by force or by deceptive plot, or preventively by the use of terror, but that he may receive the imperial authority by request and almost imposition of the citizens, and that he may consider it a personal weight and a service of which he must ultimately reckon with divine justice....This is what I mean by legality and its manifestation. Justice is that which will ensue upon the advice of the citizens and the deliberation of the optimates. It is religious piety to receive from God, entrusting all to him, the status of divine dignity among men"; "Priestly orders deserve more consideration on the part of the emperor, not less, given their dignity....But even for these men it is hoped that imperial authority may concern itself only with the high priests, as these—being truly worthy of the priesthood—would verily take care in choosing and ordering the other priests of second and third rank and all the others, bearing in mind above all that criterion that, when neglected, entails an affront to the priesthood itself and, moreover, a diminution of power for all the state." Within this theoretical framework, the emperor—imitator and vicar of God on earth—personally became *lex animata, legibus solutus, soli Deo devinctus*, and his every decree became inalterable and infallible unless by his own intervention. No state power, not even that in countries of long-standing Christian background, seems today—after the end of the *ancien regime* and the collapse of totalitarian states of Hegelian ideological inspiration—to call for the restoration of such a Christian ideology of absolute and sacred political power, although it was not called into question in the era of the "most Christian," "most Catholic," "most orthodox" monarchical families.

eleventh century onwards, there is documentation attesting to the repeated official contacts between the churches of Rome and Constantinople along bilateral lines involving missions and official delegations. Generally, it could be said that there was never a period longer than twenty-five years between such encounters. At Lyon in 1274 or at Constance and later at Ferrara-Florence in 1438/1439, the united effort to celebrate a new ecumenical council, after the seven ancient, reached the organizational stage. Also, there was even an attempt at the Council of Trent to have the patriarchate of Constantinople, at the time under the Ottoman Empire, participate in the work, although this is generally unfamiliar to historians.[20] These endeavors were always informed by the requisites either traditionally held or established in fact by the ecumenical councils. But in no case, not even in Florence, where success was most likely, was there a stable final outcome in terms of the reestablishment of the unity of the Church in visible and canonical communion. The reasons, accumulated by now throughout the centuries, adopted by historians on both sides to explain these failures have been polemical and moralistic, basing themselves on reciprocal accusations of bad faith and dishonor, or of carelessness in the observance of traditional norms and mutual commitments, on the part of individual protagonists, whether Eugene IV or Marcus Eugenicus, who, quite to the contrary, had tenaciously pursued the outcome of unity.

The reason for the failure of the two churches to celebrate and accept an eighth ecumenical council (despite the declared intention of celebrating Florence with this official title) is more clearly visible today. The political, administrative, and cultural structure of the Christian Roman Empire—and even the sacred theory of its definitive and universal affirmation by divine will—had disintegrated to the point of oblivion in the overall geopolitical picture and even in the very thought of the dominant culture in the West. The original mechanism underlying the synodal and hierarchical system aimed at ensuring the unity of the public profession of faith and visible communion of all the Christian churches was able to endure in the type of an

---

20. V. Peri, "Il Concilio di Trento e la Chiesa greca," in *Il concilio di Trento nella prospettiva del terzo millennio*, ed. G. Alberigo and I. Rogger (Brescia: Morcelliana, 1997), 403–41, here 414–28.

"imperial" ecumenical council as long as the empire itself remained in some way a reality; with the decline of the empire, it became increasingly difficult to aspire to effectively respecting all the practical and legal requisites for the celebration, reception, and implementation of an ecumenical council. It could only be appealed to in an abstract, formal, and conventional way. The impetus, however, to restore the synodal and hierarchical system in a single venue for consultation and dialogue for all Christians and for all humans (etymologically "catholic") has left its trace in tradition and appears to be particularly alive in our own age of global transformation with the diffusion of the ecumenical movement.

In numbers 6 and 7 of the abridged list of eight themes proposed by the *Plan to Set Underway the Theological Dialogue between the Roman Catholic Church and the Orthodox Church* we find "the sacraments in their relationship to history and to eschatology" and "the sacraments and the renewal of mankind and of the world." In the paragraph preceding the second of these we read: "The anthropological question...should not be neglected in studying the sacraments. For example, the question could be raised as to what is the new reality (the 'new creation') which the sacramental life creates. In what does the new creation consist? Consideration must be given to the fact that for theology and tradition [or, more precisely, tradition and theology (author's note)], the sacraments, in the light of the holy eucharist, contain dimensions wider than the psychological and individual levels and reach out even unto the transformation of the social milieu as well as of the natural and cosmic milieu of mankind. How is this transformation conceived of, and what consequences can such a consideration have for the life of the faithful in the Church?" (§7c). One need, however, only read the official communiqués after each session of the Theological Dialogue from 1980 to date, without even turning to the bilateral trilingual proceedings that were in any case not published after the initial decision, to see that these significant themes—emerging with force in Catholic and Orthodox theology of the nineteenth century and brought to the attention of all Christians by the "signs of the times" now dramatically unfolding—have not in the least been dealt with in this first phase of the Dialogue, while historical events have increasingly brought them to the forefront of the consciousness of all those seeking unity and accord in humanity today.

4. The Church as Chorus, Orchestra, Symphony of Lived Faith

The Bible and tradition have offered many models drawn from the common experiences of the individual and social life of humans in order to evoke an image of the Church, of its intimate nature, its activities, and its united, organic, and hierarchical structure so that through a familiar and accessible reflection they might enable one to approach, in an analogical way and in faith, its mysterious reality and action in the world. The constitution *Lumen gentium* also proposed the most recurrent images: fold, farm, vineyard, building, city on a hill, temple, body, community, perfect society, a structural unity bearing the banner of Christ, his kingdom among us. By calling to mind experiences of human life, each of these images helps us to sense, without detracting from the mystery, some aspect or function of Christ our Redeemer and Lord of history.

Yet the image that bishop Ignatius of Antioch, martyr under Trajan (98–117), offers of the Church as chorus, orchestra, symphony—capable of lifting its voice to sing of Jesus Christ in harmonic accord, with interpreters, instruments and chords all in harmony—seems to be the one that can be best adapted to contemporary ecumenical ecclesiology. This Eastern Father and martyr, so often cited for his living testimony and for the original and monarchic conception of the ancient episcopacy and of its role in the subapostolic Church, wrote to the Christians of Ephesus: "So then it becometh you to run in harmony with the mind of the bishop; which thing also ye do. For your honourable presbytery, which is worthy of God, is attuned to the bishop, even as its strings to a lyre. Therefore in your concord and harmonious love Jesus Christ is sung. And do ye, each and all, form yourselves into a chorus, that being harmonious in concord and taking the key note of God ye may in unison sing with one voice through Jesus Christ unto the Father, that He may both hear you and acknowledge you by your good deeds to be members of His

Son. It is therefore profitable for you to be in blameless unity, that ye may also be partakers of God always" (Eph 4).[21]

Study and reflection on our musical experience helps us to distinguish the reality of instruments, scores, vocal tones, and acoustic environment. Analogically in the Church, these are comparable to the ecclesial means of salvation, and to certain permanent and ordered roles in executing and directing that belong to the members as a whole and are required of each one of them individually. Bearing in mind the merciful and providential universal *exousia* of God over creation or the *exousia* (or *kratos* or *dynamis* active in the history of humanity) given by him to his Son over every creature so that it may be exercised for the benefit of all, the Christian recalls that every existing power, even that exercised by Pilate and the tyrants or the crucifying mob, comes from God. Thus, the power and rights of those who rule may indeed constitute a reference point and an allusion to divine authority, but only on the condition that one does not lose sight of the fact that his kingdom is not of this world and that its exercise remains radically incompatible with every form of tyranny, domination, and abuse.

The image of the Christian community as a chorus and orchestra, with the rigorous internal order that this perceptible reality imposes on each, but above all with the compelling and intimate force that both liberates and communicates, seems in our own age to evoke the mysterious reality of the Church much more than an analogy with a political state or a civil and administrative system. The universal and profound condition required of each and all, including the audience, would be a sense of music and song, or what would commonly be known as having an ear. In order to take delight personally and ineffably in the Church, all must come to an understanding, through faith in Christ, of the gift and significance of the Holy Spirit. The applications and deeper reflections, in specific terms of the visible unity of the Church and its traditional structures, are innumerable and can be made in the light of the bimillennary historical experience of ecclesial life. The adverb that best evokes the spiritual

---

21. As cited in *The Apostolic Fathers, Comprising the Epistles (Genuine and Spurious) of Clement of Rome, the Epistles of St Ignatius*, ed. J. B. Lightfoot and J. R. Harmer (London: MacMillan, 1891), 138.

mood with which the first Christian community maintained its perseverance in the teaching of the apostles and in communion (*koinônia*), in the breaking of bread and in prayer, recurs throughout the Acts of the Apostles, namely, "of one accord" (*homothymadon, unanimiter*). Particularly in compound constructions, the typical adverbial preposition of the evangelical and Pauline vocabulary, and hence Christian ecclesiology, is *syn/cum* rather than *ypo/sub*, and the most recurrent adverbial expression, *pros allêlous/ad invicem*.

Capturing the catholic sense of the Church in its profound "liturgical" root—which is at the same time a distinctive aesthetic and representative experience, involving each individual's intimate and community sphere—and thus making his own the instructions of the council, John Paul II writes in the encyclical *Slavorum apostoli* (n. 18): "The Church is catholic also because she is able to present in every human context the revealed truth, preserved by her intact in its divine content, in such a way as to bring it into contact with the lofty thoughts and just expectations of every individual and every people." And also: "In virtue of this catholicity each individual part of the Church contributes through its special gifts to the good of the other parts and of the whole Church. Thus through the common sharing of gifts and through the common effort to attain fullness in unity, the whole and each of its parts receive increase....Such a traditional and at the same time extremely up-to-date vision of the catholicity of the Church [could be compared to] a symphony of the various liturgies in all the world's languages united in one single liturgy, or a melodious chorus sustained by the voices of unnumbered multitudes, rising in countless modulations, tones and harmonies for the praise of God from every part of the globe, at every moment of history."

Ignatius is the first known source to designate the totality of Christians with the name "catholic Church": "Wheresoever the bishop shall appear, there let the people be; even as where Jesus may be, there is the universal Church" (*Smyrn.* 8.2).[22] To Ignatius can also be traced the first specific acknowledgment that the church of Rome "presides in the territory of the Romans" and "was president in charity." Modern discussion and debate on the paternity and the precise ecclesiastical, institutional, and even canonical significance of such

---

22. Ibid., 158.

Ignatian expressions do not diminish the historicity or value for those who read them in the light of the vision itself of the Church, which the martyr bishop perceived and experienced as a chorus of voices, an orchestral symphony in which all are called to play a part in Christ and for Christ, interpreting their respective and personal parts rigorously and creatively under his ineffable direction. Among these parts, the role of the bishop of Rome—the church to which the apostles Peter and Paul had entrusted, according to Ignatius, their sacred legacy—seems to endure, so that the communion of charity may be visibly encouraged and sustained in the catholic Church of Jesus Christ, synodically and hierarchically structured on free consent, in order that it may visibly realize and be present everywhere and at all times as the revealed and partially visible pattern of human coexistence.

Summary of Discussion

Several interventions stressed the importance of a historical approach. One should avoid treating theology and related issues as abstract, nontemporal, preexisting realities. Church institutions often follow secular patterns in their development. The only possible theology is a theology embedded in history, in human society, and in the world.

The ecumenical councils of the first millennium did not develop a specific theology of the ecumenical councils; they only offered a list of conditions that allow us to discern when a council can be considered ecumenical.

The conditions for celebrating an ecumenical council have changed in the course of the second millennium, just as the relationship between the bishop of Rome and the ecumenical council has changed from the ninth century onwards.

From the Orthodox side, it was requested not to oversimplify the relationship between the Byzantine emperor and the ecumenical councils by linking them too closely. There is no exclusive doctrine concerning the relations between Church and state, since such a doctrine would need to be assessed according to the changeable course of historical circumstances.

The "Petrine Primacy": The Role of the Bishop of Rome according to the Canonical Legislation of the Ecumenical Councils of the First Millennium, an Ecclesiological-Canonical Evaluation[*]

V. Nicolae Durã

Introduction

In 1492, the metropolitan of Moscow declared his see to be the "new Constantinople,"[1] the third Rome. In turn, at the beginning of the sixteenth century, the monk Philotheus declared that "the two Romes have fallen, but the third still remains standing, while the fourth shall never be."[2] Are there two or "three Romes"?![3]

---

[*] May 23, 2003 (afternoon session). Original text in French.

1. *Russkaya storiceskaya Bibliotheka* (St. Petersburg, 1880), 6:799.

2. V. Malinin, *Starets Eleazorova monastyria Filofey i ego poslaniya* (Kiev, 1901), 50–55.

3. See C. Melnik, *La troisième Rome* (Paris: Grasset, 1986); A. Wenger, *Les trois Rome* (Paris: Desclée de Brouwer, 1991).

At the beginning of the third millennium, we are here together, from East and West, in the one Rome, the see of the apostles Peter and Paul, to discuss the theme of the "Petrine primacy," which shows that evidently there is but one Rome and one "primacy" for ecumenical Christian unity.

I come from a land with an "Orthodox majority," where "Christianity was brought"—as Pope John Paul II recalled during his apostolic visit to Romania (May 7–9, 1999)—"by the apostle Andrew, Peter's brother....The seed of the gospel, fallen on fertile soil, produced...many fruits of sanctity and many martyrs. I am thinking"— said the "Roman pontiff"—"of Saint John Cassian and Dionysius Exiguus, who contributed to the diffusion of the spiritual, theological, and canonical treasures of the Greek East and of the Latin West."[4]

According to the witness of the apostolic bishop of Rome, I come therefore from a country baptized by the apostle Andrew and where Dionysius Exiguus, the father of Latin canon law, was born.[5] This is a further reason why my witness on the "Petrine primacy," and ipso facto on the role of the bishop of Rome for ecumenical unity, rests on the canonical legislation of the ecumenical councils of the first millennium, which was studied and translated by the father of all canonists from East and West—among whom we count ourselves— that is, by Dionysius Exiguus.

Is it possible to prepare the way for a common understanding of the papal primacy? Our thinking on this burning and most crucial question for our churches has drawn us to focus our attention on two documents of utmost importance. The first, written by the Pontifical Council for Promoting Christian Unity, was kindly put at our disposal by His Eminence Cardinal Walter Kasper. The text of this document is considered as "a first reflection" on the question of the Petrine min-

---

4. "Discours de Jean–Paul II lors de la cérémonie d'arrivée à l'aéroport de Baneasa," *L'osservatore romano*, cahier spécial (1999): 37.

5. N. V. Durā, "Dionysius Exiguus (Denys le Petit) (465–545): Précisions et correctifs concernant sa vie et son œuvre," *Revista española de derecho canonico* 50 (1993), 269–290; "Dionysius Exiguus and His Canonical Work: A Canonical Evaluation concerning His Contribution to the Development of Church Law" (in Romanian), *Ortodoxia* 41, no. 4 (1989): 37–61; "Denys the Minor, Father of Western Canon Law" (in Romanian) *Studii teologice*, 43, nos. 5–6 (1991): 84–90.

istry. The second is the text itself of the ecumenical canonical legislation of the first millennium, which is also the subject of study and research in my country by the students of both the Faculty of Theology and the Faculty of Law.

It has rightly been said that theology has no meaning if it is presented "merely as speculation. It is alive only if applied to the life of man."[6] The unity of our churches, Orthodox and Catholic, concerns precisely the life of man, the human condition, which has a privileged place in all interventions of the Holy Father, Pope John Paul II. One can therefore affirm that he is "the premier humanist of the planet, and [that]—as an Orthodox theologian has said—if the 'natural law' of the whole of humanity could have but one voice, today it would come from the mouth of the supreme pontiff."[7]

But what does the supreme pontiff, the humanist John Paul II, say regarding the unity of our churches?

First of all, the pope says that "the Church must breathe with her two lungs" (encyclical letter *Ut unum sint* [= *UUS*]); in other words, he urges us to declare our own ecclesial identities, Oriental (Orthodox) and Western (Roman Catholic), which should finally recover their *unitas in diversitate*.

But does not this unity need a center of ecclesial unity? What was the reality of the first millennium? What does the canonical legislation say regarding the exercise of the ministry of unity and, therefore, of the role of the bishop of Rome?

These are a few questions that we shall try to answer—from the point of view of Orthodox canonical doctrine—by examining first the text of the Pontifical Council and then the text of the canonical legislation of the ecumenical councils of the first millennium, substantiated of course by the elements provided by Orthodox and Catholic ecclesiology.

---

6. V. Zielensky, *Dincolo de ecumenism* (Beyond ecumenism), trans. C. Dobre (Bucharest, 1998), 73.
    7. Ibid., 58.

1. The Role of the Bishop of Rome in the Light of the Text of the Pontificium Consilium ad Christianorum Unitatem Fovendam

As we know, the official theological dialogue between the Orthodox Church and the Catholic Church has not yet taken up formal discussion on the question of the primacy of the bishop of Rome, which is, moreover, the most difficult to solve.

The text on the "Petrine ministry"—drawn up by the Plenary Assembly of the Pontifical Council for Promoting Christian Unity—provides a first official point of view of the Catholic Church on the "Petrine primacy"; hence the need to examine and evaluate it also from the point of view of Orthodox ecclesiology and canonical doctrine. All the more so because that text—which considers all aspects of the problem of the "Petrine primacy"—offers also the possibility to reflect "together" on the role of the bishop of Rome for "the unity of all Christian communities" (*UUS*, 95).

The Pontifical Council "ad Christianorum Unitatem Fovendam" calls attention, among other things, to "the difficulty in finding an immediate foundation for the ministry of the Bishop of Rome in the New Testament."[8] It furthers recalls that "the Catholic Church considers the primacy of the Bishop of Rome as 'de jure divino' instituted and therefore belonging to the essential and irrevocable structure of the Church." Finally, it affirms that "all ecumenical partners traditionally contested or rejected this 'de jure divino' institution."[9] The Pontifical Council also considers that "a clearer distinction can and should be made between the doctrinal essence of papal primacy and its contingent historical styling or shaping," in other terms "what pertains to the order of 'de jure divino' and what does not pertain to it."[10]

The same text reminds us that "regarding the jurisdiction of the Bishop of Rome, Vatican I defined the ordinary and immediate Episcopal jurisdiction of the Pope over all churches and their bish-

---

8. "Petrine Ministry: A Working Document," *Information Service* (Vatican City) 109, nos. 1–2 (2002): 32.

9. Ibid., 33.

10. Ibid., 33.

ops,"[11] and makes clear that "for the Bishop of Rome to exercise his ministry of unity in a more collegial or synodical way, a clearer distinction will be required between his complementary responsibilities."[12]

Thus, we take it from the last clarification that the bishop of Rome actually can exercise his ministry of unity in a more collegial and synodical way, as has already been sought by a number of Catholic bishops, theologians, and canonists; hence, the need also to act through strictly and specifically collegial actions and arrive at a clearer distinction between his responsibilities, required above all by this ministry of ecumenical unity, the scope of which is certainly larger and therefore difficult to consider.

Moreover, the need for the Roman pontiff to exercise his "plenary and supreme" power (cf. canons 331–332 of canon law) through strictly and specifically collegial actions was referred to even by the Fathers of Vatican II.[13] But today some Catholic canonists see that such "exercise of power...is not frequent...; the college still exists, but for all that it does not act permanently in a strictly collegial way, as it emerges from the tradition of the Church. In other words, it is not always 'in full exercise,' and even more, it acts only at intervals in a strictly collegial action."[14] Hence, there also emerges the role of the tradition of the ecumenical Church of the first millennium[15] as the point of reference in the application of the fundamental canonical principles of collegiality[16] and synodality by the Petrine ministry.

"The Bishop of Rome acts simultaneously," continues the text of the Pontifical Council, "at once as bishop of a local diocese, as 'patri-

---

11. Ibid., 34.

12. Ibid., 34.

13. *Relatio circa principia quae Codicis juris canonici recognitionem dirigant* (Vatican City: Typis Polyglotis Vaticanis, 1967), 5–18.

14. J. L. Gutiérez, "Le commentaire au canon 337," in *Code de droit canonique*, ed. L. Caparros et al. (Montreal, 1990), 221. (French translation based on bilingual annotated Spanish edition published by the Institut Martin De Azpilcueta.)

15. See N. Durā, *Le régime de la synodalité selon la législation canonique conciliaire œcuménique, du 1er millénaire* (Bucharest, 1999), 497–531.

16. Ibid., 119–37; 223–66; "Principiile canonice, fundamentale, de organizare si functionare a Bisericii Ortodoxe" (Fundamental canonical principles in the organization and operation of the Orthodox Church), *Revista de teologie Sfântul Apostol Andrei*, 5, no. 9 (2001): 129–40.

arch' of the Western or Latin Church, and as the universal minister of unity."[17] But first of all, we can ask ourselves—as the Pontifical Council itself has already done—"Under which of these responsibilities will be entered the Churches interested in restoring full communion with the Bishop of Rome?"[18]

We have here an area still open for our common work to find satisfactory answers and solutions!

As we know, during the first millennium, the bishop of Rome acted as the bishop of a local diocese and as patriarch of the Western Church, that is, of the *pars Occidentis* of the Roman Empire (cf. canon 3 of the First Council of Constantinople; canon 28 of the Council of Chalcedon; canon 36 of the Sixth Council in Trullo; canons 17 and 21 of the Council of Constantinople of 869–870; and canon 1 of the Council of Constantinople of 879–880), and not as head of a pontifical state. In any case, during the first millennium, at least in the East, no one honored the pope as "head" of a pontifical state, but as the bishop of Rome and patriarch of the West.

Regarding his ministry of unity, it was clearly recognized by the East despite moments in which Byzantine imperial politics intended to subdue the papacy to its own political and ecclesiastical interests. But the content of this ministry of unity and the forms of its manifestation—in the first millennium—differ greatly from those referred to by our Catholic colleagues today, who express them usually in terms of "administration" and of "exercise of authority and power," and not in terms of a sui generis evangelical "responsibility," the only one, by the way, that could link it to the ministry of Peter and give a meaning to the words "Feed my lambs," and really make the Pope *servus servorum Dei*.

If, on the one hand, we Orthodox intend and wish to define the papal primacy with the words of Pope Gregory the Great—who put himself in the service of the Petrine primacy as *servus servorum Dei*—on the other hand, the document of the Pontifical Council challenges us by saying that "primacy is more than government, authority is more than power, and jurisdiction is more than administration."[19]

---

17. "Petrine Ministry," 34.
18. Ibid.
19. Ibid.

Undoubtedly, we are no longer spoken to with the same language used in the first millennium, when—whether we like it or not—we were all together in dogmatic, canonical, and liturgical unity. Of course, such language shows that one is pledged to the Roman juridical thinking and to the ecclesiological conceptions expressed by canon law rather than to the conception of a "service of charity," like the one lived by the popes of the first millennium, as in, for example, the happy case of Saint Gregory the Great.

The text of the Pontifical Council observes also, rightly, that the definition of Vatican I regarding papal infallibility is found by "non-Catholics...in contradiction with both the Scripture and the Tradition" and remains "the most difficult and controversial one" because "many reactions to *Ut unum sint* still take a strong stand on this point and they consider the Vatican I definition of papal infallibility as the major obstacle to an ecumenical rapprochement. They consequently plead for a serious re-reading of this dogmatic definition."[20]

In this connection, it is known that the Orthodox Church has never sought such a rereading; on the contrary, it has resolutely rejected the text of such a definition, which is found to be scandalous and contrary to biblical and patristic teaching as well as to the canonical legislation and doctrine of the first millennium, the period of our ecumenical unity. This is why this definition remains rather foreign to the spirit of the Orthodox tradition, now and in the past.

Of course, this does not mean that we are a priori opposed to any rereading of the definition given by Vatican I, even if it is rightly considered to be "the most difficult and most subject to controversy." On the contrary, in our opinion it is absolutely necessary to discuss precisely these difficult problems that are subject to controversy. To hide them during our theological dialogue—as has been done up to now—leads to nothing other than sterile ecclesiastical diplomacy, and "Cui prodest?"

As far as we are concerned, we are convinced that, through a rereading and, if necessary, a redefinition of the dogma of papal infallibility—as defined by Vatican Council I—we may be able to express

---

20. Ibid., 35.

it in a language appropriate to our own ecclesiological and canonical doctrines, in order to reach a theological consensus at least on what the text of the Pontifical Council distinguishes between "the invariable essence and what can be considered as historical, contingent and variable characteristics of papal primacy."[21]

From the same text—which represents the result of a first reflection worked out by the Pontifical Council—we read that "the person who exercises a universal ministry of unity also disposes of a particular teaching authority."[22]

Thus, the bishop of Rome, as "universal primate," exercises a particular doctrinal authority. But of what does it consist exactly? The text does not explain it and merely recalls that "the Vatican I definition declared that the Bishop of Rome can promulgate doctrinal definitions which are infallible *'ex sese, non autem ex consensu ecclesiae.'*"[23]

Although the word *infallibility* does not exist in the text of the ecumenical canonical legislation of the first millennium, it must nevertheless be recognized that at that time the bishop of Rome indeed enjoyed a special doctrinal authority but he could not, for all that, claim to have some sort of infallibility in matters of orthodox faith, as demonstrated quite evidently by the condemnation of certain popes by Eastern and Western councils.

As to the alleged papal right to promulgate infallible doctrinal definitions, it is known that the Orthodox do not even want to hear of it because—in their view—this excludes a priori any form of expression of collegial-synodical authority as well as the process of reception of the dogmatic definitions promulgated by the ecumenical councils.

The same text of the Pontifical Council tells us that Pope John Paul II did not use the term *infallibility* in his encyclical *Ut unum sint* because "of its problematic resonance, by reminding of the restrictive conditions laid down by the Vatican I definition and by combining a possible ex cathedra teaching with the principle of communion."[24]

But what kind of communion? If one follows literally the Latin Code of Canon Law, it is the "right" of the Roman pontiff "to deter-

---

21. Ibid., 40.
22. Ibid., 45.
23. Ibid., 36.
24. Ibid.

mine the personal or collegial way to exercise that function," that is, "in lieu of communion with the other bishops and with the whole Church" (canon 333 § 2). And if we believe what our Catholic colleagues say, "the Pope's primacy extends not only to the universal Church as a whole, but also to each of the persons."[25] We can therefore ask under what kind of primacy are placed the members of the churches interested in the restoration of full communion with the bishop of Rome. Is it a "primacy" of charity, of service for unity, or a primacy that "is more than government"?

Of course, "in terms of communion there was a mixture of good and bad experiences in both the first and the second millennium."[26] Yet the first millennium can be considered "as a possible model for restoring full communion, without either glamorising the first millennium or disdaining the second millennium,"[27] because it was in the first millennium that the *communio in sacris*, a full and authentic communion, was really lived out in spite of all the bad experiences in the area of canonical relationships between the sees of the two Romes (the "old" and the "new") (cf. canon 28, Council of Chalcedon, etc.). Furthermore, it is precisely this kind of *communio in sacris* that has been missing since the Great Schism of 1054, that is to say, from the beginning of the second millennium to our days.

In any case, we cannot arrive at a true *unitatis redintegratio* without passing through a *communio in sacris*,[28] at least between Orthodox and Catholics, already engaged in a theological dialogue.[29]

---

25. Ibid.

26. J. L. Gutiérez, op. cit., 218.

27. "Petrine Ministry," 37.

28. N. V. Durā, "Intercomuniune sau comuniune sacramentala? Identitatea ecleziala si unitatea în credinta" (Intercommunion or sacramental communion? Ecclesial identity and unity of faith), *Ortodoxia* 38, no. 4 (1998): 15–58; "Consideratii canonico–ecleziologice privind Documentul de la Lima (BEM)" (Canonical-ecclesiological considerations on the Lima Document [BEM]), *Ortodoxia*, 38, no. 2 (1986): 119–47.

29. "Dialogul teologic ortodox–romano-catolic si implicatiile sale ecleziologice" (The Orthodox–Roman Catholic theological dialogue and its ecclesiological implications), *Mitropolia Banatului* 36, no. 1 (1986): 24–41; "Primatul papal în perspectiva dialogului ortodoxo–romano-catolic: Consideratii ecleziologice" (Papal primacy in the perspective of the Orthodox–Roman Catholic dialogue: Ecclesiological considerations), *Mitropolia Banatului* 37, no. 5 (1987): 23–30.

Aware of this ecclesiological reality, Pope John Paul II asked the Catholic Eastern patriarchs to help him to achieve "full communion with the Orthodox Churches," or "complete communion with the Orthodox Churches..., so much hoped for between the Catholic Church and the Orthodox Churches" (*La documentation catholique* 2192, Nov. 15, 1998).

To arrive at this "full communion" so much hoped for by our churches,[30] we must first overcome the difficulties created by our own ecclesiological and canonical doctrines regarding the "Petrine ministry" and ipso facto the role itself of the bishop of Rome in the universal Church. But to do that, we must certainly "overcome inappropriate confessional preconceptions and move," as suggested by the Pontifical Council, "towards a common understanding of this particular ministry," hence also the urgent necessity to pay "particular attention...to hermeneutics and to historic developments which have taken place,"[31] which is what we too have tried to do in the second part of our canonical-ecclesiological study, in which we look at the text of the canonical legislation of the ecumenical councils of the first millennium.

2. The "Petrine Primacy" and the Role of the Bishop of Rome for Christian Unity according to the Canonical Legislation of the Ecumenical Councils of the First Millennium

For the Second Vatican Council, "the Roman Pontiff, as the successor of Peter, is the perpetual and visible source of the unity" (*Lumen gentium*, 23). Similarly, for Catholic canonists, in our days, the pope,

---

30. This is the case of the Romanian Orthodox Church, whose theologians and canonists have for a long time highlighted this need. See N. V. Durã, "Relatiile ecumenice actuale dintre Biserica Ortodoxa si Biserica romano-catolica si bazele lor ecleziologice" (Current ecumenical relations between the Orthodox Church and Roman Catholic Church and its ecclesiological foundations), *Mitropolia Banatlului* 36, no. 1 (1986): 24–41.

31. "Petrine Ministry," 41.

as "principium et fundamentum unitatis," exercises "a primatial mission of unity."[32]

When we read the text produced by the Pontifical Council, we see that "the primacy of the Bishop of Rome" is "'de jure divino' instituted" and that, consequently, it belongs "to the essential and irrevocable structure of the Church" but that "all ecumenical partners traditionally contested or rejected this 'de jure divino' institution"; hence the need to make "a clearer distinction...between the doctrinal essence of papal primacy and its contingent historical styling or shaping."

Regarding the jurisdiction of the bishop of Rome, it is affirmed that it was defined by "Vatican I," hence the need also to make "a clearer distinction" between the "complementary responsibilities [of the Bishop of Rome]" regarding "his ministry of unity."

At the same time, we learn that "the Bishop of Rome acts simultaneously at once as bishop of a local diocese, as 'patriarch' of the Western or Latin Church, and as the universal minister of unity," which requires, quite evidently, a clarification of the "responsibilities" that our respective churches recognize in the bishop of Rome as "universal minister of unity."

It has also been specified that the universal ministry of unity exercised by the bishop of Rome is expressed in terms of "administration," of "authority," and of "power," that is, in terms of jurisdictional universal "primacy" and papal "infallibility."

No wonder, then, that the question of papal "infallibility" remains "the major obstacle to an ecumenical rapprochement" and therefore "the most difficult" to solve, and ipso facto "the most controversial one."

We are also told that the bishop of Rome "disposes of a particular teaching authority" and that consequently he can "promulgate doctrinal definitions which are infallible" and that the "infallibility," in spite of its "restrictive conditions," is linked with "the principle of communion." As we have already observed earlier, this adds—at least for the Orthodox—further obstacles to the ecumenical efforts made

---

32. P. Valdrini, "Principii ale organizarii Bisericii catolice" (Principles of the organization of the Catholic Church), trans. N. Durā, *Biserica Ortodoxa Româna* 118, nos. 4–6 (2000): 138.

to overcome the real *causa dirimens* of Christian unity, which is the question of papal infallibility.

Finally, we read that we cannot progress "towards a common understanding" of the Petrine ministry without renouncing "inappropriate confessional preconceptions."

Of course, the most difficult issue is to arrive at such a common understanding. But how? Could the canonical legislation of the ecumenical councils of the first millennium help to reach that common understanding? What does it say of the primatial mission of unity exercised by the bishop of Rome? What role did he have in maintaining that ecclesial unity?

It should be made clear from the outset that the canonical legislation—decreed in the East under the aegis of the imperial policy[33]—speaks rather of a form of collegial government, a type of diarchy, and later of a pentarchy (cf. canon 3, Second Council; canon 28, Fourth Council; canon 36, "in Trullo"). Besides, in the eyes of the Byzantines, the role of the pope was limited to that of a *primus inter pares*, except when the imperial policy required something different.

According to current canonical legislation, today the pope is "Collegii Episcoporum caput, Vicarius Christi atque universae Ecclesiae Pastor" (the head of the college of bishops, vicar of Christ, and pastor of the whole Church) (canon 331).

Without any doubt, "every Council should be interpreted in the context of the entire Tradition of the Church, which includes both the Christian East and West, both the first and the second millennium,"[34] but here we shall expressly limit our reading and interpretation to the Eastern tradition of the first millennium only, in order to keep within the proposed subject. Moreover, "as far as the doctrine of the primacy is concerned, Rome must not require more of the East," wrote Cardinal Ratzinger, "than was formulated and lived during the first millennium."[35]

---

33. See S. N. Troianou, *The Eight Ecumenical Council and Its Legislation* (in Greek) (Athens, 1989), 6–11, 64–67.

34. "Petrine Ministry," 40.

35. J. Ratzinger, *Theologische Principienlehre: Bausteine zur Fundamentaltheologie* (Munich, 1982), 209; also "Petrine Ministry," 38.

The first canon that refers expressly to the bishop of Rome is the sixth canon of the First Ecumenical Council (Nicaea, 325). Literally, this canon requires "that the ancient customs in Egypt, in Libya, and in the Pentapolis be maintained, so that the bishop of Alexandria will have the power (*tēn exousian, potestatem*) over all those eparchies, since such a custom (*to toiouton sunēthes, parilis mos*) exists also for the bishop of Rome."[36]

Thus, the sixth canon of the First Ecumenical Council, being directed at the Egyptian schism of Meletius of Lycopolis, settled the legal solution in accordance with ancient custom, which recognized the bishop of Alexandria as protos over entire Egypt. Rome served only as an analogous situation to confirm the prerogatives of the See of Alexandria, based on the ancient customs.

Some Catholic theologians and historians of our time write that "the initiative of convening the council was certainly taken by the emperor....The presence of the Spanish bishop at the side of Constantine, while contributing to make the voice of the West also heard, did by no means imply a formal representation of Rome."[37]

They add that the sixth canon of the Council of Nicaea "referred to the preeminence of the church of Rome...in central and southern Italy, as well as in Sicily and Sardinia" and not "in the West, of which Rome will later on be the only patriarchate."[38]

We know that the major difference between the original text of the sixth canon of the Council of Nicaea and the ancient Latin versions (Priscian, Rufinus, etc.) consists in the following addition: "ut in suburbicaria loca sollicitudinem gerat." In fact, we read in Rufin's paraphrase, "ut...suburbicarium Ecclesiarum sollicitudinem gerat,"[39] and in Priscian, "ut suburbicaria loca et omnem provinciam suam sollicitu-

---

36. *Les conciles œcuméniques*, vol. 2, part 1, *Les décrets: Nicée I à Latran V*, ed. G. Alberigo et al., French edition ed. A. Durval et al. (Paris: Cerf, 1994), 41–42.

37. L. Perrone, "De Nicée à Chalcédoine, les quatre premiers conciles œcuméniques: Institutions, doctrines, processus de réception," in *Les Conciles œcuméniques*, vol. 1, *L'histoire*, 29–30.

38. Ibid., 43.

39. See F. Maassen, *Der Primat des Bischofs von Rom und die alten Patriarchalkirchen* (Bonn, 1853), 100ff.

dine gubernet."[40] Also, in the "Interpretatio Caeciliani" there has been added, "ut in suburbicaria loca sollicitudine gerat."[41] Finally, in the "Interpretatio quae dicitur Prisca"—according to a manuscript of the seventh century, revised by C. H. Turner—we read that "antiqui moris est ut urbis Romae episcopus habeat principatum ut suburbicaria loca et omnem provinciam sua sollicitudine gubernet."[42]

On the other hand, in other ancient Latin versions, which have remained faithful to the original text,[43] we find only the authentic words of the sixth canon. For example, in the "Interpretatio Attici" (edition written in Constantinople at the time of the inquiry of the church of Carthage in 419), we read that the Fathers of the Council of Nicaea did not decide "that the ancient customs used in Egypt...be maintained..., quia et urbis Romae episcopo similes mos est" (since a custom of the same kind exists also for the bishop of Rome). The same words are found in the "Interpretatio Dionysii Exigui prima"[44] and in the "Interpretatio Dionysii Exigui altera."[45]

Thus, in the Latin versions, in which falsifiers have made additions and interpolations to the text of canon 6 of the Council of Nicaea, it was just a "sollicitudo" for the bishop of Rome and not a "jurisdiction," and even less a "jurisdictional primacy." Furthermore, this "sollicitudo" was exercised only on those "suburbicana loca" and "omnem provinciam suam" (his entire province), not on Italy and even less on the entire West.

Besides, this reality is confirmed also by other Latin writings, for example, by the "Interpretatio quae dicitur Gallo-Hispana," which specifies that it was a matter of "vicinas sibi provincias."[46]

---

40. See H. Leclercq, "Les diverses rédactions des canons de Nicée" (appendix 5), in C. J. Hefele, *Histoire des conciles d'après les documents originaux*, (Paris, 1907), 1:1145, n. 3.

41. See C. H. Turner, *Ecclesiae occidentalis monumenta juris antiquissima* (Oxford, 1904), 120.

42. Ibid., 121.

43. See H. Leclerq, op. cit., 1139.

44. C. H. Turner, op. cit., 260.

45. Text published in PL 67:147; J. D. Mansi, *Sacrorum conciliorum nova et amplissima collectio*, Florence; new ed. Paris—Leipzig, 2:177.

46. See C. H. Turner, op. cit., 196.

Thus, we see that even for the authors of those additions, the bishop of Rome exercised just a solicitude or a canonical pastoral authority on his "suburbicarian churches" and on "his whole province."

What should we understand by "loca suburbicaria"? Much ink has flowed in the vain effort to demonstrate that the term applied to the whole of Italy, and even to the entire West.

We know that following the administrative and territorial reformation undertaken by the emperors Diocletian (284–305) and Constantine (306–326 in the West), the Italian peninsula was divided between the *vicarius Italiae* and the *vicarius urbis*. But Rome continued to form a distinct government under the *praefectus urbis*. The *vicarius urbis*, who had received ten provinces in central and southern Italy, was designated with the name of *suburbicariae* or *suburbicariae regionis vicarius*.

The jurisdictional territory of the bishop of Rome, too, was limited by the borders of those suburbicarian regions.

By confirming the process of adaptation of the Church's organization to the types of the state administrative and territorial organization system (cf. canon 4), the Fathers of the Council of Nicaea had therefore recognized in the bishop of Rome a suprametropolitan right (of an exarchal type) over these territories of the suburbicarian diocese, which he already administered in accordance with the ancient custom.

Consequently, at the time of the Council of Nicaea (325), as a Catholic canonist observed, we are "not in a position to prove that the bishop of Rome exercised on the whole West a supremacy identical to that which he exercised on the territories adjoining Rome or to that of his colleague of Africa, to mention only the latter."[47]

And yet, at the sixteenth session of the Fourth Ecumenical Council (Chalcedon), the papal legate (Bishop Paschasinus) read the introduction of the sixth canon of the Council of Nicaea in the following terms: "Ecclesia Romana simper habuit primatum."[48] Where had the papal legate obtained the text of that canon? In the opinion

---

47. H. Leclercq, "Observations sur le sixième canon du Concile de Nicée," in C. J. Hefele, op. cit., 1:1198–99.

48. J. D. Mansi, op. cit., 7:443. For the original text and commentary on canon 6, see *Pedalion* (in Greek) (Athens, 1990), 129–131.

of Catholic canonists, Paschasinus in 451 obtained the text of canons 6 and 7 of the Council of Nicaea from the Chieti manuscript ("Interpretatio Codicis Ingilrami").[49]

At the time of his dispute with Patriarch Acacius of Constantinople (472–489), Pope Felix III (482–492) also said that the bishop of Rome "has in every synod the sovereign authority *(to kyros)*, as provided by the canon of the Council of Nicaea," that is, canon 6.[50]

In the Isidorian version, written around 636,[51] the first part of canon 6 has been replaced by the passage of another version, that of the Chieti manuscript, in which we read that "Ecclesia Romana semper habuit primatum."[52] These words have also been reproduced in the Gallic version. According to H. Leclercq, "the same hand that drew the first part of canon 6 from the ms. of Chieti brought the rubrics and the division of the canons from that version into the Isidorian version."[53]

In the collection of the Saint-Maur manuscript[54] (eighth century), the Nicaea canons come after the Sardica canons.[55] This again provides undeniable evidence that the canons of the Council of Sardica were still in circulation, even in the eighth century, under the Nicaean appellation, and that the Petrine primate—enunciated by the Fathers of the Council of Sardica (343) (cf. canons 3, 5)—had been attributed to the Fathers of the Council of Nicaea.

According to Greek canonists, the sixth canon of the Council of Nicaea obviously proves that "the diocese of Rome is limited, like also that of Alexandria, and consequently the Romans think in vain that

---

49. H. Leclerq, "Les diverses rédactions des canons de Nicée," 1157.

50. Commentary on canon 6 of Nicaea, in *Pedalion*, 130, n. 1.

51. According to G. M. Diéz, the Isodorian version—Hispana edition—was drafted "más probablemente el 634" (*La colección Hispana I* [Madrid, Barcelona, 1996], 218).

52. See H. Leclerq, "Les diverses rédactions des canons de Nicée," 1152–53.

53. Ibid., 1154.

54. Cf. Ms. de l'Abbaye de Saint-Maur-des-Fossés (now in Paris, Fonds. lat. 1451).

55. Cf. H. Leclerq, "Les diverses rédactions des canons de Nicée," 1173.

they are authorized by that canon to exercise unlimited *[aperioriston]* power *[exousian]* over the whole world *[eis holon ton kosmon]*.["56]

Regarding the title of the bishop of Rome, the same canonists remind us that at the time of the Council of Nicaea (325), one could not speak of a patriarch because the custom *(synêtheia)* of designating a bishop with the name of patriarch *(to tou patriarchou onoma)* did not yet exist.[57] Indeed, the appellation "patriarch" appears only at the time of the Fourth Ecumenical Council, and it came into general use—in both the East and the West—only after the Council of Chalcedon (451).[58]

The second canon that refers expressly to the bishop of Rome is canon 3 of the Second Ecumenical Council (Constantinople, 381). It states that "the bishop of Constantinople should have the primacy of honor *[ta presbeia tês timês, honoris primatum]* after *[meta]* the bishop of Rome, that city being the new Rome."[59]

Thus, the only reason that determined the Fathers of the Second Ecumenical Council to recognize this "honorary primacy"[60] in the bishops of Rome and Constantinople was of an eminently political nature. In this case, the political principle acquired a preeminence to the detriment of the affirmation of the apostolic principle,[61] known and observed up until that time.

It is usually written that in the West the council held in Constantinople in 381 was not recognized as ecumenical "until the

---

56. Commentary on canon 6 of Nicaea, in *Pedalion*, 130, n. 1.

57. Ibid., 129.

58. See N. Durā, *Le régime de la synodalité selon la législation canonique conciliaire œcuménique, du 1er millénaire*, 641–60, 759–802; "Legislatia canonica a Sinodului II ecumenic si importanta sa pentru organizarea si disciplina Bisericci" (The legislation of the Second Ecumenical Council and its importance for the organization and discipline of the Church), *Glasul Bisericii* 40, nos. 6–8 (1981): 630–71; "Întâistatatorul în Biserica Ortodoxa: Studiu canonic" (The *prôtos* in the Orthodox Church: Canonical study), *Studii teologice* 40, no. 1 (1988): 15–50.

59. See *Les conciles œcuméniques*, 88–89 (see note 36).

60. See L. Perrone, 64.

61. See N. Durā, "Biserica crestina în premele patru secole: Organizarea si bazele ei canonice" (The Christian Church in the first four centuries: Its organization and canonical foundations), *Ortodoxia* 34, no. 3 (1982): 451–69; "Principiile canonice, fundamentale, de organizare si functionare a Bisericii Ortodoxe," 129–140.

Lateran Council of 649."[62] Now, we know that Dionysius Exiguus (towards 545) had introduced the canons of the first four ecumenical councils as early as his first canonical collection.[63]

But whereas Dionysius translated the words *ta presbeia tês timês* as *privilegia honoris,* the *Versio Dionysio-Hadriana* expressed them through the slant of the syntagma *honoris primatum.*

In fact, according to the *Versio Dionysiana,* "Constantinopolitanae civitatis episcopus habeat privilegia honoris post Romanum episcopum, eo quod sit ipsa nova Roma" (canon 3, Second Council).[64] On the other hand, according to the *Versio Dionysio-Hadriana,* the third canon of the Second Ecumenical Council (Constantinople, 381) provides that "Constantinopolitanus episcopus habeat honoris primatum post Romanum episcopum: propterea quod urbs ipsa sit junior Roma."[65]

The syntagma *honoris primatum* was to be taken up again by most Latin canonical collections, from the *Versio Dionysio-Hadriana* up to our time. The text of the canonical collection established by G. Alberigo and others, for example, reproduces literally the text retained by the *Versio Dionysio-Hadriana,* including the syntagma *honoris primatum,*[66] which proves clearly that the canonical-ecclesiological conception of the papal primacy forged at the time of Pope Hadrian I (772–795) has remained in force in the Roman Catholic Church up to our days.

A further canon of an ecumenical council to refer expressly to the bishop of Rome is canon 28 of the Fourth Ecumenical Council (Chalcedon, 451), which became known in the West—for the first time—thanks to the *Versio Dionysiana.*

As far as Rome is concerned, the Fathers of the Fourth Ecumenical Council stated that the "one hundred and fifty bishops," gathered in Constantinople in 381, "have rightly granted prerogatives [*ta presbeia*] to the See of old Rome because that city was the imperial city; moved by that same reason, the hundred and fifty

---

62. A. García y García, *Historia del derecho canonico,* (Salamanca, 1967), 1:162.

63. See *Codex canonum ecclesiasticorum,* in PL 67:169–72.

64. *Codex canonum universae Ecclesiae,* in PL 67: 78.

65. Ibid., 172.

66. See *Les conciles œcuméniques,* 88–89 (see note 36).

bishops...granted the same prerogatives *[ta presbeia]* to the very holy
See of the new Rome, judging rightly that the city honored by the
presence of the emperor and of the senate and enjoying the same civil
prerogatives as the ancient imperial city of Rome, should have equal
stature also in ecclesiastical matters, being the second after it."[67]

Yet the word *ta presbeia* was translated in Latin by *primatum* (primacy) and not by *privilegia*.[68]

Catholic theologians and canonists have rightly noted, however, that actually canon 28 of the Fourth Ecumenical Council had
simply taken up "the honorary primacy already recognized in the See
of Constantinople (after the church of Rome)....Moreover, the assimilation to the privileges of the Roman See rests on a motivation that
underlines the political basis more explicitly than it was implied by
the canon of 381. The primatial position of Rome is in fact considered as the consequence of its role as capital of the empire....It is true
that the reasons put forward to support the privileges of
Constantinople ignored completely the apostolic recognition and
were in fact against the Petrine doctrine....But the Fathers of
Chalcedon only confirmed the principle on which rested, in large
part, the identification between the imperial administrative structures
and the ecclesiastical districts."[69]

The "primatial" position of Rome was due, then, to its role as
capital of the Roman Empire, like that of Constantinople. Indeed, it
was again underlined that the political importance of a city was the
sole criterion for establishing the honorary order of the main primatial sees of the ecumenical Church at that time.

The truth is that it was only a matter of honorary primacy for
both primatial sees, "old Rome" and "new Rome."

Canon 28 ascribes to the See of Constantinople a jurisdiction
only on the territory of the three dioceses, namely, Asia, Thrace, and
Pontus,[70] where the archbishop of the "new Rome" could consecrate

---

67. Ibid., 225–227.

68. Ibid.

69. L. Perrone, op. cit., 102.

70. Regarding the illegitimate claims of the See of Constantinople to exercising canonical jurisdiction over the entire Orthodox diaspora, see also N. Durã,
"Comunitatile române de peste hotare, o preocupare permanenta a Bisericii ortodoxe

"also the bishops of the barbarian areas of those dioceses,"[71] but not beyond their limits, as affirmed by the upholders of the Greek pentarchy of Constantinople since the beginning of the twentieth century.[72] Of course, these hegemonic affirmations about the Orthodox diaspora[73] can have serious consequences for the relations between the autocephalous Orthodox churches and the "ecumenical patriarchate."[74] As for Rome, it exercised its jurisdictional primacy on the entire West, namely, on the *pars Occidentalis* of the then Roman Empire. But in addition, Rome enjoyed the Petrine privilege, since its see had an apostolic origin, which was missing in the "new Rome"; hence the legend created in the fourth century, according to which the apostle Andrew had been the apostle of "Byzantium."[75]

In any case, the same cannot be said about Rome, whose apostolic origin is even twofold (Peter and Paul), in spite of all steps taken by some of our colleagues with the purpose of minimizing, and even rejecting, the Petrine privilege of the "old Rome."[76]

Regarding the Apostolic See of Rome, neither can one mask the fact that "the church of Rome, in the most perilous situations, against Origen of Alexandria, against Arius, against Apollinarius of Laodicea,

---

romane" (The Romanian Orthodox communities outside the borders—a constant preoccupation of the Romanian Orthodox Church); "Legislatia canonica a Sinodului II ecumenic si importanta sa pentru organizarea si disciplina Bisericci."

71. I. N. Floca, *Canoanele Bisericii Ortodoxe:. Note si comentarii* (The canons of the Orthodox Church: Notes and commentaries) (Sibiu, Romania, 1991), 90.

72. See H. K. Papthanasiou, *Diorthodoxa ke dieklisiastika temata* (in Greek) (Athens, 2000), 10–27.

73. The "Holy and Great Synod"—envisaged by Constantinople—has in effect no other purpose than to ratify its hegemonic pretensions on the entire Orthodox diaspora.

74. See L. Stan, "Despre autocefali" (On autocephaly), *Orthodozia* 8, no. 3 (1956): 369–96; I. D. Ivan, "Raporturile Bisericilor ortodoxe autocefale locale între ele si fata de Patriarhia ecumenica, dupa canoane si istorie" (The relation of the autocephalous local churches and the ecumenical patriarchate according to history and the canons), *Mitropolia Moldovei si Sucevei* 49, nos. 7–8 (1973), 465–78.

75. See H. K. Papathanasiou, op. cit., 9–12.

76. See, e.g., H. Papadopoulos, *The Primacy of the Bishop of Rome: Historical and Critical Study* (in Greek), 2nd ed. (Athens, 1964), VII–XIIf.; Arch. Chrysostomos, *Orthodox and Roman Catholic Relations from the Fourth Crusade to the Hesychastic Controversy*, trans. R. Popescu and N. Precup into Rumanian (Bucharest, 2001), 35, 222–23.

against Eutyches, has always kept, despite all the obstacles, the pure Hebrew doctrine, the pure and strict monotheism, and the original Christology, that of Peter, John, and Paul."[77]

The last canon of an ecumenical council of the first millennium to refer explicitly to the canonical status of the bishop of Rome is canon 36 of the Seventh Ecumenical Council ("in Trullo," 691/692).[78]

This canon too reaffirms that the sees of the "old Rome" and the "new Rome" enjoy the "same honorary prerogatives" *(tôn isôn presbeiôn)* and that the three other patriarchal sees, of Alexandria, Antioch, and Jerusalem, follow them within that honorary order (canon 36).

The "same equal privileges"[79] were thus recognized in both Rome and Constantinople. In addition, the administrative system of collegial government of the ecumenical Church under the five patriarchs was confirmed. This system has been known as the "pentarchical system."

In the opinion of earlier and modern Orthodox, "the principal sees of Christianity, such as those of the old Rome, Constantinople, Jerusalem, Antioch, and Alexandria, have only precedences and primacies of a purely honorary character among them, based on certain dispositions of the early periods of the Church."[80]

Some contemporary Catholic theologians and historians write that these canons, namely, canon 28 of the Fourth Council and canon 36 of the Council "in Trullo," "had never been esteemed in Rome, where they were ignored when not openly opposed."[81]

Certainly, it must be admitted that these canons, hardly esteemed and even ignored by Rome, were nonetheless introduced

---

77. C. Tresmontant, *La pensée de l'église de Rome: Rome et Constantinople* (Paris, 1996), 8.

78. We are in fact dealing with the second session of the Sixth Ecumenical Council. On the ecumenicity of the Council "in Trullo," see N. Durā, "The Ecumenical Council in Trullo (691–692): The Canonical Tradition's Evidences from East and West," in *The Council in Trullo Revisited*, ed. G. Nedungatt and M. Featherstone, Kanonika 6 (Rome, 1995), 229–62.

79. *Pedalion*, 1990, 252.

80. Alexandre de Sturdza, *Considérations sur la doctrine et l'esprit de l'Église Orthodoxe* (Stuttgart, 1816), 122–23.

81. P. A. Yannopoulis, "Du deuxième concile de Constantinople (553) au deuxième concile de Nicée (786–787)," in *Les conciles œcuméniques*, vol. 2, 134.

into the Latin canonical collections as early as the beginning of the sixth century. In fact, they were found in the *Dyonisiana* (version 2).[82] They were later taken up again and published in the canonical collection written by another canonist among our Daco-Roman ancestors, namely, Saint Martin of Bracara[83] (Braga, in Portugal), after 550, and also in the *Hispana* (Isidorian version, seventh century).

On the other hand, in the *Dionysio-Hadriana* (Codex canonum ecclesiasticorum, sive Codex canonum vetus Ecclesiae Romanae) (cf. PL 67:170–72)—sent by Pope Hadrian I (772–795) to Charlemagne, king of the Franks—canon 28 of the Fourth Ecumenical Council (cf. PL 67:176) cannot be found, and even less so canon 36, because the ecumenicity of the Council "in Trullo" had been totally rejected from that canonical collection.

On the contrary, we find the canons of the Council of Sardica (343), which were missing in the *Dionysiana* (version 2) and which had been included after the canons of the Fourth Ecumenical Council (cf. PL 67:176–182).

Some Catholic historians and canonists attest that the said canons (canon 3 of the Second Ecumenical Council; canon 28 of the Fourth Council "in Trullo") were known in the West. For example, Professor G. M. Diéz writes that these canons were known in Spain and in other Western countries, thanks also to the *Hispana* (Isidorian version), written during the second half of the fourth century, which uses the canonical sources offered in the *Dionysiana*. The same researcher of ancient canonical collections writes that even the coun-

---

82. Cf. *Codex canonum Ecclesiae universae*, ed. C. Justellus, in PG 47:76–80, 84–90.

83. He was born at the beginning of the sixth century in Pannonia, a territory then inhabited by the ancestors of the modern Romanians, i.e., Daco-Romans. At that time, Pannonia was also in canonical communion with Rome, as were all the other churches of the Daco–Romans to the south and north of the Danube. See N. Durã, "Biserica 'Vlahilor' (românilor) din Nordul Dunarii si relatiile ei canonice cu principalele Scaune episcopale din Sudul Dunarii (sec. IV–XIV)" (The church of the 'Vlahilor' [Romans] on the north of the Danube and its canonical relations with the main episcopal sees on the south of the Danube [4th–14th centuries]), in *Anuarul Facultatii de Teologie Ortodoxa* (University of Bucharest) (Bucharest, 2002), 353–67. A cleric during the reign of the Franks in the eighth century provides evidence for relations in the church of Saint Martin's homeland (Pannonia) and Rome (see M. Andrieu, *Les ordines Romani du haut moyen âge* [Leuven, 1985], 4:495).

cils of Spain—for example, the one gathered in Barcelona in 540—cite expressly the canons of the Fourth Ecumenical Council.[84]

In our days, Orthodox canonists write that the Lord Jesus Christ did not institute honorary prerogatives or privileges among his apostles, and consequently that "among the holy apostles there was no honorary primacy, and even less any primacy of another nature."[85]

Of course, the apostles received the same apostolic charisma and were therefore equal from the point of view of grace and, for this very reason, of power. Yet, their charge was different; hence, the difference of the honor attributed to them. The apostle Peter, for example, was given the charge to "feed my sheep" (John 21:15–17). It is in accordance with this special responsibility that he speaks on behalf of the Twelve (cf. Acts 1:23, 26; 2:3–7, 47, etc.). Therefore, it is not a matter of "primacy of age,"[86] as affirmed by some biblicists of the Orthodox Church, but of a real "Petrine primacy."

Some Catholic canonists affirm that the papal primacy is one "de las piedras angulares des sistema ecclesiologico y juridico" ("of the cornerstones of the ecclesiastical and juridical system").[87] But they also recognize that, according to the father of catholic (orthodox) ecclesiology, Saint Cyprian of Carthage (†258), the bishop of Rome does not detain "un poder jurisdictionnal sino solamente directivo y honorifico" ("a jurisdictional power, but only a power of a directive and honorary nature").[88]

Regarding the "Roman primacy"—exercised by the bishop of Rome during the period of the ecumenical councils of the first millennium—the same Catholic canonists write that both the Orthodox and the Protestant "seem to confuse between two causes: the right and its exercise, recognized or not at a given time. The councils, and all the more so the juridical texts do not and cannot give a primacy of

---

84. G. M. Diéz, op. cit., 282.

85. N. I. Floca, "Întâietatea, întâietate jurisdictionala, si primat de jurisdictie universala" (Primacy, jurisdictional primacy, and universal primacy), *Studii teologice* 41, nos. 5–6 (1989): 6.

86. I. Mircea, *Dictionar al Noului Testament* (Dictionary of the New Testament) (Bucharest: Edit. Inst. Biblic, 1995), 393.

87. A. García y García, op. cit., 85.

88. Ibid., 91.

divine right to the bishop of Rome; this is why they limit themselves to recognizing it."[89]

Now, unfortunately, these councils and their canonical legislation not only did not limit themselves to merely recognizing it; on the contrary, they condemned any claim to a primacy of a universal jurisdictional nature.

Besides, the canons of the first millennium use the term *potestas* (power) rather in the sense of *auctoritas* (cf. canon 6, First Council); hence also the concept of moral person emerges, of the public canon law attributed to the organs of the Church that exercise that power, that is, the bishops.

At any rate, the term *potestas* contains undoubtedly "el elemento màs juridico" ("the most juridical element"),[90] which is at the same time the most coveted in the world.

As for the two terms, *potestas* and *auctoritas*—drawn from Roman law—they were used in Rome to replace ancient notions, of canonical-pastoral origin: *cura* and *sollicitudo*. Whereas the former notions expressed "the powers of the *superior* (the head)," the latter referred only to the qualities of a "pastor." Therefore, *cura* and *sollicitudo* were not reserved only to the popes but to all bishops.[91]

We know that it is only from the fifth century that the term *papa* was reserved to the bishop of Rome in the expressions *Romanus papa* or *urbis papa*, and only with Pope Gelasius I (492–496) was the title of *Pontifex Maximus* given to the pope. We also know that the Fathers of the Roman council held in 495 designated the pope as "Vicarius beati Petri Apostoli" and "Vicarius Christi." Finally, some Catholic historians and canonists tell us that "from the fifth century on, the appellation *Sedes Apostolica* was reserved only to Rome."[92]

Yet, in the first millennium, the new *Pontifex Maximus* had not forgotten the condition of Christian humility, as Pope Hadrian II demonstrated when, on February 13, 868, he organized a great feast in honor of the brothers Cyril and Methodius in his Palace of the Lateran, to which he invited all Greek monks of Rome. The pope did

---

89. Ibid., 199, n. 11.
90. Ibid., 59.
91. J. Gaudemet, *L'Église dans l'Empire romain* (Paris, 1958), 412–16.
92. A. García y García, op. cit., 197.

not only share the meal with them; what is more, he himself served at the table.[93]

Indeed, through this gesture, the pope showed himself in the true hypostasis of *servus servorum Dei*. In any case, we know that no "ecumenical patriarch" of that period had ever showed such evangelical humility in serving his brothers in Christ.

In the Code of Canon Law we read, "Prima sedes a nemine iudicatur" ("The first see is judged by no one") (canon 1404). Such a syntagma goes back to the Symmachian apocrypha, which "endeavored to demonstrate through false precedents that the pope could not be judged by any man."[94]

This syntagma was pronounced for the first time at the synod held by Pope Symmachus on October 23, 502, which decided that no human court could judge the *prima sedes*, that is, the pope; therefore, the judgment had to be left with God.

Father Salvatore Vacca, OFM Cap, who made a pertinent historical study on the genesis and the evolution of this axiom of Latin canonical ecclesiology of the Middle Ages, has aptly shown that this syntagma expressed "an ideology" and that the sources "of canonical law cannot be fully expressed without referring to it."[95]

Without entering into the details, it must nevertheless be clarified that such an axiom expresses actually a whole ideology loaded with a corresponding canonical-ecclesiological doctrine and that even Latin canon law cannot be correctly understood without referring to its contents, although it is only a product of the Symmachian apocrypha.[96]

According to modern Catholic canonists, these words form part of canon 1404 of the current canonical code. "The pontiff, to whom the words *prima sedes* refer, cannot be judged in this world by any

---

93. See P. Devos, "Le dîner au Latran d'Hadrien II avec les Grecs en 868, sexta feria septuagesimae: Quel jour? Quels préliminaires?" *Analecta bollandiana* 108 (1990): 183–91.

94. J. N. D. Kelly, *Dictionnaire des papes*, trans. C. Friedlander from the English (Brepols, 1994), 100.

95. S. Vacca, *Prima sedes a nemine iudicatur: Genesi e sviluppo storico dell'assioma fino al Decreto di Graziano* (Rome, 1993), 4.

96. See J. Rambaud–Buhot, "La critique des faux dans l'ancien droit canonique," *Bibliothèque de l'École des Chartres* 126 (1968): 5–62.

human power. The pope is the supreme judge in the Church and God alone can judge him. This prerogative is a matter of divine right, so that the pope himself cannot renounce it. And when it is said that the first see cannot be submitted to the judgment of any human power, it is to be understood as referring to both the decisions pronounced by the pope and to those he makes his own by expressly and positively approving and accepting them."[97]

In this light, it is therefore a prerogative of divine right, but no ecumenical synod of the first millennium knew of it. On the contrary, the canons of those councils speak only of an honorary prerogative of human right (cf. canon 6, First Council; canon 28, Fourth Council; canon 36, "in Trullo"; etc.). What can be done then? There is a choice to be made: either to still credit the authenticity of the "Symmachian apocrypha" or to follow literally the spirit of the canonical and ecumenical legislation of the first millennium.

By Way of Conclusion

The two possibilities envisaged above do not help us to overcome the impasse today regarding the "Petrine primacy" and the role of the bishop of Rome in the process of restoration of ecumenical Christian unity. Therefore, in our opinion, this canonical legislation of the ecumenical councils of the first millennium concerning the canonical status of the bishop of Rome is to be read and assessed through the prism of the data offered by the biblical witness on the "Petrine primacy." In other words, the question is to assess and corroborate the dispositions of divine right with those of human right and vice versa, in order to overcome that impasse.

Of course, no one can deny that the apostle Peter—the date of his martyrdom "remains uncertain (64 or 67)"[98]—confessed his messianic faith on behalf of all the apostles (Mark 8:29); that he appears as the spokesman of the Twelve (Mark 10:28–30); that Jesus, when he preached on his boat, ordered him to move into deep waters; that

---

97. *Code de droit canonique,* ed. L. Caparros et al., 813.

98. "Pierre," in *Petit dictionnaire encyclopédique de la Bible* (Brepols: Centre Informatique et Bible [Maredsous], 1992), 729.

Jesus made a special prayer for his conversion and gave him the duty to strengthen his brothers in the faith (Acts 22:31; 24, 34); and so forth. Yet "the Beloved Disciple is the confidant of Jesus (13:23ff.), and Peter must go through him," write Catholic biblical theologians, "to learn who is the traitor. The disciple alone is at the foot of the cross, while Peter has denied his Master (John 18:15–18 and 25–27)." Finally, "at the appearance by the lake, the Disciple is the first who recognizes Jesus."[99]

It is also unanimously recognized that "with James and John, the apostle Peter constitutes one of the columns of the Church," but "he will arrive in Rome only after the writing to the Romans," that is, Paul's letter to the Romans.[100]

Nevertheless, it cannot be denied that the Lord entrusted to Peter the task to strengthen his brothers…

In what does the "Petrine primacy," which is the subject matter of our symposium, consist? What is its nature and how does it manifest itself in its content?

From the study of the text of the canonical legislation of the ecumenical councils of the first millennium, it is evident that no canon makes any mention or allusion to it. This legislation speaks neither of the "Petrine primacy" nor of a primatial office of the bishop of Rome as successor of Saint Peter.

Regarding the term *primate,* the Code of Canon Law tells us that it is an honorary title that does not usually include a power of government or of jurisdiction in the Latin Church (cf. canon 438). Does it mean for the bishop of Rome "an apostolic privilege or an approved custom" (canon 438)?

According to canon 331, it is in "the Bishop of the Church of Rome that rests the office *[munus]* given by the Lord in a singular manner to Peter, first among the Apostles *[singulariter Petro, primo Apostolorum].*" Likewise, canon 333 §1 specifies, "Romanus Pontifex…in universam Ecclesiam potestate gaudet" ("The Roman Pontiff has power over the whole Church"), and that he "obtains also on all particular Churches *[super omnes Ecclesias particulares]*…the primacy of ordinary power *[ordinariae potestatis principatum]*" (canon 333 § 1).

---

99. Ibid., 728.
100. Ibid., 729.

Consequently, in the Latin Code of Canon Law it is a question of *principatus*, that is, of "supremacy," of a "primacy" of the Roman pontiff. But as we have seen, nothing of this is in the text of the canonical legislation of the ecumenical councils of the first millennium, where it is only a question of an honorary primacy of the church of Rome and, ipso facto, of an honorary preeminence in the canonical order of the principal episcopal sees of the ecumenical Church. This is why we should not limit ourselves to the text of that canonical legislation. The whole tradition of the Church, Orthodox and Catholic—biblical, liturgical, patristic, historical, and so forth—must be taken into account, from the apostolic period up to our time, in order to better discover the principal role of the bishop of Rome at the service of the unity of the ecumenical Church.

But shall we Orthodox be able to recognize in the bishop of Rome a primatial mission of unity, so as to rebuild the ecclesial unity torn in 1054?

In our opinion, this is possible provided that the nature of that primatial mission of unity is better clarified. In other words, provided that we succeed in specifying better "the concerns of the primacy" (*UUS*, 95) and, finally, that we reach a "consensus" on the interpretation of the words that Jesus said to the apostle Peter: *Boske ta arnia mou* ("Feed my lambs"). Then we shall be able to say that we have succeeded in specifying accurately the nature and the content themselves of the "Petrine primacy" and, through it, of the *principatus* of the bishop of Rome, referred to in the Latin Code of Canon Law.

In concluding this brief look at the text of the Pontifical Council for Promoting Christian Unity and of the canonical legislation of the ecumenical councils of the first millennium, we come to the conclusion that the theme of our symposium, the "Petrine Primacy," needs a comparative study that can evaluate—*sine ira et studio*—all Orthodox and Catholic ecclesiological and canonical data.

Finally, for our Orthodox-Catholic theological dialogue to lead to a positive result, it needs to be animated with passion, "the passion of unity." It is with that hope and passion, of which Yves Congar has spoken in times past, that we have come to Rome, the city of the apostles Peter and Paul, to contribute to the return of our union lost in 1054—as our ancestor Dionysius Exiguus did at the time of the Acacian schism—and also to bring our respects to him who is at the "service" of the "Petrine primacy" for this ecumenical unity, the bishop of Rome.

Summary of Discussion

Several interventions pointed out that one should not limit oneself to the canons in the strict sense of the word when one wants to study the role of the bishop of Rome in the ecumenical councils. Other related documents (minutes, letters, speeches) should also be taken into consideration.

One Orthodox intervention suggested that Vatican I did not intend to express the entire tradition of the first millennium but tried to answer some specific needs of the times. If that is accepted, a common discussion should be possible.

From the Orthodox side it was stated once more that the so-called primacy of honor supposes a real ministry. It is not just a question of protocol. The Orthodox should take this issue seriously. The need for a ministry of unity was supported by other Orthodox interventions; the nature and extent of the authority that would be needed for the exercise of such a ministry should be defined by something like a "pentarchy," that is, by various patriarchs in a collegial way.

In the Western tradition, during the first millennium, the ministry of the bishop of Rome was expressed more in terms of *cura* or *sollicitudo* than *potestas*. In order to be exercised in an effective way, however, *sollicitudo* needs some degree of *potestas*.

During the discussion, the affirmations regarding the canonical jurisdiction of the ecumenical patriarchate in the diaspora were refuted by the representative of the ecumenical patriarchate.

The Question of the Roman Primacy in the Thought of Saint Maximus the Confessor[*]

Jean-Claude Larchet

The question of the primacy of the Roman pope has been and remains, together with the question of the *Filioque*, one of the main causes of the separation between the Latin Church and the Orthodox churches and one of the principal obstacles to their union.

The thought of Saint Maximus the Confessor on the question is of a major interest. He is one of the few church fathers who took a clear position on the subject, with the dual characteristic that he never undertook any role in the ecclesiastical hierarchy (remaining a simple monk all his life) and that he had a deep knowledge of both the Eastern and Western churches, maintaining direct contact with their representatives at the time of the Monoenergist and Monothelite controversies (on one occasion even staying nearly seven years in Rome near the pope and the theologians of his entourage), in a historical context where the problem of the relationships between the Roman See and the Eastern patriarchates was a crucial one.

Several writings of Saint Maximus include an emphatic tribute to the church of Rome, to its function and mission, although he also presented a number of ecclesiological considerations that help to define its nature and its scope. His thought has not failed to draw the

---

[*] Original text in French.

attention of those interested in the question of the Roman primacy[1] and has continued to be of relevance as a major and inescapable reference in the debate on this subject between the Latin and the Eastern churches after their separation and with a view to their reunion. I would like to clarify here some analyses on the thought of Maximus on this matter by bringing to light the prerogatives he recognizes in the church of Rome, but also the prerequisites and conditions he sets out for them.

I. The Prerogatives Recognized in the Church of Rome

The positions taken by Saint Maximus in favor of the church of Rome, of its collocation and its role in relation to the other churches, are among the strongest in the Greek Fathers.

Elsewhere[2] I have listed and analyzed at length all the texts written by Maximus on this subject.[3] A recapitulation leads to the following principles.

---

1. Cf. G. Glez, "Primauté du pape," in *Dictionnaire de théologie catholique* (Paris, 1936), vol. 13, cols. 294–95; F. Dvornik, *Byzance et la primauté romaine*, Unam Sanctam 49 (Paris, 1964), 79–80; J.-M. Garrigues, "Le sens de la primauté romaine chez saint Maxime le Confesseur," *Istina* 21 (1976), 6–24; J. Pelikan, "Council or Fathers or Scripture: The Concept of Authority in the Theology of Maximus the Confessor," in *The Heritage of the Early Church: Essays in Honour of G. V. Florovsky*, ed. D. Neiman and M. Schatkin, Orientalia christiana analecta 195 (Rome, 1973), 277–88, partially taken up in *La tradition chrétienne*, vol. 2, *L'esprit du christianisme oriental*, 600–1700 (Paris, 1994), 157–182; V. Croce, *Tradizione e ricerca: Il metodo teologico di san Massimo il Confessore*, Studia patristica mediolanensia 2 (Milan, 1974), 115–31; K. Schatz, *La primauté du pape: Son histoire, des origines à nos jours* (Paris, 1992), 90; O. Clément, *Rome autrement* (Paris, 1997), 36–38; J.-C. Larchet, *Maxime le Confesseur, médiateur entre l'Orient et l'Occident*, Cogitatio fidei 208 (Paris, 1998), 125–201.

2. J.-C. Larchet, *Maxime le Confesseur* 127–76.

3. *Opuscula theologica et polemica* (= Th. Pol.) 10, PG 91:237C–247D; *Th. Pol.* 20, PG 91:237C, 244C, 245BC; *Ex epistola sancti Maximi scripta ad abbatem Thalassium* (= *Ep. A*), Mansi 10:677C–678B; *Epistulae* (= Ep.) 12, PG 91:464CD; *Th. Pol.* 12, PG 91:144A–D; *Disputatio cum Pyrrho* (= *Pyr.*), PG 91:352CD, ed. Doucet, 608–9; PG 91:353AB, ed. Doucet, 609–19; *Th. Pol.* 10, PG 91:133D–136B; *Th. Pol.* 11, PG 91:137C–140B; *Relatio motionis* (= *Rel. Mot.*), PG 90:120CD, CCSG (= Corpus

Maximus recognizes incontestably that the church of Rome has a privileged place and role among the churches. He sees it as "the first of the churches" (*princeps ecclesiarum*),[4] as undoubtedly the oldest and quantitatively the largest one, but also as the one that ranks first and should be considered as number one. Here *princeps* could be translated in a stronger sense, since Maximus goes as far as to consider that the church of Rome has "received from the incarnate Word of God himself, as well as from all the holy councils, according to the sacred canons and definitions, in all and for all, sovereignty and authority on all holy churches that are on earth, and that it possesses the power to bind and to unbind."[5] Maximus does not specify how he conceives the primacy he recognizes in the church of Rome, any more than how he conceives the sovereignty and authority he attributes to it. But it is clear that he sees the church of Rome as a reference and a norm in terms of faith for the other churches by affirming that "to the ends of the inhabited earth and throughout the whole earth, those who confess the Lord in a pure and orthodox way look straight and far away, as to a sun of eternal light, to the most holy church of the Romans and to its confession and faith."[6] Furthermore, he recognizes that the pope has the power to bind and to unbind, that is, to adjudicate exclusion from the Church and reintegration into it,[7] not only with regard to the bishops of his church but also with regard to the patriarchs who erred in heterodoxy: they must repent and confess the faith in front of him, and it is by his decision that they can be reintegrated into the catholic Church and be readmitted into its communion.[8]

Christianorum: Series graeca) 39:31–33; PG 90:128BC, CCSG 39:45–47; *Epistula Anastasi discipuli ad monachos Calaritanos* (= *Ep. Cal.*), PG 90:135C–136C, CCSG 39:168–69 (this was not written by Maximus, but it was inspired by him); *Disputatio inter Maximum et Theodosium Caesaerae Bithiniae* (= *Dis. Biz.*), PG 90:145C–148A, CCSG 39:95–97; PG 90:153CD, CCSG 39:113–15; *Epistula ad Anastasium monachum discipulum* (= *Ep. An.*), PG 90:132A, CCSG 39:161.

    4. *Ep. A*, Mansi 10:677C.

    5. *Th. Pol.* 12, PG 91:144C.

    6. *Th. Pol.* 11, PG 91:137C–140A.

    7. *Pyr.* 352CD, 353AB, ed. Doucet, 608–9.

    8. *Th. Pol.* 12, PG 91:144A–D; *Pyr.* 352CD, 353AB, ed. Doucet, 608–9; *Dis. Biz.*, PG 90:153CD, CCSG 39:113–15.

These positions of Saint Maximus, schematically summarized here, must be understood, however, in the light of the historical circumstances in which they were taken, on the one hand, and of the specific points and the nuances introduced by Maximus, on the other hand.

Today historians on all sides agree in recognizing that the Latin Church, especially from the ninth century on, understood the papal primacy in a way that was clearly different from that of the earlier centuries, inasmuch as it gave it a political and juridical turn, where power took the place of authority, where primacy was conceived as superiority, where centralism supplanted collegiality.[9] Dialogue became more and more difficult, as Latin theologians tended to reinterpret the whole history of the papacy of the first centuries in the light of this new model and to justify it by showing its continuity with its origins, while the Eastern theologians reacted by going so far as to refuse to acknowledge the existence of any form of primacy in the first centuries, interpreting in a restrictive and minimalist way the patristic and canonical texts but also the historical facts that might be understood in that sense. Within the current ecumenical dialogue, Maximus's very clear affirmation of the prerogatives of the church of Rome deserves utmost attention on the part of Orthodox theologians in order to examine the validity of those prerogatives, while the conditions he sets deserve utmost attention on the part of Latin theologians so as to reconsider the way and the conditions in which those prerogatives should be exercised.

2. The Foundations of the Prerogatives Recognized in the Church of Rome

Maximus recalls several characteristics of the church of Rome that are the foundation of its particular importance and of the prerogatives he recognizes in it.

First, the church of Rome is the largest of all churches,[10] and it is the church of the ancient capital city.[11] This criterion, according to

---

9. On the Catholic side, cf. in particular K. Schatz, *La primauté du pape*.
10. *Ep. A*, Mansi 10:678B.
11. *Ep. Cal.*, PG 90:136A, CCSG 39:169.

which the Eastern patriarchates have for many centuries recognized in the church of Rome a primacy of honor, deserves to be placed first, for it has a significant and deep-rooted conciliar basis and was therefore unanimously accepted.[12]

Second, the church of Rome was founded by Saints Peter and Paul,[13] it received their teaching, they lived there, and it is the place of their martyrdom and where their tombs are found.[14] This repre-

---

12. The primacy of honor of the church of Rome is implicitly recognized by canon 3 of the First Council of Constantinople (381): "That the bishop of Constantinople should have the primacy of honor [*ta presbeia tês timês*] after the bishop of Rome, since this city is the new Rome" (*Les conciles œcuméniques*, vol. 2, *Les décrets* [Paris, 1994], 88). The Council of Chalcedon (451) reaffirmed this by confirming in its canon 28 the canon 3 of Constantinople I : "The Fathers have rightly granted prerogatives to the See of the old Rome, since that city was the imperial city; prompted by that same motive, the hundred and fifty bishops beloved by God have granted the same prerogatives to the Most Holy See of the new Rome [Constantinople], judging rightly that the city honored by the presence of the emperor and of the senate, and enjoying the same civil prerogatives that the ancient imperial city of Rome, should also be magnified like the former in ecclesiastical matters, being the second after it" (ibid., 226). A further confirmation is found in *Novellae* 131 of the emperor Justinian: "We decree, according to the decisions of the councils, that the Most Holy Pope of the old Rome is the first of all hierarchs and that the Holy Archbishop of Constantinople, the new Rome, occupies the second see, after the holy and apostolic See of Rome, but with precedence over the other Sees" (*Corp. jur. civ.*, ed. G. Kroll, 3:655). The interpretation of theses canons, however, raises a certain number of problems, and it remains difficult to define what that primacy of "honor" (or prerogatives) consists of exactly. Cf. J. Meyendorff, "La primauté romaine dans la tradition canonique jusqu'au concile de Chalcédoine," *Istina* 4 (1957), 474–81; F. Dvornik, *Byzance et la primauté romaine*, 9–84; W. de Vries, *Orient et Occident: Les structures ecclésiales vues dans l'histoire des sept premiers conciles œcuméniques* (Paris, 1974); K. Schatz, *La primauté du pape*; A. de Halleux, "La collégialité dans l'Église ancienne," *Revue théologique de Louvain* 24 (1993), 433–54; O. Clément, *Rome autrement*, 33–64; P. Maraval, *Le christianisme de Constantin à la conquête arabe* (Paris, 1997), 204–13. The rank of capital that the Byzantines (who continued to call themselves "Romans") have never ceased to assign to Rome in a somewhat honorary manner, even after the transfer of the capital of the empire to Constantinople (cf. F. Dvornik, *Byzance et la primauté romaine*, 33–50), is found again in the expression, used several times by Maximus (and common in his time and in the previous centuries), of "old Rome" (cf. among others *Th. Pol.* 20, PG 91:244C; *Ep. Cal.*, PG 90:136A, CCSG 39:169), Constantinople being the "new Rome."

13. *Ep. A*, Mansi 10:678B; *Th. Pol.* 12, PG 91:144C.

14. Cf. *Pyr.*, PG 91:353A, ed. Doucet, 609.

sents the second of the criteria according to which the church of Rome was recognized, in the East itself, as the first among the churches.[15]

Third, Maximus considers that the church of Rome proved itself unfailingly faithful to the orthodox faith from its very origins up to his own time. He sees in it "the truly solid and immovable 'stone,'"[16] and he celebrates its faithful, clergy, and theologians, who are "pious and firm as stones" and "the very fervent champions of the faith."[17]

3. The Limits and the Conditions of the Prerogatives Recognized in the Church of Rome

1. The Position of Maximus Relativized through the Historical Context of His Time

Unquestionably, Maximus's strong emphasis on the church of Rome depends in large measure on the historical context in which he found himself, at a time when the Monoenergist and Monothelite heresies obtained the approval and the support of the Eastern patriarchs.

The sole purpose of the support given by Maximus to the ambiguous formulations of Pope Honorius[18]—which leads him to develop an argumentation that seems often to be forced, without in any case convincing the Fathers of the Sixth Ecumenical Council who condemned Honorius—was to deprive the Monothelites of a weighty support they claimed for their theses.

The emphatic praise of the church of Rome and the affirmation of its primacy found in *Letter A (To the Priest Thalassios)* is intended to support this church at a time when the emperor was aiming to make it accept the *Ekthesis* (of Monothelite inspiration) in exchange for the ratification of the election of Pope Severinus.[19]

---

15. Cf., among others, F. Dvornik, *Byzance et la primauté romaine*, 21–50; K. Schatz, *La primauté du pape*, 16–23, 26–27, 53.
16. *Ep. A*, Mansi 10:678B.
17. *Ep. Cal.*, PG 90:136AB.
18. *Ep. A*, Mansi 10:677–78.
19. *Ep. A*, Mansi 10:677–78.

The special insistence of Maximus, in *Opusculum* 12,[20] on the notions of sovereignty and authority (the use of the first term was not very common in the East) and on the pope's power to bind and to unbind, finds an explanation mostly in the context concerning the person (Pyrrhus) holding the rank not only of patriarch but of "ecumenical patriarch" with the primacy of honor among the Eastern patriarchs, and therefore a person who would have to answer for his faith and to ask to be reintegrated into the church communion only before an authority at least equal to his own and whose foundation is recognized and authority unquestionable.

The recognition by Maximus, in *Opusculum* 11, of the church of Rome as reference and norm in dogmatic matters,[21] is closely linked to the fact that, during the Monoenergist and Monothelite controversy, the successive Roman popes (including, according to him, Honorius) had never deviated from the orthodox faith whereas the Eastern patriarchs were heretics.

In a controversy in which he was opposed to all the Eastern patriarchs, the interest of Maximus in obtaining the support of the church of Rome, but also in emphasizing its authority to the maximum, is obvious, and it does not allow us to evaluate exactly his ecclesiological conception of the place and role of the church of Rome among the other churches. For example, it is impossible to describe exactly to what extent he recognizes its privilege (a right or power that the other churches would not have) to act as authority of appeal and judgment or as holder of the power to bind and to unbind, since it alone is in a position to exercise these roles. The same applies to its authority in dogmatic matters, since in that period it alone holds an exclusivity, among the churches, in the confession of the orthodox faith and is the only one that represents the catholic Church. In these circumstances, with the church of Rome in a monopoly situation, it is difficult even to strictly speak of primacy, for any comparison with the other churches, and any evaluation of its place in relation to them, is impossible.

---

20. *Th. Pol.* 12, PG 91:144C.
21. *Th. Pol.* 11, PG 91:137C–140B. Cf. also *Ep.* Cal., PG 90:136AB, CCSG 39:169.

2. *The Conciliar and Canonical Foundation of the Primacy of Rome Is Primordial*

As F. Dvornik has pointed out, Maximus insists on the conciliar and canonical origin of the prerogatives recognized in the church of Rome.[22] In this he expresses the Eastern point of view, which is at odds with the Western one, which the papacy had been developing since the end of the fourth century and according to which the precedence of the church of Rome over the other churches is not dependent on conciliar decisions but on institution by the Lord (primacy by "divine right").[23] The reference to the conciliar and canonical origin is indeed much more indisputable in the eyes of the East than the reference to Matt 16:16–19, a text over which the exegetes have always been divided and that some Latin theologians, from the third century on, have interpreted in a way (i.e., the succession and subsequently the vicariate of Peter by divine right) that has encountered the reluctance of the East.

3. *Maximus Has in Mind the Church of Rome More Than the Person of the Pope*

A study of the texts of Maximus shows that generally he has more the church of Rome in mind than its representative, the pope. When he mentions the latter, he often includes also the Roman theologians and the faithful, indicated as a whole as "the Romans," "those of Rome," or "the pious men of ancient Rome."[24]

4. *The Apostolic Foundation of the Church of Rome Refers to Both Saint Peter and Saint Paul*

Maximus, like many Fathers, refers at the same time to both Saint Peter and Saint Paul when he mentions the apostolic foundation

---

22. F. Dvornik, *Byzance et la primauté romaine*, 80.

23. Ibid.

24. Cf. *Rel. mot.*, PG 90:120D, CCSG 39:33; PG 90:121B, CCSG 39:33; *Ep. Cal.*, PG 90:136A, CCSG 39:169.

of the church of Rome.[25] When this is not explicit, he speaks in a general way of the "apostolic" origin of the church of Rome,[26] but he never links that origin to Saint Peter only.

Thus, by associating Saint Peter and Saint Paul, Maximus takes up an ancient tradition found in Eusebius of Caesarea who, in this case, refers to several ancient sources: Dionysius of Alexandria, Origen, and Clement of Alexandria.[27] We could also name Irenaeus of Lyon, who mentions "the very great, very ancient, and well-known church that the two very glorious apostles Peter and Paul founded and established in Rome."[28]

When Maximus mentions "the stone" on which the Church is firmly founded, he does not yet have the person of Peter in mind but Peter's upright profession of faith in Christ,[29] and he believes that it is against this upright profession of faith that the gates of Hades will not prevail,[30] according to an interpretation of Matt 16:16–18 that would become classical among Byzantine theologians,[31] but is already found, as far as the Greek Fathers are concerned,[32] in Origen,[33] John Chrysostom,[34] or Cyril of Alexandria.[35]

Thus, according to Maximus's conception, it is impossible not only to see the pope as successor or "vicar" of Peter but even to speak of the function of the pope as of a "Petrine ministry."

---

25. *Pyr.* 352D–353A, ed. Doucet, 609.

26. Cf. *Ep.* A, Mansi 10:678B.

27. *Hist. eccl.*, 2.25.8, SC (= Sources chrétiennnes) 31:93; 3.1.2, SC 31:97; 6.14.6, SC 41:107.

28. *Adv. haer.*, 3.3.2, SC 211:32.

29. *Ep. Cal.*, PG 90:136A, CCSG 39:169; *Ep. An.*, PG 90:132A, CCSG 39:161.

30. We find the confirmation of this interpretation of the words of Christ in *Ep.* 13 : "the pious confession [of the faith] against what the perverse mouths of the heretics, open like the gates of hell, shall never prevail" (*Ep.* 13, PG 91:512B).

31. Cf. J. Meyendorff, "Saint Pierre, sa primauté et sa succession dans la théologie byzantine," in N. Afanassieff, N. Koulomzine, J. Meyendorff, and A. Schmemann, *La primauté de Pierre dans l'Église orthodoxe* (Neuchâtel, 1960), 93–115.

32. This interpretation is also found in the Latin Fathers prior to Maximus, among them Saint Hilary of Poitiers, Saint Ambrose of Milan, and Saint Augustine.

33. Cf. *In Mat.* 12.10, ed. Klostermann (Leipzig, 1935), 85–89.

34. Cf. *In Mat.* 54.2.

35. Cf *In Is.* 4; *De Trinitate* 4, SC 237:148–50.

Moreover, it should be noted that neither Saint Irenaeus nor the various sources mentioned by Eusebius of Caesarea[36] indicate Peter as having been bishop of Rome. Saint Irenaeus writes that "after they had founded and built the church, the blessed apostles [Peter and Paul] handed the responsibility of the episcopate over to Linus."[37] The first lists of bishops indicate Linus as the first bishop of the capital. It seems, then—especially if we take the witness of Clement of Rome and of Hermas—that originally the episcopate was collegial in Rome.[38] As F. Dvornik points out: "The first Christians would never designate an apostle as first bishop of the city where he had implanted the faith. It was the one ordained by him who was considered the first bishop. That custom was in use also in Rome."[39]

The conception by which the pope is linked to the person of Peter and that makes him a direct successor of Peter, or his vicar, or considers Peter's personal charisma as being hereditary within the papacy, is a later development and is of Latin origin; the idea of the succession was expressed in the West in the middle of the third century by Pope Stephen, and the concept of vicariate appeared in the West with Pope Leo the Great (440–461).[40] These ideas were developed by the papacy to strengthen its authority in the sense of a less collegial and more autocratic conception of the Church as being more exclusively centered on the person of the pope himself; but on the whole they remained foreign to the Christian East.

The reference to Peter and Paul as common foundations of the authority of the church of Rome in no way restricts that authority; quite on the contrary, for it gives it, as it were, twofold support. On the one hand, the apostolic origin was rather common in the East, and many churches could claim it; on the other hand, Peter had founded the church of Antioch before taking part in the foundation of the church of Rome, and therefore, from that point of view, the church of Antioch had the right to assert its priority. But Rome had

---

36. Cf. n. 27.

37. *Adv. haer.* 3, SC 211:32–34.

38. Cf. Clement of Rome, 1 *Clem.* 44, SC 167:172; Hermas, *Past.*, Vis., 2.2.6, SC 53:92; 3.9.7, SC 53:124.

39. F. Dvornik, *Byzance et la primauté romaine*, 33–34.

40. Cf. in particular K. Schatz, *La primauté du pape*, 55–58.

the unique privilege (1) of having as founders and teachers two of the most illustrious apostles, Peter and Paul; (2) of being the place where Peter spent the last period of his life (whereas he had only gone through the other Eastern cities where he founded a church); (3) of being the place where the two great apostles were martyred; (4) and, finally, of being the place where their tombs are kept.[41]

Yet the dual reference allows one to adhere to a more collegial conception, more in keeping with the ecclesiological conception of the Christian East.[42]

5. Confessing the Orthodox Faith and Being Faithful to It as the Criterion of Authority

When he praises this or that pope, Maximus shows that the value he attributes to him depends less on that pope's function than on his piety[43] and his faithfulness to the orthodox faith.[44] He states quite clearly that he loves the church of Rome insofar as it confesses the orthodox faith.[45] And "it is the orthodoxy of the doctrinal position of Rome that is regularly invoked in favor of its particular apostolic situation,"[46] and not the latter in favor of the former.

The church of Rome is a reference and a norm in matters of faith as long as it confesses the orthodox faith defined by Christ, by the apostles, by the Fathers and the councils.[47]

---

41. Cf. Eusebius of Caesarea, *Hist. eccl.* 2.25.5–7, SC 31:92–93.

42. On the ecclesiology of Rome and of the Eastern churches, cf. F. Dvornik, *Byzance et la primauté romaine*, 21–87; W. de Vries, *Orient et Occident*, 13–194; K. Schatz, *La primauté du pape*, 15–90; A. de Halleux, "La collégialité dans l'Église ancienne"; J. Pelikan, , *L'esprit du christianisme oriental*, 600–1700, 157–82; O. Clément, *Rome autrement*, 17–64; P. Maraval, *Le christianisme de Constantin à la conquête arabe* (Paris, 1997), 189–213.

43. *Th. Pol.* 12, PG 91:143A.

44. See *Th. Pol.* 15, PG 91:168A.

45. *Rel. mot.*, PG 90:128C, CCSG 39:47.

46. J. Pelikan, "Council or Father or Scripture," 287.

47. *Th. Pol.* 11, PG 91:137C–140B.

6. The Principle of Church Unity Is Not the Pope but Christ

The idea, emphasized in Latin ecclesiology, that the pope is a principle of unity or a visible center of unity for the Church is foreign to Maximus's thinking, in the same way that it remained generally foreign to the Christian Eastern conception, in which the unity of the Church is expressed through the unity of the faith and the communion in Christ.

In fact, for Maximus the principle of Church unity is Christ,[48] and it is through the common confession of the same faith in the same Trinity and in the same Christ that the local churches and their faithful are united in the same catholic Church.[49] Maximus writes that in the Church "all are in affinity with one another and bound with one another in one and the same grace and in the simple and indivisible power of the faith. 'Now the whole group of those who believed were of one heart and soul' [Acts 4:32], so that there was and could be seen but one body, made of different members, worthy of Christ himself, our true head."[50]

It is by this confession of the same faith, which unites all the Christians dispersed throughout the world and throughout the centuries that, as Maximus has written, "[the catholic Church] gathers in itself everything under the skies, and continues to add what remains to what it has already gathered, showing through the Spirit, from one extreme of the earth to the other, only one soul and only one language, through the unanimity of the faith and agreement in its expression."[51]

---

48. See *Thal.* 48, PG 90:433C, CCSG 7:333; 53, PG 90:501B, CCSG 7:431.

49. On the confession of the orthodox faith as the principle of unity in the Church, cf. *Myst.* 1, PG 90:668A, ed. Sotiropoulos, 132; *Thal.* 53, PG 90:501B, CCSG 7:431. For Maximus, the confession of the faith is a principle of unity before communion, which is conditioned by it (cf. *Rel. Mot.* 6, PG 90:120CD; *Dis. Biz.*, PG 90:140C–140D, CCSG 39:83; PG 90:161D–164A, CCSG 39:131). Cf. V. Croce, *Tradizione e ricerca*, 69.

50. *Myst.* 1, PG 90:668A, ed. Sotiropoulos, 132.

51. *Ep.* 18, PG 91:584A.

7. The Catholicity of the Church Lies Not in a Universality of Jurisdiction or of Authority but in the Unanimous Confession of the True Faith

For Maximus, the catholic Church identifies itself neither with the local church, nor with any particular church,[52] nor with the universal Church; the problem of modern ecclesiology concerning the relations of the local church with the universal Church is foreign to him, as is the Latin conception that the catholic Church, as the sum or the totality of the local churches, is the universal Church. "The catholic Church," for Maximus, "is the Church founded by God,"[53] the Church of Christ, of which he is the cornerstone [Eph 2:20],[54] or of which he is the head and which is his body [Col 1:18, 24],[55] which he has himself established on the basis of the authentic confession of faith in him,[56] and which is one and unique.[57] It is fundamentally characterized, as catholic, by the fact that it confesses the orthodox faith, as can be seen in several texts[58] and very clearly in the following affirmation uttered before the patriarch Peter and reported in the *Letter to the Monk Anastasius:* "The catholic Church is the rightful and salvific profession of faith in the God of the universe."[59] Most of the other passages of Maximus's corpus that use the expression "catholic Church" do so in a context in which the orthodox faith is advanced and opposed to heretical conceptions.[60] To one of his accusers who

---

52. In the way he expresses himself, he makes the distinction between "the catholic Church" and the local churches (for the designation of these, see, e.g. *Th. Pol.* 7, PG 91:77B; 10, PG 91:136C; 19, PG 91:229C; 20, PG 91:237C; *Dis. Biz.*, PG 90:148A, CCSG 39:97).

53. *Ep. Cal.*, PG 90:136A, CCSG 39:169.

54. Cf. *Thal.* 63, PG 90:501AB, CCSG 7:431.

55. Cf. ibid., PG 90:672BC, CCSG 22:155.

56. Cf. *Ep. An.*, PG 90:132A, CCSG 39:161.

57. Cf. *Thal.* 63, PG 90:685C, CCSG 22:77.

58. *Th. Pol.* 12, PG 91:144AB; *Th. Pol.* 11, PG 91:140B; *Ep.* 12, PG 91:464 D; *Rel. mot.*, PG 90:120C, CCSG 39:31; *Ep. Cal.*, PG 90:136A, CCSG 39:169; *Ep. An.*, PG 90:132A, CCSG 39:161.

59. *Ep. An.*, PG 90:132A, CCSG 39:161.

60. Cf : *Th. Pol.* 11, PG 91:140AB; 7, PG 91:84A, 88C; 8, PG 91:89CD, 92D; 9, PG 91:116B, 128B; 12, PG 91:141A, 143CD, 144A; 15, PG 91:160C; 17, PG

said to him, "By affirming these things; you have put schism into the Church!" Maximus answered: "If one who speaks the words of the Holy Scriptures and of the holy Fathers puts schism into the Church, what will one who abolishes the dogmas of the saints do to the Church, which cannot even exist without them?"[61] It can therefore be said that in Maximus there is an "identification of the catholic Church with the rightful confession of faith,"[62] and this for him "is the confession of the orthodox faith, which grounds and constitutes it."[63]

Therefore, "catholic" (*katholikòs*) does not mean "universal" (*oikoumenikòs*): Maximus, like the ancient Fathers, distinguishes clearly the two notions and concurs with their ancient use.[64] If the catholic Church is universal, its universality is not a geographical one nor one of jurisdiction or of authority but a universality that includes, in time and space, all truths that constitute always and everywhere the orthodox faith as well as all the people who have always and everywhere confessed that faith.[65]

91:209D; *Ep.* 11, PG 91:461BC; 12, PG 91:464D, 465AB; 13, PG 91:532CD; 17, PG 91:580C, 581CD; 18, PG 91:584D–584A; *Ep. Cal.*, PG 90:136A, CCSG 39:169; *Rel. mot.*, PG 90:120C, CCSG 39:31. In *Ep.* 15, PG 91, Maximus quotes a passage of Saint Basil of Caesarea where the expression has the same connotation.

61. *Rel. mot.*, PG 90:117D, CCSG 39:29.

62. V. Croce, *Tradizione e ricerca*, 70; see also 71–72, 79–80.

63. Ibid., 80.

64. Indeed, observes pertinently G. Florovsky, "in the oldest documents, the term *ekklêsia katholikê*...meant...the integrity of faith or of doctrine, the faithfulness of the 'Great Church' to the plenary and primitive tradition, as opposed to the sectarian tendencies of the heretics, who separated themselves from that original plenitude, each following his particular and particularistic line, and therefore it meant 'orthodox' rather than 'universal'" ("Le corps du Christ vivant," *Cahiers théologiques de l'actualité protestante* HS 4 [1948], 24). See also V. Lossky, *À l'image et à la ressemblance de Dieu*, ch. 9, "Du troisième attribut de l'Église," 170–73. V. Lossky writes in particular: "Catholicity appears to us as an inalienable attribute of the church as possessing the Truth" (170) Paris: Aubier-Montaigne, 1967.

65. On this point see also Cyril of Jerusalem, *Cat.* 18.23, PG 33:1044A. This explains that at a given historical moment, if heresy spread in all or almost all churches—which happened several times and is a possibility that Christ himself contemplates: "When the Son of Man comes, will he find faith on earth?" (Luke 18:8)—the catholic Church could find itself reduced to a few faithful, indeed to one only. Thus, V. Lossky writes: "Each part, the smallest one of the church—even only one faithful—can be called 'catholic.' When Saint Maximus, to whom the ecclesiastical tradition attributes the title of confessor, answered to those who wanted to force him

In confessing and defending the orthodox faith, Maximus is well aware that he is confessing and defending "the dogma...that is common to the catholic Church,"[66] that is to say, the faith that the apostles, the Fathers, the councils, the clergy, and the orthodox faithful have confessed always and everywhere. He who confesses the orthodox faith integrates or reintegrates the catholic Church and its communion;[67] he who professes a doctrine not in accordance with the orthodox faith excludes himself from the catholic Church[68] and must be excluded from it.[69] This principle applies to individuals, but also to the particular churches: they belong to the catholic Church, or rather they identify themselves with it inasmuch as they confess the orthodox faith; they are excluded from it (even if they continue institutionally to be churches and to bear the name of church) if the doctrines they profess are foreign to the orthodox faith as defined by the apostles, the Fathers, and the councils. Thus, Maximus identifies the church of Rome with the catholic Church for the sole reason that it confesses the orthodox faith[70] and that, during the period of the Monothelite controversy, it was even the only one that confessed

---

to take communion with the Monothelites: 'Even if the whole universe [*oikoumenê*] took communion with you, I alone shall not take communion,' he opposed his catholicity to an ecumenicity presumed heretical" (*À l'image et à la ressemblance de Dieu*, ch. 9, "Du troisième attribut de l'Église," 173).

66. *Rel. mot.*, PG 90:120C, CCSG 39:31.

67. Cf. *Th. Pol.* 12, PG 91:144B (4) (concerning Pyrrhus); *Ep.* 12, PG 91:464D, 465AB (concerning the sisters of Alexandria who had taken refuge in the region of Carthage).

68. See *Th. Pol.* 12, PG 91:144A (4).

69. Cf. *Th. Pol.* 7, PG 91:88C, in which Maximus, addressing heretics, writes: "We reject in wisdom those who are opposed both to themselves and to each other as well as to the Truth; let us courageously throw them out of our house, the holy catholic and apostolic church of God, and let us give no entrance to those who, against the orthodox faith, plot like brigands to move the boundaries set by the Fathers." In *Th. Pol.* 8, PG 91:92A, Maximus says that with his fight, he tries "courageously to chase away those who rise up against the Lord with their words and their doctrines, and to eliminate them from the good soil that is our Lord himself and the orthodox faith." Here the good soil symbolizes the Church, identified with both Christ and the faith that confesses him rightfully.

70. Cf. *Th. Pol.* 12, PG 91:144A. Moreover, it is indicated as a local church among the others; cf. *Th. Pol.* 12, PG 91:237C; *Dis. Biz.*, PG 90:148A, CCSG 39:97.

it.[71] On the contrary, at the time of Maximus, the churches of Constantinople, Antioch, Alexandria, and Jerusalem were outside the catholic Church and its communion (although they were in communion among themselves) because they adhered to the Monoenergist and Monothelite heresies.[72] Inversely, all churches that confess the orthodox faith are considered as "holy catholic churches."[73]

It is true that the gates of hell cannot prevail against the Church established by Christ, but this does not means that a particular church that represents it could not fall into heresy because it retained a special charisma, or power or privilege, for no particular church is identified a priori or definitively with the Church. All churches, as history has shown, have at a time been heretical, and the catholic Church existed in only a few faithful who continued to confess the orthodox faith. Thus, if the gates of hell cannot prevail against the Church, it is through the grace of God that it receives as a body of which Christ is the head,[74] or as the bride of Christ. Thus, Maximus writes that "the catholic Church, the bride of the Lord," is guarded "by the Lord himself in security so that we might be saved from the aggression of the enemies."[75] If the catholic Church cannot lose its integrity and its catholicity, it is because fundamentally it is a mystical reality identified with the body of Christ.[76]

---

71. Thus, when the Roman apocrysaries seem ready to accept the heretical doctrine of the patriarch Peter, Maximus considers that "because of that, the affairs of almost the whole catholic and apostolic church founded by God are seriously in danger" (*Ep. Cal.*, PG 90:136A, CCSG 39:169).

72. Cf. *Ep. An.*, PG 91:132A, CCSG 39:161.

73. *Th. Pol.*, 16, PG 91:209B.

74. See *Thal.*,63, PG 90:672B–D, CCSG 22:155–57.

75. Cf. *Th. Pol.* 8, PG 91:92D.

76. This ideal vision of the Church appears in *Thal.* 63, PG 90:672B–673B, CCSG 22:155–57.

8. *The Doctrinal Authority Belongs to the Tradition: The Pope Is Not Infallible*

For Maximus, the source of the truth of Church dogmas is therefore Christ himself.[77]

The orthodox faith is not defined by a particular church, by its clergy, its pope, its patriarch, or its faithful but by the whole tradition of the catholic Church. The criterion of the orthodoxy of faith, as Maximus states on several occasions,[78] is its agreement with tradition as expressed by the teaching of the Scripture, the apostles, the councils, and the Fathers. Not only the dogmatic positions of the popes and patriarchs and bishops but the councils themselves must be received and ratified according to the orthodox faith[79] as defined by tradition in all its components.

In the Church, says Maximus, "we are taught at the same time by Holy Scripture, Old and New Testament, by the holy doctors and the councils."[80] No one of these components of tradition as such has any absolute authority taken individually, but only in agreement with the others and with the whole.[81]

Maximus acknowledges and appreciates highly the fundamental role played since the origin of the Church, especially in the defense of dogma, by the church of Rome and the popes who led it (he shows high regard, for example, for Pope Leo I on account of his decisive action for the victory of orthodoxy at the Council of Chalcedon),[82] and he expresses the hope that they will continue to play that role. Nonetheless, for him there is no a priori papal infallibility. When told

---

77. *Ibid.*, PG 90:433CD, CCSG 7:333.

78. *Th. Pol.* 10, PG 91:136A; *Ep. Cal.*, PG 90:136B, CCSG 39:169; *Dis. Biz.*, PG 90:144C, CCSG 39:91; PG 90:145C–148A, CCSG 39:95–97. Other references in J. Pelikan, "Council or Father or Scripture." See also the excellent study by V. Croce, *Tradizione e ricerca.*

79. *Dis. Biz.*, PG 90:145C, 148A, CCSG 39:95, 97.

80. *Rel. mot.*, PG 90:124A, CCSG 39:37. These different elements as Maximus understands them are analyzed at length in V. Croce, *Tradizione e ricerca.*

81. See J. Pelikan, "Council or Father or Scripture," 287.

82. See *Th. Pol.* 15, PG 91:168A.

that the pope has accepted the heresy to which the other patriarchs have adhered, he does not find it impossible.[83]

And we must recall here that if Maximus made efforts to interpret the positions of Pope Honorius in an orthodox sense (with the purpose of depriving the Monothelites of an authority to which they were referring), the Sixth Ecumenical Council (Constantinople III) a few decades later did not follow Maximus and placed Honorius among the condemned heretics, showing that the council fathers did not acknowledge an automatic infallibility of the pope of Rome.[84]

9. *The Confession of the Orthodox Faith as Ecclesiological Criterion*

Maximus maintains that the church of Rome is the head of the churches, but the fact remains that, in his eyes, all churches are fundamentally on an equal footing[85] and that none of them prevails over the others.[86]

The fundamental criterion of the hierarchy that Maximus establishes among the churches and their representatives is whether they confess the orthodox faith.[87]

The churches that confess the orthodox faith belong to or, more correctly, are the catholic Church; those that do not confess it are outside the catholic Church. In Maximus's view, the church of Rome is assimilated to the catholic Church[88] insofar as it confesses the orthodox faith[89]—and was indeed at that moment of history the only one to do so—since the catholic Church, as we saw earlier, is there where the orthodox faith is confessed.

Every pope, patriarch, or bishop who is at the head of a church, and not only the pope of Rome, presides over the faith.[90]

---

83. *Rel. mot.*, PG 91:121BC, CCSG 39:33–35; *Ep. An.*, PG 91:132A, CCSG 39:161.

84. *Les conciles œcuméniques*, vol. 2, *Les décrets*, 280.

85. *Th. Pol.* 12, PG 91:143B.

86. Ibid.

87. Ibid., 143BC.

88. Ibid., 144A.

89. Ibid., 144B.

90. *Th. Pol.* 12, PG 91:245BC.

In the troubled period in which Maximus lived, the pope of Rome, after the death of Sophronius of Jerusalem, was the only one among the patriarchs of the pentarchy to confess the orthodox faith. Hence his privileged role, recognized by Maximus, in the defense and exposition of that faith. But as a matter of principle, he has no privilege in the definition of that faith. The decisions in matters of faith are taken collegially by the councils or the synods, and the validity of these synods depends on the approval, by all bishops, metropolitans, and patriarchs, of their gatherings and their decisions.[91]

Even outside these synods, the dogmatic positions taken by the pope, and those of any other patriarch, must be received by all the churches that confess the orthodox faith and are therefore subject to their approval. In the ancient Church, and even at the time of Maximus, it was customary for every patriarch, but also for every newly elected pope, to share the content of his faith with his brothers in a synodal letter and to submit it for their agreement, which conditioned the validity of his consecration and allowed communion to be established.

A famous text of Maximus even shows that the theological positions of the pope, far from being normative and indisputable, were discussed by the theologians of other churches, and he considered it quite normal that he should justify them.[92]

Decisions in matters of ecclesiastical discipline are also taken collegially.[93]

Whether dogmatic or disciplinary, the decisions of Rome, as of any other church, must be in agreement with the orthodox faith, the councils, and the canons.[94]

If the church of Rome, as says Maximus, is the one "that has received from the incarnate Word of God himself, as well as from all the holy synods, according to the sacred canons and definitions, and possesses, in all and for all, sovereignty and authority over all holy churches of God that are on earth, and the power to bind and to

---

91. Cf. *Pyr.*, PG 91:352CD, ed. Doucet, 608–9.

92. *Th. Pol.* 10, PG 91:133D–136C.

93. *Ep.* 12, PG 91:464CD.

94. *Th. Pol.* 12, PG 91:144C; *Dis. Biz.*, PG 90:145C, CCSG 39:95; PG 90:153CD, CCSG 39:113.

unbind,"[95] this can only be, as indicated in the text itself, on the basis of "the stone" that is the confession of the true faith in Christ, and within the limits of what was defined by the councils and the canons, that is to say, of what all churches have collegially willed and accepted. The notions of sovereignty, of authority, and of the power to bind and to unbind (to exclude from the Church or to reintegrate into the Church) must be understood in their historical context, when these notions, in the consciousness of both the Western and Eastern churches, did not have the political and juridical connotations they took on in the image formed subsequently by the Roman papacy (particularly from the ninth century on) of its place and its function.[96] One could not advance the argument that the power to bind and to unbind belonged exclusively to the pope because it had been entrusted to Peter by Christ (Matt 16:19) and that the pope is the successor of Peter. Apart from the fact that Maximus, as we noted earlier, does not see in the pope a successor or a fortiori a vicar of Peter (the latter being mentioned either in relation to Paul as founder of the church of Rome or regarding his confession of true faith in Christ), he could not forget that the power to bind and to unbind had also been entrusted by Christ to all apostles (Matt 18:18)[97] and that all bishops have it. Moreover, for Maximus, fundamentally it is Christ who is "the door," and those who desire true life must enter into the Church through it.[98]

In the eyes of Maximus, what creates union (or reunion) and communion with the Church is the confession of the orthodox faith; what causes and maintains the rupture of this communion is the profession of a heterodox faith.[99] The role of the pope, as shown in the case of Pyrrhus (who in that case, we should not forget, could deal only with a peer), is to pronounce exclusion from, or reintegration into, the Church and communion, not through an arbitrary decision of, or proceeding from, his own authority but as witness and guaran-

---

95. *Th. Pol.* 12, PG 91:144C.

96. See K. Schatz, *La primauté du pape.*

97. "Truly I tell you, whatever you bind on earth will be bound in heaven, and whatever you loose on earth will be loosed in heaven."

98. *Thal.* 48, PG 90:433C, CCSG 7:333.

99. *Th. Pol.* 12, PG 91:144A–D; *Pyr.*, PG 91:353AB, ed. Doucet, 609; *Rel. mot.*, PG 90:120CD, CCSG 39:31–33; PG 90:128B, CCSG 39:45–47; *Dis. Biz.*, PG 90:145B, CCSG 39:93; *Ep. An.*, PG 90:132A, CCSG 39:161.

tor, on behalf of the Church, of the confession of faith that is certainly made in his presence but also and above all before God and before the apostles, as highlighted by Maximus.[100] The pope himself, in his power to bind and to unbind, is subject to the confession of the orthodox faith,[101] which determines whether he himself belongs to the catholic and apostolic church and conditions his authority.

Conclusion

To conclude, regarding the present ecumenical reflections and dialogue on the Roman primacy and the function of the pope, it can be said that the position of Saint Maximus constitutes, on the one hand, for the Eastern churches, a strong reminder of the church of Rome's essential role that they had recognized before the schism and of the role it should play again if communion is reestablished. On the other hand, it is also a reminder of the conditions under which such a role was, and could again be, recognized.

Two points particularly emerge from an analysis of the positions of Saint Maximus:

First, Maximus recognizes that the role of the church of Rome and of the pope is closely linked to their confession of the orthodox faith. This means that the reestablishment of a faith common in every respect between the Catholic Church and the Orthodox Church is an inescapable prerequisite for the recognition, by the Eastern churches, of a primacy of the church of Rome among the churches and of the pope of Rome among the patriarchs.

Second, Saint Maximus insists strongly, on the one hand, on the collegial character of the relations among the churches, and on the other hand, the function itself of the pope within the church of Rome. Over the years, the patriarchs of the Orthodox churches have preserved this collegial character in their relations with the other bishops within their respective churches whereas the Latin Church evolved in the direction of an increasingly marked centralization around the person of the pope, up to an autocratic and almost monar-

---

100. *Th. Pol.* 12, PG 91:144B; *Pyr.*, PG 91:252D–253A, ed. Doucet, 609.
101. *Th. Pol.* 10, PG91:133D–136B; 12, PG 91:144B.

chical conception of his function. An analysis and a critique of this trend have already been considerably developed within the Latin Church itself,[102] and correctives have been introduced, especially by the Second Vatican Council and by the efforts of the popes Paul VI and John Paul II, for more collegiality and for a conception of the papal function as a "service of love." But regarding what the Roman Church itself sees as the model of the first millennium (see the conciliar decree *Unitatis redintegratio* and the encyclical *Ut unum sint*), a model considered normative by the Orthodox Church, several new insights remain to be brought into consideration. The "Petrine" conception of the papal function maintained by the church of Rome remains foreign to the exegetical and ecclesiological tradition of the Orthodox Church. As to the idea of papal infallibility, which was dogmatized at the First Vatican Council (itself a recent introduction in the Latin Church that has never ceased to raise objections), it appears unacceptable under any form to the Orthodox Church, insofar as it is incompatible with certain basic principles of its ecclesiology. The way the papacy conceives its function as a "ministry of unity" remains also questionable because it is still dependent on the Latin idea according to which the pope is the "vicar" of Peter and, directly or through Peter, the "vicar" of Christ. Thus, the formulation found in the encyclical *Ut unum sint*: "All the Churches are in full and visible communion, because all the Pastors are in communion with Peter and therefore united in Christ" (§ 94), remains quite distant from the Orthodox ecclesiology.

On these and on other points, a deeper study of the model of the first millennium, as expressed by the voice of the Fathers, should enable us to pursue this new direction and to rediscover a wider common ground under the weight of our history.

---

102. I think particularly of the excellent book of the Jesuit Klaus Schatz, *La primauté du pape*, which I have mentioned several times in my account.

RECENT DISCUSSIONS ON PRIMACY IN RELATION TO VATICAN I[*]

Hermann J. Pottmeyer

1. The Recent Discussion

If one compares theology with a landscape, the theological tradition surrounding the Petrine office resembles a frontier zone between long-hostile countries. At every step one encounters traces and residues of military conflicts: old trenches and bunkers and—as a particularly dangerous legacy—land mines. It is generally considered that the most dangerous mine lurking here is the dogma of the First Vatican Council concerning the primacy of the successor of Peter. It is no wonder therefore that ecumenical dialogue between the long-hostile churches has until now given this danger zone a wide berth. But if any further convergence is to be achieved, it is imperative that this mine, which has until now seemed an insuperable obstacle, be defused. As with every mine, its deactivation presupposes the will to put an end to the hostility, and demands a method of approach combining expertise and precision.

No other dogma has its identity designated so distinctly by a double hallmark. The same is true of its rejection. Both have been decisively shaped by a polemical debate which reaches back many centuries and has its basis in conflicting human interests rather than in theological distinctions. Both have been equally decisively shaped by the separate evolutionary paths taken by the churches in the East and in the West, as determined by their history and established long before the

---

[*] May 24, 2003 (morning session). Original text in German.

Great Schism in 1054. To be sure, that schism facilitated the separate evolution of the ecclesiastical tradition in the West, which culminated in the dogma of Vatican I. But even within the ecclesiastical tradition of the West, this dogma bears yet another hallmark. It was also decisively shaped by the religious and political situation in Europe in the eighteenth/nineteenth centuries.

This factor is in turn the reason why controversy surrounds the dogma not only in an ecumenical context. Even within the Catholic Church there is debate, not regarding the primacy of the bishop of Rome itself, but certainly regarding the formulation and interpretation of the dogma, and the form taken by the exercise of the primacy as a consequence of the dogma. To continue the analogy between this dogma and an explosive mine, the explosive effect which this subject has had and continues to have is demonstrated not least by the history of the First and Second Vatican Councils. At Vatican I, the formulation led to the brink of a breach, and subsequently to the secession of the Old Catholics. At Vatican II, the failure of the Constitution on the Church was only avoided by the concession made to the minority by Paul VI with a binding text interpretation. The minority at Vatican I feared the betrayal of the ancient tradition of the Church, the minority at Vatican II feared a betrayal of the dogma of Vatican I.

Therefore, when the Roman Catholic Church today engages in a process of rapprochement on the primacy of the successor of Peter, it should in my view at the same time or—even better—beforehand clarify those critical questions which have been posed within the Catholic Church itself regarding the long-standing customary interpretation of this dogma, and the exercise of primacy validated by that interpretation. For if we Catholics are convinced that the Petrine office is a gift and an aid which Christ handed down to the community of all Christians, we are called upon to first of all clear away everything which obscures this divine gift and gives rise to misunderstandings.

That does not, however, mean that we should postpone the ecumenical dialogue on Petrine ministry until we have accomplished our own "purification of the memory," which Pope John Paul has invited Catholics to undertake.[1] Rather, we Catholics need the ecumenical

---

1. John Paul II, apostolic letter *Tertio millennio adveniente* (November 10, 1994), nos. 33–36; apostolic letter *Novo millennio ineunte* (January 6, 2001), no. 6.

dialogue in order to achieve this goal. For it is a common human experience that a different perspective and the experience of others can be helpful in clarifying one's own self-understanding, particularly when the matter at issue is one of common concern, namely, recognizing the will of God for his Church. This insight forms the basis of the invitation by the current pope to other churches and other Christians in *Ut unum sint*, to assist him and the Catholic Church in dealing with the pressing question of the primacy.[2] Bound up with this invitation is naturally the hope that the "purification of the memory" by Catholics in ecumenical dialogue may at the same time clear the vision of other Christians regarding this divine gift.

As far as the dogma of Vatican I is concerned, the critical questioning within the Catholic Church was already initiated by the minority at Vatican I. That questioning intensified during Vatican II, and has intensified to an increasing degree since that last council. Today, a *re-lecture* or re-reception of the dogma of 1870 is demanded within the Catholic Church—a *re-lecture* within the framework of the *communio* ecclesiology which Vatican II wished to reestablish.[3]

That statement identifies the major reason why a discussion of the dogma of 1870 arose within the Catholic Church immediately before, during, and after Vatican II. This was the rediscovery of the sacramental *communio* character of the Church, and the *communio* structure and praxis of the as yet undivided Church of the first millennium. The Catholic Church owed this rediscovery to the burgeoning and deepening study of the Bible, of the church fathers, and of the development of the early Church. It broke the bonds of the one-sided

---

2. John Paul II, encyclical *Ut unum sint* (May 25, 1995), nos. 89, 95–96.

3. Hans Urs von Balthasar, *The Office of Peter and the Structure of the Church* (San Francisco, 1986); Joseph Ratzinger, ed., *Dienst an der Einheit* (Düsseldorf, 1978); Jean Tillard, *L'évêque de Rome* (Paris, 1982); Patrick Granfield, *The Limits of Papacy* (New York, 1987); Yves Congar, *Église et papauté: Regards historiques* (Paris, 1994); Wolfgang Klausnitzer, "Die Diskussion innerhalb der römisch-katholischen Kirche um das Papstamt," *Una sancta* 53, no. 1 (1998): 21–29; Michael Buckley, *Papal Primacy and the Episcopate* (New York, 1998); Hermann J. Pottmeyer, *Towards a Papacy in Communion: Perspectives from Vatican I and II* (New York, 1998); John R. Quinn, *The Reform of the Papacy* (New York, 1999); Paul Tihon, ed., *Changer la papauté?* (Paris, 2000); Congregazione per la dottrina della fede, ed., *Il primato del successore di Pietro nel mistero della chiesa* (Vatican, 2002).

apologetic and juridical focus of the ecclesiology of nineteenth-century Neoscholastic theology. The understanding of the primacy which had prevailed in the Catholic Church since Vatican I and was grounded in that council could only with difficulty be reconciled with *communio* ecclesiology. This problem also set in motion an intensified study of the history of papal primacy. That led in turn to the discovery that the still undivided Church was indeed already aware of the primatial position of the bishop of Rome and successor of Peter, but had interpreted and exercised the primacy in differing ways in different epochs, and that the interpretation and the exercise of the primacy at any particular time had been influenced by both the prevailing concept of the Church and the contemporary political context.[4]

It was not surprising that the problem experienced by the Fathers of Vatican II in reconciling *communio* ecclesiology with the current interpretation of the dogma of 1870 awakened a special interest in the history of Vatican I. The study of this history led to a twofold discovery. First came the discovery of the degree to which the dogma of primacy and its formulation had been influenced by the historical situation of the eighteenth and nineteenth centuries in Western and Central Europe. The dominant interpretation of the dogma up until Vatican II had not taken this historical factor into account. That interpretation saw the dogma as the result of a logical development of the biblical data and as the perfected formulation of papal primacy. All previous versions were therefore seen as merely preliminary stages in the developmental process of the primacy, and deficient forms of its exercise. From this perspective, the dogma of Vatican I was indeed irreconcilable with *communio* ecclesiology. It was this interpretation of the dogma which led to the opposition by the minority at Vatican II against the doctrine of the collegial structure of the supreme authority in the Church.

At this point a second discovery advanced the discussion. It was established that alongside the long-standing prevailing interpretation, oriented towards the one-sided formulation of the dogma, there had been and still was another interpretation. It is the interpretation

---

4. Klaus Schatz, *Papal Primacy from Its Origins to the Present* (Collegeville, MN, 1996).

of the minority of Vatican I, which—and this can be proven historically—was recognized as legitimate, even if it was virtually ignored following Vatican I. In this interpretation, the dogma of 1870 is open to a *communio* ecclesiology. It therefore appears possible to integrate this dogma into a *communio* ecclesiology.

We have so far sketched in brief outline the progress of the recent discussion within the Catholic Church on the dogma of Vatican I. The results can be summarized as follows: just as we have learned to draw a distinction in the history of the primacy between the abiding commission of Peter and his successors and its changing modes of formulation and realization depending on the current situation, we must also view the dogma of Vatican I in a similarly differentiated manner. In that which it says, it expresses the evolved and abiding belief of the Catholic Church regarding the primacy of the successor of Peter. But the manner in which the council formulates this belief is guided by a particular situation and intention, which lends its formulation a historical aspect and a certain one-sidedness. This one-sidedness means that the formulation is indeed capable of being overhauled and improved, as are the monarchical structure and the centralist exercise of the primacy, which are supported by that one-sidedness. If the *necessitas ecclesiae,* for whose benefit Christ intended the ministry of Peter and his successors, demands it, we can and must alter the formulation and the exercise of the primacy, without calling into question the truth of the dogma, that is, the perpetual commission of Peter. If the *necessitas ecclesiae* today requires the reestablishment of unity, modeled on the tradition of the still undivided Church, then this dogma can and must be integrated into a *communio* ecclesiology.

It is precisely this insight of the recent Catholic discussion on the dogma of Vatican I which found expression in two recent documents of the Catholic magisterium, namely, in the encyclical *Ut unum sint* (= *UUS*) of 1995 and in the document *The Primacy of the Successor of Peter in the Mystery of the Church,* which the Congregation for the Doctrine of the Faith published in 1998.[5] In his encyclical, Pope John Paul II distinguishes between "what is essential to the mission" of the

---

5. Congregation for the Doctrine of the Faith, *The Primacy of the Successor of Peter in the Mystery of the Church* (October 31, 1998).

primacy and the various ways it is exercised, which are to correspond to the current needs of the Church. He refers expressly to the way the primacy was exercised in the still undivided Church, which he does not characterize as deficient or as merely a preliminary developmental phase, as was the practice before the last council (*UUS* 95).

The Congregation for the Doctrine of the Faith takes up this distinction. It distinguishes between the "unchanging nature of the primacy of the successor of Peter" and its historical forms, the changing ways it is exercised. And it sets down criteria for the forms of exercise appropriate to the particular situation. As criteria it designates on the one hand the intended purpose of the primacy, that is, the unity of the Church, and on the other the *necessitas ecclesiae*, which can differ according to place and time (no. 12). In addition, the Congregation emphasizes that the bishop of Rome should in each instance clarify in fraternal dialogue with the other bishops the appropriate extent of the application of his powers (no. 13). Beyond that, the document, which is designated as "Reflections of the Congregation," contains initiatives towards integrating the doctrine of papal primacy into a *communio* ecclesiology. It is an attempt to defuse the tension between primacy and collegiality, which was still felt to exist at Vatican II. These reflections by the Congregation have as yet had no effect on the legal structure and practical exercise of the primacy. But they open up perspectives for the future.

2. The Hermeneutics of the Dogma

The preceding sketch of recent Catholic efforts to evaluate the dogma of 1870 has demonstrated that a perception is beginning to gain ground that this dogma is indeed open to a *communio* ecclesiology. This perception still encounters skepticism, not only outside the Catholic Church. Reservations regarding the possibility of reconciling the two have been raised and still are raised within the Catholic Church itself. I have already mentioned the fears of the minority at Vatican II. And I would also remind you of the discussion aroused by Hans Küng immediately after the council.[6] He claimed

---

6. Hans Küng, *Infallible? An Inquiry* (New York, 1971).

that only the annulment of the dogma could clear the way for a *communio* primacy. Vatican I had defined the primacy as an absolute monarchy of the pope, and papal infallibility as an a priori infallibility—concepts which could not be reconciled with the Bible or with the history and tradition of the Church. Küng was supported in this by the work of August Bernhard Hasler on Pius IX and the First Vatican Council.[7] Both claimed that the dogma was in fact null and void on formal grounds, because the council had not been free in its definition.

Küng's thesis did more than simply spark off a vehement controversy. It also prompted a series of studies of the history of Vatican I. The result: Küng's thesis is false. I will mention here only the most comprehensive and detailed study, namely, the three-volume work by Klaus Schatz, *Vaticanum I*, which appeared in 1992–1994.[8] Was Küng's thesis so difficult to disprove that it necessitated such comprehensive studies? In a certain sense, Yes! Catholic apologetics had over a long period presented and interpreted the dogma of 1870 in a way which seemed to confirm Küng's thesis. It is this long-standing prevailing apologetic-maximalist interpretation which to this day determines the image of the dogma both within the Catholic Church and without. An added difficulty arises because the one-sided formulation of the dogma does not make sufficiently clear that this maximalist interpretation does not fully convey the intended meaning of the council. That meaning can only be inferred from the council files and from several official documents which followed Vatican I in order to protect the dogma from misunderstanding. In the following discussion I will therefore elaborate on the results of the more recent studies, which demonstrate that the dogma of 1870 did remain open to a *communio* ecclesiology.[9]

The hermeneutics of dogmatic conciliar texts, in this instance those of Vatican I, is well known. To be more precise, the dogmatic constitution *Pastor aeternus* of the First Vatican Council deals with two

---

7. August Bernhard Hasler, *Pius IX. (1846–1878), päpstliche Unfehlbarkeit, und 1. Vatikanisches Konzil: Dogmatisierung und Durchsetzung einer Ideologie* (Stuttgart, 1977).

8. Klaus Schatz, *Vaticanum I, 1869–1870*, 3 vols. (Paderborn, 1992–1994); see also Ulrrich Horst, *Unfehlbarkeit und Geschichte* (Mainz, 1982).

9. See for the following Hermann J. Pottmeyer, *Towards a Papacy in Communion*.

dogmas which are closely linked to one another.[10] The first defines the jurisdictional primacy of the bishop of Rome as the legitimate successor of Peter, the second the infallibility of his teaching office under certain conditions. The interpretation of both dogmas takes as its starting point the respective thetic definitions at the end of the relevant chapters, the canons. The canonical definitions are to be interpreted in the light of the corresponding chapter, which supplies the theological exposition. A further aid to interpretation can be found in the council files. These consist primarily in the commentaries by the speakers of the responsible commission on the proposals of the council fathers and on the concluding text. Important indications of the intended meaning of the council can be discerned from these commentaries. Further clarification of the intended meaning of the council is also provided by the textual history of the two dogmas, and the council debates.

In order to understand the historical context of the dogma of the primacy, which had a formative influence on its formulation, we will begin with the latter, namely, the relevant council debates and the textual history.

3. The Struggle between Two Conceptions at the Council

To be clear at the outset: at the council there was no dispute about two points, *first,* that Christ himself had appointed Peter as the first among the apostles and as visible head of the Church here on earth and, *second,* that the bishop of Rome is the successor of Peter, and as such holds the primacy over the whole Church. On those points there was undivided consensus. There were, however, critical questions by the council fathers regarding the extent and form of exercise of the primacy. How was the relationship of the primacy to the authority of the college of bishops and to the individual bishops to be defined more precisely? These questions were prompted by the fears of the minority that at the council the pope was to be declared universal bishop and absolute monarch and sovereign of the Church,

---

10. Denzinger-Schönmetzer (DS) 3050–75.

so that the other bishops would be reduced to representatives of the pope.

There were good reasons for these fears, for precisely this concept of the primacy had found broad acceptance in the Catholic Church during the nineteenth century. It did not originate in Rome, but from the so-called Ultramontane movement. Catholic laypeople and clergy in Europe were striving for a strengthening of the papacy because they saw it as the only hope of protecting the Church against encroachments by the rulers in the evolving nation states. For them, only the sovereignty of the pope could embody and guarantee the autonomy and independence of the Church from the state.[11]

A brief explanation of this point. The modern state began with the concept of sovereignty and the model of absolute monarchy. Sovereignty meant the absolute independence of the monarch internally, and of the state itself externally. By appealing to its sovereignty, the state claimed the right to direct the Church within its territory according to its own interests. That threatened the Church with disintegration into national churches. As a countermove, the Ultramontane movement maintained the sovereignty of the pope over the Church, that is, the complete independence of his powers of jurisdiction internally within the Church, so that it could secure its independence externally. Any claim that the episcopate should also participate in the governing of the universal Church was seen as dividing or detracting from papal sovereignty, because that sovereignty had always been interpreted as absolute. The bishops, often bound by national or feudal interests, or exposed to the pressure and influence of the secular powers, were neither in a position nor willing to assert the autonomy of the Church.

The classic example of the dominance of the state over the Church was France, which is also the land where the modern state originated. The king nominated the bishops and prevented the exercise of papal jurisdiction. Thus, for example, he prevented the implementation of the reforms of the Council of Trent within France. The French Revolution assumed the state's claim to power over the Church, as did the restored French monarchy subsequently. Other

---

11. Hermann J. Pottmeyer, *Unfehlbarkeit und Souveränität: Die päpstliche Unfehlbarkeit im System der ultramontanen Ekklesiologie des 19. Jahrhunderts* (Mainz, 1975).

European states also introduced this system. The ideology of this system was so-called Gallicanism.[12] Gallicanism was therefore the real opponent which the dogma of Vatican I was intended to combat and eliminate. The dogmatization of the papal primacy as sovereignty was at the heart of the Ultramontane strategy in the battle for the freedom of the Church.

But it was not only state dirigisme which the Ultramontane movement rebelled against. The intellectual developments in Europe caused no less consternation: rationalism, materialism, atheism, and liberalism called the foundations of the Christian faith into question.[13] In response to this threat too, the Ultramontanes placed their hopes in strengthening the authority of the pope as the representative of the authority of God and his revelation. Therefore the dogmatization of papal infallibility became the second central objective of the Ultramontane movement. Rome did not take the lead in this movement until the time of Gregory XVI and Pius IX.

This brief excursion into the prehistory and the historical context of Vatican I is essential to an understanding of the council. It was not a lust for power on the part of the popes which led to the two dogmas of the primacy and the infallibility of the pope, but the very real threat to the Church, its unity and its autonomy vis-à-vis the state, and the fact that the faith was in danger. The endeavors to strengthen the authority of the pope were initiated at the grass roots of the Church. However, the desire to counter an extreme challenge with an extreme reaction gave rise to a new danger. To declare the pope absolute and sovereign monarch of the Church would have meant a break with the divine constitution and the tradition of the Church.

That is the background to the fears held by the theologically better-educated of the bishops among the council fathers, who formed the minority and rejected the extreme conceptions of the primacy and infallibility of the pope. There was every indication that

---

12. Louis Châtellier, *L'Europe des dévots* (Paris, 1987).

13. Hermann J. Pottmeyer, *Der Glaube vor dem Anspruch der Wissenschaft: Die Konstitution über den katholischen Glauben "Dei Filius" des 1. Vatikanischen Konzils* (Mainz, 1968).

the council should and would define these conceptions. It is due to the minority that this was prevented.

The first draft of the text which was presented to the council fathers for discussion did indeed take the extreme conception of the primacy as monarchical sovereignty as its starting point. The following critical objections were raised during the discussion of the draft:

- The Church is not an absolute monarchy. Beside the supreme authority of the pope there is also the supreme authority of the college of bishops and the authority of the individual bishops, which are no less a part of the divine constitution of the Church. The bishops are not vicars of the pope.
- The projected image of the primacy resembles too closely a secular model of power rather than a gift of divine love.
- Not the pope but Christ is the unifying principle of the Church. The pope is merely the "visible foundation" of her unity.
- While it is claimed that the primacy defends the rights of the bishops, those rights are nowhere defined, nor are the limits to the exercise of the primacy, or the existence of intermediate authorities.

The focus of the criticism by the minority was the designation of papal jurisdiction as an "ordinary, immediate, and truly episcopal" power. Papal jurisdiction thus appeared to be a rival jurisdiction which superseded the equally ordinary, immediate, and episcopal power of the bishop within his diocese. The minority demanded that the subsidiary character of an immediate intervention by the pope in the local churches should be given prominence. And as far as the definition of papal jurisdiction as an episcopal power was concerned, it must be made clear that the pope was not a universal bishop and the entire Church was not his diocese.

Of particular significance for the interpretation of the dogma is the reply of the speaker of the responsible commission to the criticisms of the council fathers. It can be summarized in the following points:

- The Church is indeed not an absolute monarchy under the pope. The primacy has to observe the divine constitution of the Church, including the authority of the college of bishops and the individual bishops, and it must take as its guiding principle the welfare of the Church which it is to serve. All of that is assumed to be taken for granted and is not a subject for debate. The sole issue here is the question whether there is any human authority beside or above the pope which can limit his authority. That is precisely what is to be excluded.

- It is true that the full and supreme jurisdictional power of the Church exists in a twofold manner. On the one hand it pertains to the college of bishops with its head, the bishop of Rome, and also to the bishop of Rome as the visible head of the Church, independently of his acting together with the other bishops. For Christ's commission was given both to all the apostles together with Peter, and to Peter alone. This twofold structure becomes problematic only when the two forms, which are bound together by the same apostolic commission and the same sacrament, are considered as separate powers competing with one another, as they are regarded by conciliarism and Gallicanism.

- The definition of papal jurisdiction as "ordinary" power does not mean that it should be considered normal for the pope to constantly intervene in the dioceses. Rather, the word "ordinary" is used as the opposite of "delegated" and means: the primacy is grounded not in a delegation by the Church, but in Christ's commission to Peter.

- It is designated as "immediate" power because the pope—if the *necessitas ecclesiae* demands—can intervene everywhere within the Church, directly and without the mediation or permission of any other authority.

- The designation as "truly episcopal" power is intended to counter the Gallican error that the pope infringes the sacramentally transmitted rights reserved for the responsible bishop when he intervenes in a diocese. The pastoral power of the pope and the bishops is based on the same sacrament, the only difference being that the pope is endowed with the *episcopê* for the entire Church and in its supreme form, while that of the bishops is valid only for their diocese and in hierarchical subordination beneath the pope.

These frequently overlooked statements by the speaker of the responsible commission are nothing less than an official commentary on the dogma and a guide to its interpretation. They allow the intended meaning of the council to become clear. They allow us to recognize what the council did not intend and what it did intend. The council did not wish to limit the divinely guaranteed rights of the episcopate, and therefore did not intend to define the primacy as an absolute monarchical sovereignty. But on the other hand, it did want complete freedom of action for the pope when the *necessitas ecclesiae* demanded it, and it wished to teach the inappellability of his decisions. In other words: it did not want to deny the limits to the primacy set by God, but it certainly wanted to establish that no human authority, whether it be a council or the state, could set limits to his commission.

How was this intention expressed in the definitive text which the council accepted? To be clear at the outset: what the council did not wish to deny and presupposed to be true, was written into the prologue to the constitution and the chapters of exposition, but not into the canon itself, as the minority wished. But what it wished to teach as a dogma was expressed in the canon, in order to condemn Gallicanism. In detail it can be summed up as follows:

- The prologue begins with the will of Christ that the Church should be one, and with the mission of all the apostles to serve the unity of the Church as pastors and teachers (DS 3050).
- This is followed by the mission of Peter and his successors as the abiding principle and visible foundation of Church unity,

to serve directly the unity of the episcopate, and indirectly—
together with the bishops and priests—"the unity of faith and
communio" (DS 3051). Thus the immediate purpose of the primacy is the unity of the episcopate, and together with them
the pope serves the unity of the Church, which is designated
as a *communio* in faith.

- It is repeatedly stated that the council wishes to define the
  primacy and infallibility of the pope with respect for the universal tradition of the Church, including the tradition of the
  still undivided Church of the first millennium (DS 3052,
  3059, 3065). The council thereby implicitly acknowledges
  the plurality of shapes in which the primacy is manifested
  and realized in the past and in the future.

- A separate paragraph in the third chapter emphasizes that the
  primacy does not threaten the ordinary and immediate jurisdiction of the bishops—the most important point raised by
  the minority in its criticism. The fact that this paragraph was
  inserted into the third chapter, which deals with the nature of
  the primacy, represents the most important achievement of
  the minority. The paragraph reads as follows:

  > This power of the Supreme Pontiff is far from standing
  > in the way of the power of ordinary and immediate
  > jurisdiction, by which the bishops, who under appoint-
  > ment of the Holy Spirit succeeded in the place of the
  > apostles, feed and rule individually, as true shepherds,
  > the particular flock assigned to them. Rather this latter
  > power is asserted, confirmed, and vindicated by this
  > same supreme and universal shepherd; as in the words
  > of St. Gregory the Great: "My honor is the honor of the
  > whole Church. My honor is the firm strength of my
  > brethren. I am truly honored, when due honor is paid to
  > each and every one." (DS 3061 ND 827)

For the rest, this chapter clearly states the true objective of the dogmatization of the primacy: It is intended as a condemnation of Gallicanism, because the latter legitimizes the view that the state is permitted to impede the free communication between the pope and the bishops, and to annul papal decrees within its territory (DS 3062). The assertion made by Gallicanism of the possibility of appealing against papal judgments to an ecumenical council meant in practice that state jurisdiction took the place of papal jurisdiction, which was rendered ineffective by this reservation. Because the inappellability of the primacy was therefore the real bulwark against encroachments by the state—that is also made clear by chapter 3—the dogma takes aim at precisely this point, but not at the relationship between papacy and episcopate.

This is expressed in the corresponding canon, which reads:

> And so, if anyone says that the Roman Pontiff has only the office of inspection and direction, but not the full and supreme power of jurisdiction over the whole Church, not only in matters that pertain to faith and morals, but also in matters that pertain to the discipline and government of the Church throughout the whole world, or if anyone says that he has only a more important part and not the complete fullness of this supreme power, or if anyone says that this power is not ordinary and immediate either over each and every Church or over each and every shepherd and faithful, *anathema sit.* (DS 3064 ND 830)

4. Results of Recent Discussion and Research

It is time to take stock. In judging the dogma of the primacy of the successor of Peter one arrives at a negative and a positive conclusion. The deliberate one-sidedness of the concluding definition is to be assessed as negative. In juridical language—which, it must be said, does serve to make the statement clear—exclusive prominence is given to the primacy, its universality and its unlimited freedom from any human authority. Neither its intended purpose nor other criteria for an appropriate exercise which respects the jurisdiction of the bishops are mentioned here. This one-sidedness of the definition itself subsequently enabled the maximalist interpretation of the primacy as absolute sovereignty to substantiate its claim on the basis of this dogma.

In turn, the maximalist interpretation justified the increasingly centralist exercise of the primacy as the only form which complied with the dogma of 1870. Finally, the maximalist interpretation influenced the legal structure of the primacy established in the codex of 1917. Conversely, the increasing centralism supported the general impression that the dogma had in fact defined the primacy as absolute sovereignty. Did the pope, as the sole legislator, not in fact intrude into the ordinary and immediate jurisdiction of the bishops?

As we have seen, it is only the council files—in particular the commentary by the speaker of the responsible commission—which allow us to infer that the definition's silence regarding the collegial coresponsibility of the bishops for the government of the whole Church in no way means a rejection of that responsibility. On the contrary, the doctrine of the simultaneous full and supreme authority of the college of bishops is presupposed as a self-evident component of the tradition. This doctrine was not disputed by anybody. What was disputed on the part of the Gallicans, and what therefore had to be defined, was the simultaneous full and supreme authority of the pope, which empowered him to act independently of the collaboration of the episcopate. For this reason, any proposals by the minority which wished to have the appropriateness of the collaboration of the episcopate also mentioned in the canon were rejected. Such a reference was not rejected because of any intention to deny that appropriateness, but because it was feared that such a reference could be understood in the sense of Gallicanism.

There is yet another reason for this silence, which was not intended to be a rejection. The doctrine of the episcopal office and the college of bishops was to be dealt with in a second constitution on the Church. This second constitution did not come to pass, because the council was suspended ahead of time because of the Franco-Prussian War. But we know the draft for this constitution.[14] In

---

14. Fidelis van der Horst, *Das Schema über die Kirche auf dem I. Vatikanischen Konzil* (Paderborn, 1963).

it, the full and supreme authority of the college of bishops is designated as "fidei dogma certissimum." When the responsible commission rejected the corresponding proposals of the minority, it had in mind that the collegial coresponsibility of the episcopate was to receive due recognition of its rights in the projected second constitution.

Even more important for the interpretation of the dogma are of course the preceding chapters and the prologue. These texts contain sufficiently clear signals that the dogma did not intend to detract from either the tradition of the Church or the rights of the bishops and the college of bishops. The citation from Gregory the Great referred to was a sentence with which that pope had refused the proposed title of *universalis papa*.

Nevertheless, the fact remains that the one-sided formulation of the dogma itself and the maximalist interpretation, based on this one-sidedness, by those for whom the strengthening of papal authority could never go far enough, gave rise to the impression among the general public that the council had in fact declared the pope to be the absolute and sovereign monarch of the Church. That is precisely what the German imperial chancellor Bismarck maintained in his circular of 1872 to the European governments. He warned them that the bishops in their countries had by this dogma been made mere tools of the pope. That prompted the German bishops to issue a collective declaration in 1875 in which they rejected this accusation. They declare expressly that this dogma has not made the pope an absolute sovereign of the Church, nor the bishops papal officials without any personal responsibility.

This document is also important for the interpretation of the dogma, since Pius IX twice gave it official approval, in an apostolic brief of 1875 (DS 3117) and in a consistorial address of the same year (DS 3112). The collective declaration of the German episcopate states: "It is a complete misunderstanding of the Vatican decrees to believe that because of them 'the episcopal jurisdiction has been absorbed into the papal,' that the pope has 'in principle taken the place of each individual bishop,' the bishops are now 'no more than tools of the pope, his officials, without responsibility of their own'" (DS 3115 ND 841).

On the positive side, we can therefore draw a threefold conclusion.

- The maximalist interpretation of the dogma of 1870 and a centralist exercise of the primacy cannot be substantiated by Vatican I. That is confirmed by Vatican II, which in its Constitution on the Church repeatedly took up the commentary by the speakers of the responsible commission of Vatican I in order to give expression to the coexistence of primacy and collegiality, and to the appropriateness of the participation of the episcopate in the governing of the Church.

- The dogma of 1870 is open to the possibility of different forms to exercise primacy because it refers also to the tradition and practice of the yet undivided Church of the first millennium.

- The dogma of 1870 is open to a *communio* ecclesiology. In designating the primacy as a "truly episcopal" authority, it binds the pope into the sacramentally instituted *communio* of the college of bishops. As its head, the pope is to serve the unity of the episcopate and together with the episcopate the unity of the Church. The pope does not stand above the Church but within the *communio* of the Church, which is designated by Vatican I as *communio* in faith. The question of how the relationship between primacy and collegiality or synodality was to be structured in concrete terms, the constitution *Pastor aeternus* did not intend to answer. Vatican II therefore wished to confront this question, precisely because it had remained open at Vatican I.

This last point, that is, the openness of the dogma to a *communio* ecclesiology, is confirmed by two recent documents of the Catholic teaching office which have already been mentioned above.

- In his encyclical *Ut unum sint* Pope John Paul II says: "When the Catholic Church affirms that the office of the bishop of

Rome corresponds with the will of Christ, she does not separate this office from the mission entrusted to the whole body
of bishops, who are also 'vicars and ambassadors of Christ.'
The bishop of Rome is a member of the 'college,' and they are
his brothers in the ministry" (*UUS* 95). This language does
indeed differ considerably from the maximalist interpretation
of the dogma, but not from the prologue of the constitution
Pastor aeternus of Vatican I, nor from the commentary of the
speaker of its commission.

• With deliberate one-sidedness the dogma of 1870 gave special prominence to the inappellability of papal judgments
according to the principle "Prima sedes a nemine iudicatur."
The maximalist interpretation of the dogma had deduced
from that the absolute sovereignty of the pope. In contrast,
the "Reflections" of the Congregation for the Doctrine of the
Faith of 1998 state: "That does not however mean that the
pope has absolute power. For it is a characteristic of the service of unity, and also a consequence of the communion of the
college of bishops and the *sensus fidei* of the whole people of
God, to listen to the voice of the particular churches....The
final and inalienable responsibility of the pope finds its best
guarantee on the one hand in his integration into the tradition and into the fraternal communion, and on the other
hand in trust in the support of the Holy Spirit who guides the
Church" (no. 10). This clarification is to be welcomed. It
accords both with the characterization of the primacy as a
"truly episcopal" authority by Vatican I and the commentary
of the speaker of the council commission, and with the
understanding of the minority of the council.

In a word: the dogma of 1870 did not deserve the bad reputa-
tion which its maximalist interpretation in theory and practice has
earned it. It is not the insuperable obstacle to the unity of Christians

which it has long been considered to be. And one further point: in the "Hall of Fame" of the ecumenical movement, the minority of Vatican I deserves a place of honor, because it was able to win over the council to keep this dogma open to a future *communio* primacy.

DS = *Enchiridion symbolorum, definitionum, declarationum, de rebus fidei et morum.* Edited by H. Denzinger and A. Schönmetzer. Freiburg: Herder, 1976.
ND = *The Christian Faith in the Doctrinal Documents of the Catholic Church.* Edited by J. Neuner and J. Dupuis. New York: Alba House, 1995.

Summary of Discussion

The general feeling was that with this presentation the symposium had reached a critical point of discussion.

Concerning Vatican I, two main points were made by Orthodox participants:

- The interpretation of Vatican I in the light of Vatican II opens real possibilities for further discussion and understanding;
- If the Vatican I definition was to a large extent conceived as a protection against extreme nationalism, the Orthodox Church was confronted with similar problems in the nineteenth century, related to the upsurge of nationalism in several countries of Central and Eastern Europe.

Catholic representatives were asked what they consider as a necessary reform in the exercise of primacy today.

In reference to Church as communion, it matters where one puts the real emphasis: on the bishops or on the local churches. Communion can be related primarily to the unity of the college of bishops, succeeding to the college of the apostles, with and under the bishop of Rome, exercising a Petrine ministry *(communio ecclesiae)*. Or communion can be related primarily to the local churches, representing the one apostolic tradition and celebrating the one Eucharist *(communio ecclesiarum)*. How to mediate between both models of *communio* ecclesiology? In the exercise of primacy, what really matters is not so

229

much whether the bishops are involved, but whether the local churches are involved.

As to the homework to be done by the Catholics, one Catholic participant suggested mainly the following two points:

- A clear distinction should be made between the authority exercised by the bishop of Rome in the West, on the one hand, and in the East, on the other.
- An ecclesiology that approaches the Church as a communion of local churches should be developed, together with a corresponding church practice.

The question of the authority and competence of bishops and bishops' conferences in the Catholic Church was raised in this context (with reference to the definitions of Vatican I and the insertion of the "Nota praevia" of Pope Paul VI).

Questions raised by Orthodox participants: Is it possible to think of a primacy based on canon law only and not on dogma (Vatican I)? To whom applies the anathema of Vatican I? Is the acceptance of primacy seen as necessary for salvation?

RECENT DISCUSSIONS ON PRIMACY IN ORTHODOX THEOLOGY*

Ioannis Zizioulas

Introduction

I should like to begin by expressing my deep appreciation of the invitation to participate in this symposium. The issue of primacy is perhaps the most important ecumenical problem. The recent papal document *Ut unum sint* makes mention of the seriousness of the problem and invites all Christians to study it. The present conference is meant to be part of such a study in response to the invitation of His Holiness. We cannot but regard this as a positive sign of the seriousness with which the Roman Catholic Church approaches the problem of church unity and of the openness to the view and positions of the other Christian communities, including, perhaps in a special way, the Orthodox Church.

The question of primacy undoubtedly lies at the very heart of Roman Catholic–Orthodox relations. Historically, it was this issue that led to the gradual estrangement and the final division between the two churches. Ever since the tragic event of 1054 AD the issue of papal primacy has deepened and strengthened more and more the division between Roman Catholics and Orthodox, accompanied most of the time with a polemic that loaded psychologically the debate concerning the issue. Discussion of this matter became finally a heated controversy, particularly during and after the First Vatican

* May 24, 2003 (afternoon session). Original English text.

Council, and continued to be so until recently when the Dialogue of Love was initiated, and a more irenic spirit prevailed in the discussions between the two sides. It is in such a spirit that we approach this thorny issue today, and we must continue to do so until some kind of rapprochement is reached. For we cannot but continue our efforts until this happens.

I have been asked to present the views of modern Orthodox theologians on the question of primacy. This is a formidable task, and it is doubtful that I can fulfil it in any satisfactory way. What I can only hope to do is to give *some typical examples* of how modern Orthodox theology approached the question of primacy in the Church in reacting against the claims of the church of Rome. I shall limit myself chronologically to some twentieth-century theologians, as they seem to be representative of the positions that still, in one way or another, dominate the theological scene. I shall not follow a strict chronological order, classifying the various theologians according to their positions rather than according to the historical period in which they have lived, although, interestingly enough, in most cases the various theological positions coincide with a certain historical period. Finally, you will allow me to say something about my personal position on the subject.

There may be different ways of classifying the views of modern Orthodox theologians on the question of primacy. The way I see things leads me to the following classifications:

a) There is a group of theologians who see little, if any, connection between primacy and the nature of the Church. For them the office of primate is a matter of the *bene esse* and not of the *esse* of the Church, that is, a matter of *canonical* rather than *ecclesiological* necessity.

b) There is another group of theologians who regard primacy in the Church as belonging to the Church's *esse*, that is, as being a matter of ecclesiology and not simply canonical order.

It is with the help of this classification that we shall try to understand the Orthodox position with regard to the primacy of the bishop of

Rome. I strongly believe that the subject of primacy is a question not only with regard to the claims of the bishop of Rome, but also within the Orthodox Church itself.

1. PRIMUS INTER PARES or Primacy of Honor

> Because of the political importance of Rome and the apostolicity of this church, as well as the martyrdom in it of the apostles Peter and Paul and its distinction in works of love, service, and mission, the bishop of Rome received from the councils and the Fathers and the pious emperors—therefore by human and not divine order—*a simple primacy of honor and order*, as first among the equal presidents of the particular churches, since basically the popes and patriarchs and archbishops and metropolitans are simple bishops, equal with their fellow-bishops from the point of view of priesthood *(hieratikos)*.

These words of one of the leading Orthodox theologians, the late Professor Ioannis Karmiris,[1] sum up the position of the greatest number of Orthodox theologians in the first half of the twentieth century, and echo the views of the late Professors Alivisatos, Mouratides, Archbishop Chrysostomos Papadopoulos, and others, to limit our references only to Greek theologians,[2] with whom Orthodox theologians writing in other languages at that time would undoubtedly agree.

---

1. I. Karmiris, *Orthodox Ecclesiology* (in Greek) (1973), 590.
2. See A. Alivisatos, "The Polity of the Church, the Metropolitan Bishop, and Especially [the Bishop] of Rome" (in Greek), *Epistemoniki Epeteris Theologikes Scholes Athenon* (1956–1957): 25–34; K. Mouratides, *The Essence and the Polity of the Church according to the Teaching of John Chrysostom* (in Greek) (1958); *Differentiation, Secularization, and Modern Developments in the [Canon] Law of the Roman Catholic Church* (in Greek) (1961); Chr. Papadopoulos, *The Primacy of the Bishop of Rome* (in Greek) (1930); *The Third Ecumenical Council and the Primacy of the Bishop of Rome: A Response to the Encyclical of Pius XI "Lux veritatis"* (in Greek) (1932); P. Trembelas, *On the Primacy of the Bishop of Rome* (in Greek) (1965).

If we attempt a theological analysis and commentary on the passage quoted above, we are bound to make the following observations:

(a) The existence of primates in the Church is not, according to this view, a matter of divine but of human right. This means that the Church could exist without primacy, although she could not exist without bishops or synods, the latter being *iure divino* and part of the Church's *esse*.[3]

(b) The actual structure of primacies, which resulted originally from the Byzantine pentarchy and was complemented later by the rest of the patriarchates and autocephalous churches in the East, is due simply to historical circumstances, such as political importance of the capital cities, distinction in service to the other churches, and so on, that is, to entirely human and transitory factors.

(c) The primacy of this kind is "a simple primacy of honor and order." This is an ambiguous expression which can be understood not so much by what it means positively, but what it intends to exclude. What this expression intends to exclude seems to be the following:

1) *The exercise of jurisdiction beyond the primate's local church.* Karmiris is clear about that: by speaking of "primacy of honor" he wants to exclude the right of the primate to exercise jurisdiction over the rest of the bishops. This is a principle accepted by all the Orthodox churches, and it is, indeed, a stumbling block for them in relation to the claims of the bishop of Rome. In spite of many examples of interventions by Orthodox patriarchs and heads of autocephalous churches in the affairs of the other bishops, no Orthodox would admit such interventions as acceptable canonically and ecclesiologically.

   While this is true, the description of this principle as "a simple primacy of honor" is ecclesiologically and canonically

---

3. There appears to be a logical contradiction with this position in the above quotation from Karmiris: if the synods are part of the Church's *esse*, how can we say that their decisions concerning primacy are "therefore by human and not divine order"?

questionable. "Simple honor" seems to suggest no power and authority at all, whereas it is known from experience that the person who chairs a meeting of any kind exercises powers of great significance, including the right to convoke and discuss the meeting, to form the agenda, and so on. With regard to the Church, such a description of primacy as "simple honor" seems to contradict basic canonical principles, such as the ones contained in the thirty-fourth Apostolic Canon which states that in every region (presumably a metropolitan district, but by extension in all forms of primacy) there *must* be a primate *(prôtos)* without whom the bishops of the district can do nothing, while he himself can do nothing without them. This seems to imply that the *primus* can even block the deliberations of the synod, if he chooses to do so *without the rest of the bishops being able to function synodically in his absence.* It is, for example, a well-known canonical provision in the Orthodox Church that in the absence of the patriarch or during the vacancy of his throne there can be no episcopal elections or the performance of any "canonical acts." Is this "a simple honor"? It appears that this phrase is useful with regard to what it intends to exclude (jurisdictional intervention, etc.) but very misleading if it is taken literally. There seems, in fact, not to exist, even in the Orthodox Church, "a simple primacy of honor."

2) *The sacramental or priestly superiority of the primate.* The expression "simple primacy of honor" is meant to stress the fact that all bishops, from the pope and the patriarchs down to the least of bishops, are equal. This is a fundamental principle for both Roman Catholic and Orthodox, however with a fundamental difference between them, namely, that the Roman Catholics would apply this equality only to the level of sacramental grace, which does *not* involve automatically the exercise of jurisdiction (the *missio canonica*), while the Orthodox would

make no such distinction. It is at this crucial point that Roman Catholic theology would feel free to reconcile its idea of equality of all bishops with the exercise of jurisdiction over the rest of the bishops by the pope. The fact, therefore, that for the Orthodox too, all bishops are equal sacramentally does not in itself justify the rejection of papal primacy, unless it is supplemented by the idea that episcopal sacramental grace is inconceivable without automatically involving jurisdictional power. But if that is the case, how can the Orthodox account for the existence in their church of "titular" bishops, that is, bishops who are equal with the rest of the bishops sacramentally but with no right of jurisdiction? It seems that the Orthodox contradict themselves fundamentally and thus weaken seriously their argument against Roman primacy. By borrowing from the West with such a light conscience the institution of titular bishops, they did not realize that they also borrowed the distinction between episcopal grace and jurisdiction (*missio canonica*), which distinction allows the pope to exercise jurisdictional authority beyond his own diocese without contradicting the principle of sacramental equality of all bishops.[4]

(d) It is noteworthy that the argument against papal primacy promoted by Karmiris and his contemporary Orthodox theologians rests upon a clear-cut distinction between *dogma* and *order*: whereas the episcopal and synodical structure of the Church is a matter of dogma (ecclesiology), primacy is not. This raises the question whether there

---

4. This is the most serious implication of the ecclesiological and canonical anomaly caused by the institution of titular bishops in the Orthodox Church. For, although the Orthodox do not accept the distinction between *potestas ordinis* and *potestas jurisdictionis*, they ordain titular bishops who cannot exercise jurisdiction in their diocese, not because of secular law, as is the case for example with the metropolitans of the ecumenical patriarchate in Turkey, but because their diocese belongs ecclesiastically to another bishop!

can be such a clear-cut distinction between canonical order and ecclesiology, since the canons of the Church derive their authority from ecclesiological justification for them. At this point a comment is necessary. Karmiris, like Alivisatos, Trembelas, and more explicitly Mouratides (all of them drawing probably from Androutsos, who was strongly influenced by Western scholasticism), operates in ecclesiology with the idea of a distinction between the *human* and the *divine* aspect of the Church. Whatever belongs to order in the Church derives from her human aspect, and whatever pertains to the dogma of the Church exists *jure divino*. This is a curious ecclesiology based on an equally curious Christology. In ecclesiology, just as in Christology, there is an *antidosis idiomatum* between divine and human, and as there is nothing in Christ's divine nature which does not affect decisively and permanently his humanity, so also in ecclesiology we cannot say that something is of the canonical order, and therefore inevitably *de jure humano*. Primacy, like episcopacy, synodality, and so on, belongs to the canonical order but not necessarily to the "human" aspect of the Church. The view maintained by the above-mentioned theologians that episcopacy, synodality etc. exist *jure divino*, but primacy does not, requires a great deal of explanation in order to become acceptable.

The main weakness of this position lies in that it seems to overlook the simple and obvious fact that *synodality cannot exist without primacy*. There has never been and there can never be a synod or a council without a *prôtos*. If, therefore, synodality exists *jure divino*, as the above theologians would (rightly) maintain, primacy also must exist by the same right.

In order to avoid this difficulty Alivisatos maintains that it is not necessary to have a permanent *prôtos;* primacy can be exercised by rotation.[5] He refers this to the relations among the autocephalous churches, but, if this position were to be accepted, we should logically extend its application also within each autocephalous church; all bishops should become primates of their autocephalous church by rotation. This would mean the abolishment of the offices of patri-

---

5. See A. Alivisatos, "The Right Meaning and Position of an Ecumenical Council in the Christian Church, according to the Canon Law of the Orthodox Church" (in Greek), *Proceedings (Praktika) of the Academy of Athens* 42 (1967): 179.

archs, metropolitans etc., as permanent personal ministries. By rejecting primacy as a permanent personal office, Alivisatos seems to overthrow more of the ecclesiastical order than he would be probably prepared to admit himself.

Alivisatos does not conceal his philosophico-theological presuppositions in taking such a position. He strongly believes that the polity of the Church is *democratic*, and finds primacy unacceptable for this reason. Whether such a presupposition is theologically correct, and not a direct derivation from the Enlightenment and secular sociology, is a matter that deserves consideration.

Karmiris also appeals to democracy as a characteristic of the Orthodox Church. But he carefully avoids speaking of rotation of primates. He argues more on the basis of *conciliarism*: there can be no primacy by the Church because the highest authority in it is the council or synod. The real *primus* in the Church is the council. Karmiris explicitly sides with western *Konziliarismus* in his opposition to the primacy of the pope. He identifies the Orthodox position with that of Western conciliarism: the council, particularly in the form of the ecumenical council, is above any primate. This is certainly the view of all the Orthodox, but the question remains *whether any council or synod can exist without primacy*. There must, therefore, be a way of incorporating primacy into conciliarity, if we are to arrive at a theologically sound position on this matter.

2. Is There a Universal Primacy?

The arguments produced by Orthodox theologians against the Roman primacy until the 1960s were more or less of the type we have examined: the Church is in her nature "democratic" and this means in terms of canonical order that she is conciliar. There cannot be, therefore, any authority assigned to an individual which could be higher than the council synod. There is no universal primacy, therefore, other than the ecumenical council.

With the arrival of the Second Vatican Council in the 1960s the entire ecclesiological debate moved in another direction. The question that already dominated the discussions during the long period of the theological preparation of the council, when the leading figures of Congar, Rahner, Ratzinger, de Lubac, and others paved the way to the theology of Vatican II, was whether the fullness of the Church, her catholicity, coincided with her universal structure. The challenge had come from Orthodox theology, mainly through the so-called "eucharistic ecclesiology" of the Russian theologian N. Afanassieff, who lived and taught in Paris, and who put forth the axiom "Wherever the Eucharist is, there is the Church." This meant that each local church in which the Eucharist is celebrated should be regarded as a full and catholic church. The Roman Catholic theologians that influenced Vatican II took this challenge seriously and as a result a theology of the local church entered the decisions of the council and gave rise to an impressive number of studies on the local church (Lanne, etc.).

This shift of the ecclesiological debate had important repercussions on the question of primacy. If each local church is a "catholic" church, is there any need to speak of a universal primacy or even of a "universal Church"? The debate was led from the Orthodox side mainly by the theologians of Russian origin who lived originally in Paris, some of them moving later to America. Four of them, Afanassieff, Meyendorff, Schmemann, and Koulomzine, produced a collective volume with the title *The Primacy of Peter in the Orthodox Church*,[6] where the discussion of primacy is placed in the context of the spirit surrounding Vatican II. There is considerable diversity among these theologians, which is worth noting.

Afanassieff insists that universal ecclesiology is unknown in the ancient Church until St. Cyprian, and that the idea of primacy is a juridical notion contradicting the evangelical idea of grace. In this he echoes Khomiakov and to some extent liberal Protestant theology (Sohm, Sabbotier, etc.). He dislikes the term *primacy* and proposes instead that of *priority*. Given that each local church is "catholic," the only form of "primacy" on the universal level that would satisfy Afanassieff would be that of "the church that presides in love," as Ignatius says in one of his letters to the church of Rome.

---

6. J. Meyendorff et al., *The Primacy of Peter* (Bedfordshire: Faith Press, 1973). Original French title: *La primauté de Pierre dans l'Église orthodoxe* (1960).

Now the difference between "primacy" and "priority" remains an ambiguous one: why should "priority" mean necessarily "grace" and "primacy," "legalism"? But the real problem created by Afanassieff's position is that it can be understood as leading to isolationism in ecclesiology, making the local church self-sufficient and independent in relation to its sister churches. As Nicholas Lossky observes,[7] this may not derive directly from Afanassieff's position but it has led, in fact, many Orthodox churches to a form of "autocephalism" which refuses to see the importance of Orthodox unity at the universal level. As Lossky notes, combined with the fact that most of the auto-cephalous Orthodox churches coincide with some kind of national identity, such views can easily lead to the infiltration of Orthodoxy by nationalism.

Afanassieff's views about primacy do not seem to be fully shared by other Russian theologians of the emigration. Florovsky, Meyendorff, and Schmemann take a different view. Most outspoken in this respect is Schmemann, who in the above-mentioned collective volume examines the idea of primacy (he does not adopt the term "priority") at all levels and concludes with the view that the highest and ultimate form of primacy is "universal primacy." He appeals to the Orthodox to free themselves from the "age long anti-roman prejudice [that] led some Orthodox canonists simply to deny the existence of such primacy in the past or the need for it in the present." For him "an objective study of the canonical tradition cannot fail to establish beyond any doubt that, along with local 'centres of agreement' or primacies, the Church had also known a universal primacy."[8] Primacy for Schmemann is of the Church's *esse* (contrast this with Karmiris and the other theologians who deny any *jure divino* character to primacy). "A local Church," he writes, "cut from the universal *koinonia* is indeed a *contradictio in adjecto*, for this *koinonia* is the very essence of the Church. And it has, therefore, its *form* and *expression*: primacy. Primacy is the necessary expression of the unity in faith and life of all local

---

7. N. Lossky, "Conciliarity—Primacy in a Russian Orthodox Perspective," in *Petrine Ministry and the Unity of the Church*, ed. J. F. Puglisi (Collegeville, MN: Liturgical Press, 1999), 127–35.

8. A. Schmemann, "The Idea of Primacy in Orthodox Ecclesiology," in J. Meyendorff et al., *The Primacy of Peter in the Orthodox Church*, 163.

Churches, of their living and efficient *koinonia*."[9] Schmemann has for this reason a critical view of certain Orthodox positions concerning autocephaly. He writes:

> At a relatively recent date there arose among the Orthodox Churches the opinion the Church is based in her life in the principle of autocephaly....According to this position, the principle of autocephaly is not only one of the historical expressions of her universal structure, but precisely the ecclesiological foundation of the Church and her life. In other words, the unique universal organism of Roman ecclesiology is opposed here to autocephalous organisms, each one constituted by several dioceses....All these autocephalies are absolutely equal among themselves, and this equality excludes any universal centre of Primacy.[10]

This amounts, in his view, to a replacement of the universal primacy by the power of the head of the autocephalous church and his synod: "Having rejected and still rejecting it [i.e,. universal primacy] in its Roman form, i.e. as universal power, the Orthodox conscience has easily accepted it in the so-called autocephalies."[11]

Similar are the views of Meyendorff on the question of primacy. It is worth quoting from his *The Byzantine Legacy in the Orthodox Church* (Crestwood, NY: St. Vladimir's Seminary Press, 1982), 243f.:

> The very idea of the primacy was very much a part of ecclesiology itself: the provisional Episcopal synods needed a president, without whose sanction no decision was valid. Such is indeed an inevitable requirement of the very existence of the Church in the world....It is a fact...that there has never been a time when the Church did not recognise a certain order among first the apostles, then the bishops and that in this order one apostle, St

---

9. Ibid., 165.
10. Ibid., 166.
11. Ibid., 148.

Peter, and later one bishop, heading a particular Church occupied the place of primate....I would venture to affirm here that the universal primacy of one Bishop...was not simply a historical accident, reflecting pragmatic requirements....The function of the one Bishop is to serve that unity on the world scale, just as the function of a regional primate is to be agent of unity on a regional scale.

Conclusions

These are some of the views that have been expressed by Orthodox theologians at the time around and since Vatican II. They have not been fully debated as yet, and they certainly are far from being the official position of the Orthodox Church. As Schmemann observed, Orthodox ecclesiology still awaits an ecclesiological appreciation of primacy on the universal level.[12] And yet the basic ideas are there and we can work with them towards an Orthodox consensus on this matter. Let me present my own view on the subject.

The idea of universal primacy in the Church has been rejected by the Orthodox, and this rejection is deeply rooted in Orthodox consciousness. This is due to nontheological as well as to theological reasons. To the first ones belongs the spirit of polemic, which characterized Roman Catholic–Orthodox relations for centuries after the Great Schism. The Orthodox interpreted papal primacy as universal expansionism and as the attempt of Rome to put all Christians under the dominion of its power. Papal primacy became in this way synonymous with oppression and ecclesiastical totalitarianism. The reaction to this led Orthodox theologians to oppose primacy in general as incompatible with the democratic ideas of modern society, thus allowing for nontheological arguments to decide a theological issue.

In this heated debate the Orthodox have tended to overlook certain facts and ideas present in their own tradition and faith, such as the presence and function of *prôtos* in every local church and its synodical life. Synods without primates never existed in the Orthodox Church, and this indicates clearly that if synodality is an

---

12. A. Schmemann, "The Idea of Primacy in Orthodox Ecclesiology," 164.

ecclesiological, that is, dogmatic, necessity, so must be primacy. The fact that *all* synods have a primate as an ecclesiological necessity means that ecumenical synods should also have a *primus*. This automatically implies universal primacy. The logic of synodality leads to primacy, and the logic of the ecumenical council to universal primacy.

Now, primacy in the Church has *never* been exercised by rotation. This is a clear indication that primacy is attached to a particular office or ministry and to a particular person. Since, however, this office or ministry finds its *raison d'être* in the synodical institution of which it is part, it can only function *in relation to those who comprise the synod*, and never in isolation. Primacy, like everything else in the Church, even in God's being (the Trinity), is *relational*. There is no such thing as individual ministry, understood and functioning outside a reality of *communion*.[13]

This is precisely what the well-known thirty-fourth Canon of the Apostles clearly and explicitly states. This canon can be the golden rule of the theology of primacy. It requires that the *prôtos* is a *sine qua non conditio* for the synodical institution, hence an ecclesiological necessity, and that the synod is equally a prerequisite for the exercise of primacy. And all this, as the canon culminates, because God himself is Trinity.

The reciprocal conditioning between primacy and synodality has profound theological implications. It means that primacy is not a legalistic notion implying the investment of a certain individual with power, but a form of *diakonia*, that is, of ministry in the strict sense of the term. It implies also that this ministry reaches the entire community though the communion of the local churches manifested through the bishops that constitute the council or synod. It is for this reason that the primate himself should be the head of a local church, that is, a bishop. This will allow each local church to be part of a conciliar reality as a full and catholic church. Primacy will not in this case undermine the ecclesiological integrity of any local church. The primate, as the head of a local church and not as an individual, will serve

---

13. See I. Zizioulas, *Being as Communion: Studies in Personhood and the Church*, Contemporary Greek Theologians 4 (Crestwood, NY: St. Vladimir's Seminary Press, 1985), passim.

the unity of the Church as a *koinônia* of full churches and not as a "collage" of incomplete parts of a universal Church.

This last point reveals that in the end the problem of universal primacy depends on the relation between local and universal Church. Is the local church a *part* of the Church universal or a full and catholic church? Does the universal Church have ecclesiological priority over the local church or is it a *koinônia* of local churches? These questions must be answered before any theological conception of universal primacy can be formed. The brief survey on the discussions on primacy in the last century, which we tried to present here, albeit incompletely, shows that Orthodox theology is ready to accept primacy at all levels of church structure, including the universal one, as ecclesiologically justifiable. The problem that remains for discussion in the context of theological dialogue between Roman Catholic and Orthodox is *what kind of primacy* we have in mind. If we approach this problem with the help of an ecclesiology of communion, we may manage to bring the two traditions closer to each other on a subject as crucial for the unity of the Church as that of primacy.

If, therefore, we wish to sharpen the question we are confronted with, we must ask ourselves: does the Church need a universal *primus* and why? And of what kind? The answer to this question can only come as a common answer from theology, not from biblical exegesis or history. A study of modern Orthodox theology shows that the disagreement between Roman Catholics and Orthodox concerning the place of Peter in the New Testament remains deep.

Although Peter's leading position among the Twelve is recognized more and more also by the Orthodox, the particular importance attached to him by the Roman Catholics is strongly disputed by them. If we wait until biblical scholars come to an agreement on this issue, we may have to postpone the unity of the Church for another millennium, if not infinitely.

History is also an unsafe ground for *rapprochement.* The late Cardinal Yves Congar makes it clear with regard to the first millennium:

> In the East, the authority of the See of Rome was never that of a monarchical prince. The history of the Sixth Ecumenical Council (680–681) is eloquent on this point.

Pope Agathon was acclaimed not because his authority would be obeyed but because the expression of the authentic faith was recognized in his words. The theory of pentarchy…was a way of structuring communication between the churches and ensuring unity.…The pentarchy was, in its way, an expression of the collegial sense of the synodal East in so far as it was a form of communion of the churches in homophony.…The body of Christ has no head other than Christ himself.…The Byzantine theologians very rarely relate the primacy of the See of Rome to the apostle Peter, although authors of prestige like Maximus the Confessor or Theodore the Studite do, at times, say something to this effect."[14]

This was not the historical situation in the West, where everyone recognized the Roman primacy, albeit without always giving it "the significance that it was given in Rome after St. Leo."[15] Historians may disagree as to the extent to which the authority of Rome was recognized in the East, but no one can dispute the divergence between East and West on this matter long before the schism of the eleventh century.

Thus the study of history offers to help us in the present, ecumenically, only in two ways—both of them unrealistic. One is for Roman Catholics and Orthodox to return to the situation of the first millennium. This is unrealistic mainly because the Roman Catholic Church would not be prepared to eliminate her second millennium from history in order to unite with the Orthodox. The other way is to regard the differences between the Orthodox and the Roman Catholics on the subject of primacy as two parallel or complementary traditions that can exist side by side. This would also prove to be unrealistic, since it would in fact mean that the pope would have to renounce *in practice* his claim of universal jurisdiction, limiting it only to the West (or to his own flock). As a matter of fact this was proposed as a solution by Roman Catholic theologians several years ago, but nothing came out of it.

---

14. Y. Congar, *L'Église: De St. Augustin à l' époque moderne* (Paris: Cerf, 1970), 78–79.

15. Ibid., 65.

If, therefore, we cannot meet on the ground of either biblical exegesis or history, we may ask ourselves whether we can meet on the basis of certain fundamental theological principles in order to give a common answer to the question raised above, namely, whether and for what *theological* reasons we need a universal *primus*, and how we can understand his nature and function. Such theological reasons can emerge from an *ecclesiology of communion*, which is beginning to establish itself in our time as a result of the theological insights of Vatican II and the overcoming of Scholasticism in both Roman Catholic and Orthodox theology in our time. This would mean that the justification of the Roman primacy would depend on whether we agree that the Church consists of *full local churches* united into *one Church* without losing their ecclesial fullness, and that primacy at all levels is a necessary means to realize and guarantee this balance between the many and the one.

Father Congar, one of the pioneers of the ecclesiology of communion on the Roman Catholic side, believed that the papal primacy, in spite of monarchical tendencies prevailing at that time, was exercised within an ecclesiology of communion also in the West until about the sixteenth century, when the papacy succeeded in imposing monarchical primacy on the whole of the West.[16] If that is the case, the return to such an ecclesiology of communion may not be so unrealistic a proposition. I would certainly hope so.

Summary of Discussion

The ecclesiology of communion was once more at the center of several Orthodox and Catholic interventions:

Though biblical scholarship and scientific exegesis are important, they cannot be considered as the ultimate approach to the Bible; the Bible should be read in order to answer theological questions, such as those related to an ecclesiology of communion.

Though the Bible is full of communion theology, there is less evidence for the "theological" necessity of a "ministry of unity," exercised by a specific person, being invested with a "universal primacy."

16. Ibid., 78ff.

The relation between the New Testament and later ecclesial developments has to be seen in a theological or ecclesiological perspective, not in a historical one. Does the New Testament imply or lead to primacy? Is Ignatius of Antioch faithful to the New Testament in the way he speaks about the bishop? The answer of one Orthodox participant to this last question was: historically not, but theologically yes.

In this context, an Orthodox participant affirmed the necessity of an effective ministry of communion among the local churches, that should be more than vaguely spiritual.

The question of the possibility of a simultaneous (or double) communion was raised: can a local Catholic church be in full communion with a local Orthodox church before full communion is restored on the universal level between the Catholic Church and the Orthodox Church? The generally accepted answer was negative.

A Catholic participant pointed out the fundamental importance of *Unitatis redintegratio*, 14, which clearly confirms the specificity of the churches of the East and the particularity of their relations with the See of Rome. This paragraph should be our main guideline. The churches are also invited to attempt new models in the exercise of primacy. A comparison between both Catholic Codes of Canon Law—the Western and the Eastern one—could be helpful to this, at least as a starting point.

Another Catholic participant underscored the importance of clarifying the concept of "primacy of jurisdiction." Often this expression is opposed to "primacy of honor," and some Orthodox theologians affirm that, although a primacy of honor would be acceptable for them, a "primacy of jurisdiction" is not. It should be clarified that Catholic terminology knows different kinds of jurisdiction, on different hierarchical levels. Jurisdiction basically means the necessary authority given to someone in order that he may be able to fulfil his ministry in the Church. In this sense the jurisdiction of the bishop of Rome is not in opposition with, nor does it nullify the jurisdiction of, the other bishops; on the contrary. This jurisdiction would not be so radically different from the "primacy of honor" which several Orthodox theologians would be ready to accept as being more than a merely honorific position, the latter having no place in the Church.

Any renewed approach to primacy presupposes profound changes in sensitivity and mentality on both the Catholic and the Orthodox side. Theological research would be helped by new attitudes and new forms of cooperation. Within the Catholic Church, greater authority could be given to the local churches (decentralization). Between the Catholic Church and the Orthodox Church, common initiatives by the bishop of Rome and individual patriarchs could be multiplied (common messages, regular consultations, common initiatives, etc.). Much can already be done together without raising any problem related to authority; by acting together whenever possible, the question of authority might appear in a different light.

Most participants agreed on the fact that the thirty-fourth Canon of the Apostles, as presented by the speaker, could be a promising starting point for future study. Some Orthodox pointed out that this canon presents a form of primacy that makes no explicit reference to a Petrine ministry, but rather reflects a theology of communion, in the image of the Holy Trinity.

INDEX

249